THE BA

Writing

A.C. "Buddy" Krizan
Murray State University
Murray, Kentucky

Joyce P. Logan
University of Kentucky
Lexington, Kentucky

SOUTH-WESTERN
CENGAGE Learning™

Australia • Brazil • Japan • Korea • Mexico • Singapore • Spain • United Kingdom • United States

SOUTH-WESTERN
CENGAGE Learning™

The Basics Writing
A. C. "Buddy" Krizan, Joyce P. Logan

Business Unit Director: Peter McBride
Executive Editor: Eve Lewis
Project Manager: Penny Shank
Editor: Alan Biondi
Production Manager: Patricia Matthews Boies
Art/Design Coordinator: Bill Spencer
Marketing Manager: Mark Linton
Cover Design: Lou Ann Thesing
Manufacturing Coordinator: Pam Wulf
Compositor: Better Graphics, Inc.

ISBN-13: 978-0-538-72301-5

ISBN-10: 0-538-72301-7

South-Western
5191 Natorp Boulevard
Mason, OH 45040
USA

Cengage Learning is a leading provider of customized learning solutions with office locations around the globe, including Singapore, the United Kingdom, Australia, Mexico, Brazil, and Japan. Locate your local office at **international.cengage.com/region**

Cengage Learning products are represented in Canada by Nelson Education, Ltd.

To learn more about South-Western, visit **www.cengage.com/southwestern**

Purchase any of our products at your local college store or at our preferred online store **www.ichapters.com**

Printed in the United States of America
4 5 6 7 8 13 12 11 10 09

ED019

CONTENTS

PREFACE

We live in an information age. Communication skills are becoming more and more important. Writing that clearly communicates ideas is a valuable job skill as well as a useful personal skill. This book helps you become a more skillful writer.

ORGANIZATION

Basics of Writing is easy to read and and understand because the eight chapters follow the actual steps of the writing process.

- Chapter 1 helps you determine goals for written messages, analyze readers' needs, and consider different types of messages.
- Chapter 2 explains major features of computer software for composing, editing, and refining messages. In addition, this chapter covers use of the Internet as a writing resource.
- Chapters 3 and 4 guide an analysis of your writing skills and present steps to follow in the writing process.
- The next two chapters, 5 and 6, give you practice in improving writing structure of sentences and paragraphs.
- In Chapters 7 and 8, you apply your writing skills to development of essays that share your ideas and perspectives with others and to preparation of reports and proposals for a variety of purposes..

SPECIAL FEATURES

Basics of Writing is more than a textbook. It is a practical, results-oriented tool with the following features designed to help you succeed:

- ***Checkpoints*** throughout the text help you apply the ideas presented.
- ***Checkpoint solutions***, provided at the end of the book, let you verify your understanding of one section before you begin another section.
- ***Margin notes and quotations*** highlight key writing concepts in the chapter and add interest.
- ***Workplace Connections*** provide realism and offer tips for succeeding on the job.
- ***E-mail and Internet*** opportunities let you check out online resources and develop online skills.
- ***Anecdotes and cartoons*** act as relevant learning aids to bring realism and humor to your study of writing.
- ***Chapter summaries*** reinforce and help you review the principles covered in each chapter.
- ***Chapter applications and course examinations*** check your achievement of the learning objectives by using your critical thinking, composition, proofreading, and teamwork skills.

- ***Grammar workshops*** at the end of each chapter help you gain technical competence for expressing your ideas.
- ***Web- and CD ROM-based supplemental resources*** provide current and timely research and application practice.
- The ***Appendix*** serves as a reference for basic grammar.

ICONS

Basics of Writing uses icons to quickly identify some of its special features.

The team icon identifies opportunities to work with others and sharpen your teamwork skills.

The workplace connection icon identifies workplace success tips as well as information and exercises that allow you to practice the foundation skills and personal qualities employers look for when hiring.

The Internet/e-mail icon marks activities where you may practice your online computer skills.

words@work

The *words@work* icon alerts you to specific lessons and exercises from the *words@work* CD-ROM that correlate with the skills you are developing in each chapter. *Words@work* can be ordered separately from South-Western Educational Publishing/Cengage Learning.

THE SERIES

Basics of Writing may be used as a standalone resource or in conjunction with the **Basics of Communication Series**, a series of text-workbooks that helps you master the communication skills needed in the workplace. The other books in the series are *Basics of English*, *Basics of Business Communication*, *Basics of Employment Communication*, and *Basics of Speech Communication.*

ACKNOWLEDGMENTS

Thanks are extended to the following individuals for reviewing the manuscript and offering suggestions:

Katherine Ploeger, California State University Stanislaus, Turlock, CA

Laurie Shapero, Miami-Dade Community College, Kendall Campus, Miami, FL

Susan Merrill, Educational Consultant, Croton-on-Hudson, NY

If you want to become a better writer, mastery of concepts presented in this book will help you achieve your goal. Practice and feedback throughout the course will improve your writing.

A.C. "Buddy" Krizan and Joyce P. Logan

MASTERING THE FOUNDATIONS OF WRITING

CHAPTER 1

We are in a global communication age. Computer modems, electronic networks, fax machines, fiber optics, and satellites speed messages all over the world. Never before have we been able to communicate so quickly and so directly with so many people. Today, successful life management and job performance require competence in the communication skills of writing, reading, speaking, and listening. Mastery of communication skills requires continued effort and practice, based on an understanding of basic principles.

WRITING TO COMMUNICATE

LEARNING OBJECTIVES

- Recognize the importance of writing competency.
- Clarify message goals.
- Analyze readers' needs.
- Classify types of writing.

Of course you can write! Writing is an everyday activity. You write a phone message for someone, write a letter about a defective product, write an essay for a class, write your daily thoughts in a journal, write an e-mail message to respond to a question, or write a report for your employer. You may enjoy writing or you may be anxious about putting words on paper or in electronic format. This book will help you to analyze your writing and to apply proven practices for becoming a confident writer. In this chapter, you begin improving your writing skills by examining basic techniques and then practicing them.

You can become an effective writer by following and practicing basic principles of writing.

What you write represents you. When you speak, you communicate not only with words but also with voice inflection or body language. A smile, a frown, tone of voice, or hand gesture may help the listener understand the spoken message. Written communication depends on the words used, the organization of these words into sentences and paragraphs, and the message format or general appearance. Even the most published authors realize that writing involves a continual refinement process. Everyone can improve their communication through a commitment to improving writing skills.

Before writing, clarify message goals and analyze the reader's needs.

The principles of good writing apply to both your personal and business life. You will become a better writer by reviewing writing principles and practicing the writing process. In this chapter, you will apply pre-writing principles—steps you take before writing—that help plan the message content. Two pre-writing steps are essential for assuring that a message will communicate effectively: (1) clarify the message goals and (2) analyze the needs of the reader.

> "The only place that success comes before work is in the dictionary."
>
> —Vidal Sasson.

CLARIFYING YOUR MESSAGE GOALS

All messages have general and specific goals. A goal is the purpose or end result that you hope to achieve. Before writing, you should be able to state clearly the response or action you want from your reader. Clear goals help you know what to say and how to say it.

General Goals

Written communication has at least one of six general goals.

Think about why you are writing. How do you want the reader to respond? General goals for written communication fit one or more of the following six categories: (1) to inquire, (2) to inform, (3) to influence, (4) to build goodwill, (5) to entertain, and (6) to engage in personal reflection. The first five can be called transactive writing because they are an exchange or transaction between you and one or more readers. The goal of transactive writing is to get something done. The sixth category refers to personal descriptive writing which is self-directed and aimed toward understanding or documenting personal events.

Information is gained through inquiries.

TO INQUIRE. Information is important to individuals and organizations. In both personal and work life, you obtain and process information from diverse sources. You gain needed information through inquiry. When the goal of a written message is to inquire, a response that provides information is desired. The following examples illustrate written messages *to inquire*:

1. A letter to Wendy asking when she is coming to visit.
2. An e-mail to Kimitaka Matsumi asking if he will be available to conduct a workshop.
3. A memorandum to the human resources office where you work asking about company health care insurance.

Informational messages must have the same meaning for both sender and receiver.

TO INFORM. A common message goal is to share information with others. Clarity in writing to inform is important, so that the reader's understanding of the message matches what you intended to convey. When the goal is to inform, remember that timeliness is also often a consideration. The receivers may need the information by a certain time so they can take action. Examples of writing *to inform* are:

1. Informing Ted that you have made first chair clarinet in the Paducah Symphony Orchestra.
2. Submitting an article about white-water rafting to the *Waco Inquirer*.
3. Sending Mr. Short a bill for your services.

TO INFLUENCE. In a message *to influence*, the writer must present to the reader the benefits of the action suggested. Use persuasive language based on facts and logic. If the information conveyed has negative points, state them concisely and accurately, but subordinate them to the benefits. In other words, if you are writing a "bad news" message, begin by describing positive information, then state the negative points, and close on a positive note. Stressing the positive points helps convince the reader to take a certain action. Even a highly respected scholar with expertise in a subject cannot effectively influence others through writing that does not apply basic writing principles. The following examples illustrate messages with the goal *to influence*:

Messages written to influence must emphasize benefits to the reader.

1. Writing to your friend, George, to ask him to vote for Teresa.
2. Writing a poem for publication that urges the preservation of wildlife.
3. Sending your employees a message about a new labor contract.

TO BUILD GOODWILL. Goodwill messages maintain or improve the relationship between the reader and the writer. These messages recognize the reader's feelings and interests. Emphasis is placed on accomplishments or events that benefit the reader. Positive wording helps convey goodwill. The goal *to build goodwill* does not require an immediate action as a message to influence does. It aims to affect the reader's attitude toward the writer. In the broadest sense, most messages have a goal *to build goodwill*, in addition to a primary goal, such as *to inquire* or *to influence*. However, in analyzing message goals, consider the direct response or reaction intended for the message. The messages below illustrate goodwill messages:

To identify the message goal, ask yourself what response or reaction you intend from the reader.

1. A congratulatory message to your friend, Sheri, on being valedictorian of her class.
2. A note accompanying a refund check to a customer (to inform and to build goodwill).
3. A message of congratulations to a friend who has just qualified for the Boston Marathon.

TO ENTERTAIN. Writing *to entertain* means that your message is intended to bring enjoyment to the reader. This type of message may include a poem, interesting ideas, or unique experiences shared with the reader. The writer must know the interests of the reader if the message is

Reader's interests must be addressed for the message to entertain.

to entertain. Humor and wit may be used in a message to entertain. Writing *to entertain* often has a secondary goal—*to inform* or *to influence.* The following messages have the general goal *to entertain*:

1. A humorous story for publication in a magazine.
2. A poem about nature's beauty sent to a friend who likes poetry and the outdoor life.
3. A letter describing an experience about mountain climbing sent to a friend who enjoys this hobby, too.

Personal writing may be a means of clarifying your thoughts and gaining new insights.

TO ENGAGE IN PERSONAL EXPRESSION OR REFLECTION. Did you ever keep a diary? If so, you know that this kind of writing was personal and not intended for others to read. Keeping a diary of events or writing your thoughts in a personal journal helps make sense of the world around you. Writing your thoughts forces you to organize and analyze them. Educators recognize that journal writing and writing personal narratives are self-learning experiences. The following three types of writing are examples of writing *for personal expression or reflection.*

1. Writing your thoughts about the death of a loved one.
2. Keeping a personal journal or diary about daily events.
3. Writing about your relationship with a friend.

Specific Goals

Writers must know the message's objective before they begin to write.

In addition to general goals, consider specific goals when creating messages. The specific goal describes the response or action that the writer wants from the reader. Identifying the specific goal before writing the message helps you select the wording so that it helps you achieve this goal. Relating the message content to the reader's needs is a key to accomplishing the writer's goals. The following examples show the general and specific goal for each situation:

"If you commit yourself 100% to any goal or task, you will be successful,"

—Steve Mraboli.

1. An advertisement to sell your automobile.
   General goal: To influence.
   Specific goal: To sell your automobile.
2. A welcome message from a local beauty shop to new residents in the town.
   General goal: To build goodwill and to influence.
   Specific goal: To gain new patrons.
3. A message to employees in a company describing uses of a new computer system.
   General goal: To inform.
   Specific goal: To give the employees the information they need to use the computer system.

IDENTIFYING GOALS

For each communication listed below, identify the general and specific goals for the message. (1) to inquire, (2) to inform, (3) to influence, (4) to build goodwill, (5) to entertain, or (6) to engage in personal expression or reflection.

Example:
Faxing a journal article to receive suggestions for change from a co-author.

General Goal 1, 2

Specific Goal receive suggestions

1. An e-mail message requesting a price quote on computer software.

   General Goal ______________________

   Specific Goal ______________________

2. A letter explaining why merchandise that was purchased is being returned for a refund.

   General Goal ______________________

   Specific Goal ______________________

3. A letter explaining "Why Affirmative Action Makes Sense in Hiring" that is printed in a *Letters to the Editor* column of a local newspaper.

   General Goal ______________________

   Specific Goal ______________________

4. An electronic message sent to a computer "chat room" to share an animated holiday greeting.

   General Goal ______________________

   Specific Goal ______________________

5. A technical report that describes the office computer network system.

   General Goal ______________________

   Specific Goal ______________________

ANALYZING THE READER'S NEEDS

Adopt the reader's perspective when you write the message.

The reader's response or reaction is the measure of a message's success. If this response or reaction matches the writer's goal, the message is completely successful. (It is possible to be partially successful—for example, humorous political writing might entertain without influencing.) A letter of inquiry is successful when the response brings the information requested. An application letter is successful when the job interview is scheduled. Knowing the reader is key to achieving written message goals; keep the reader in mind throughout the pre-writing and writing process. Give careful consideration to the reader's needs, interests, and education. Writing from the reader's point of view assumes the "you" perspective. The writer mentally focuses on the reader and thinks about "you" rather than "I."

General Needs

General needs are human needs that apply to everyone. To address these needs, messages should have three characteristics; they should be: *respectful*, *interesting*, and *understandable*.

A successful message makes the reader feel respected and important.

RESPECTFUL. The wording of the message and the tone reflect courtesy and a positive outlook. Disrespect for the reader, in tone or in language, affects the response and goodwill. A reader who is offended by the message is unlikely to react or respond positively. Write and rewrite until you find a way to express your concerns in a positive manner. Start with what can be done or what is good about the product or the relationship. Then, accurately state your concerns and suggest positive ways to remedy them.

A successful message must be interesting to the reader.

INTERESTING. With today's glut of communication and information, the reader scans the message quickly for the bottom line: How does this communication affect me? How will I benefit from a response? Unless the beginning of the message addresses and holds the reader's interest, the reader may not finish reading it or may quickly read it and toss it away.

A highly successful written message has the same meaning for both writer and reader.

UNDERSTANDABLE. The message must be understandable. Visualize the reader and word the message as though you were speaking to the individual(s). Include essential information. Wording should be clear, complete, concise, and correct.

Specific Needs

Specific information to consider about the reader includes:
- *Education and experience*
- *Emotional state*
- *Socioeconomic and cultural background*

What specific information about the reader(s) should the writer have before writing? Begin by considering the experiences and educational background of your intended audience. Consider the reader's knowledge of the subject to be discussed. In addition, determine as well as possible the reader's level of formal education, emotional state, socioeconomic and cultural background, and interests.

EDUCATION AND EXPERIENCE. The education and experience of the audience affect the writing level and the amount of detail you need to include. Analyzing the reader's education means considering the general education and reading level. When writing for multiple readers, write for understanding by the person with the lowest level of education or knowledge of the subject. Simple, nontechnical words and short sentences increase readability. Technical words, when used, should be defined if the audience has little experience related to the topic. When considering experience, ask yourself these questions: How does the reader's experience relate to the topic? How extensive is the experience? Educational level and experience influence the reader's interpretation of the message. A message sent to a college graduate would differ from one sent to a high school teenager. If writing an appeal to support a local baseball franchise you would consider the reader's knowledge or experience related to baseball or sports in general.

EMOTIONAL STATE. Events may cause fluctuations in people's emotional states. They may be happy, sad, angry, confused, or depressed. While you have no control over the emotional state of the reader before the message is read, you must consider how your reader will react to your message. If you are responding to a complaint letter, you may assume that the reader will be angry before reading your message. One goal for your message will be to replace anger with understanding.

Socioeconomic and Cultural Background. All communication—in fact, most sensory input—passes through a series of "filters," that is, it is interpreted by the individual based on what he or she knows, believes, and values. The socioeconomic status of a group plays an important role in determining the beliefs, values, and learning opportunities of the members of that group. To analyze the socioeconomic characteristics of your audience, consider these questions: What occupation(s) are represented? What are the professional concerns? What values do they hold? How resistant are they to the ideas in the message you will write? For example, individuals whose income places them in the middle economic stratum generally value independence, hard work, and privacy. People at the upper socioeconomic level, such as corporation presidents, would be likely to value education, maintaining status in society, contributing to community life, making a profit, and finding time for leisure activities. Individuals at the lower economic level are primarily concerned with taking care of their basic needs for food, shelter, and clothing. Although values are not defined the same by all people within a particular socioeconomic group, the writer should be aware of commonly held beliefs and values for the individuals or groups to whom the message is addressed.

Effective written communication calls for finding out as much as you can about the audience for whom the message is intended. Increasingly, that audience is culturally diverse. This is due both to an increasingly multicultural society and to the rapid expansion of world-wide telecommunications. The Internet, fax, and e-mail have contributed to the speed with which information moves. These electronic messages, as well as publications and letters, span the globe. Sending messages to an audience with a cultural background that differs from yours—whether that audience is an individual or a large, multinational group—requires sensitivity to cultural differences, such as word meanings, traditions, protocol, and values.

Workplace Connections

The job market requires workers who can communicate thoughts, ideas, and information to diverse audiences.

Interest and Opinions. The interest level and opinions of your intended audience will also have an effect on how you present your message. Is the reader's opinion of the topic positive or negative? Or is he or she indifferent? If the attitude of the reader toward the subject is negative or indifferent, your first job is to generate interest. This calls for using both sensitivity and creativity. To motivate a diverse audience, you should consider interests that will be common across the group, as well as beliefs and opinions, wording the message to avoid offense. Common human concerns, such as physical, social, and achievement needs, can help give your message a stronger motivational appeal. For example, a message with the goal of influencing readers to support the local school system would highlight ways that this support would benefit both children and the community.

A reader's attitudes must be considered when composing a message.

ANALYZING THE READER'S NEEDS

Analyze the reader's needs for the following situations. Answer the questions for each situation.

1. Leroy and Sally completed high school six years ago. Leroy earned a letter in football in high school and college. Sally played softball in high school but did not play after that. You are writing a message to gain support for eliminating contact sports in high schools. How does the experience of each individual differ, and how should this difference affect the message?

2. Luisa was a member of the National Honor Society and graduated with honors from college. She never missed a rock concert on campus. Cathy was a high school band member who married immediately after graduation. If you were preparing a letter to raise funds for a community symphonic orchestra, how would the analysis for these two individuals differ?

3. Karen lived on a small farm most of her life. She enjoyed hunting and fishing. William was reared in a larger community of 125,000. During high school, he played sports and read nonfiction books. Today Karen is an office manager for a large petroleum company, and William is an insurance sales representative. You are writing a message asking for their support for limiting urban expansion to create a nature reserve. How should the message be worded differently for each reader?

CLASSIFYING TYPES OF WRITING

Written communication takes various forms and can be categorized in a number of ways. In this section, writing is examined by how it is used and by who sends the message.

Classification by Use

Writing with a purpose has three major categories: (1) reflective or expressive writing, (2) literary writing, and (3) transactive writing. The following paragraphs describe each of these categories and relate each type of writing to the general goals described earlier in this chapter: *to inquire, to inform, to influence, to build goodwill, to entertain,* and *to engage in personal expression or reflection.*

Classification of writing may be categorized as:
- ***Reflective or expressive***
- ***Literary***
- ***Transactive***

REFLECTIVE OR EXPRESSIVE WRITING. Reflective or expressive writing is a way to learn from events or introspection. It may take the form of a personal narrative that focuses on one event in the writer's life; a memoir describing relationships with people, places, animals, or things; or it may take the form of a personal essay reflecting on a central idea supported by events in the writer's life. If personal essays, journals, or memoirs are published, they become **literary writings**.

LITERARY WRITING. Short stories, books, poems, scripts, or plays are examples of literary writing. *Literary* is defined as having the characteristics of literature. The general goal for literary writing is *to entertain, to inform, to influence* or a combination of these goals. The writing style depends on the form of the particular type of literature.

TRANSACTIVE WRITING. Transactive writing is an exchange between a writer and the recipient of the writing. The message may have one or more of these goals: *to inquire, to inform, to influence,* or *to build goodwill.* The message could entertain, but this is not a major goal for transactive writing. Transactive writing is writing with a goal of "getting something done." Generally, the writer expects a response from the recipient. Figure 1-1 shows the transactive writing process.

Figure 1-1
The Transactive Writing Process

Classification by Sender

Another classification of writing depends on whom the message represents: the individual writer of the message or an organization. Effective writing is important to individuals and to organizations. Both types of writing have general and specific goals. Most writing for organizations, and much of the writing by individuals, is transactive in nature; that is, its primary goal is to get something done.

Individual goals are accomplished through personal writing.

PERSONAL WRITING. Personal writing accomplishes individual goals. Much of the writing you do is transactive. You may write a letter to apply for a job or to express thoughts to a friend who lives far away. Your personal writing could convey your point of view to a government official; place an order for items you wish to purchase; ask for information; or request a promotion. As noted earlier in the chapter, personal writing also includes reflective, expressive, or literary writing.

Whether organizational messages are internal or external, they follow the same pre-writing principles: clarify message goals and analyze the reader's needs.

WRITING FOR ORGANIZATIONS. Organizations use both internal and external messages. Both categories are equally important in an organization's daily operations. The same prewriting principles apply to each: *clarify message goals* and *analyze the needs of the reader.*

Organizations function more effectively when they listen to employee suggestions.

Internal Messages. **Internal communication** is an exchange of information among members or employees in an organization. There are three kinds of internal organizational messages—messages that flow up, down, or horizontally.

Upward messages go from the organization members to officers in the organization or from employees to supervisors or managers. The officers or managers in an organization cannot function effectively without input from the membership or employees. Listening to membership or employee suggestions may result in new ideas for organizational improvement. Promptly addressing areas of concern helps keep them from becoming major problems. An organization that receives and responds to feedback from all levels is more likely to accomplish its goals. Examples of upward messages are informal reports, employee suggestions, formal complaints, and inquiries about operations.

Horizontal communication occurs between peers in an organization. Completion of important projects requiring teamwork depends on effective horizontal communication. Departments working on joint projects within an organization use horizontal communication. Employees communicate with co-workers to share information or to solve problems. Memoranda to justify spending resources, instructions for operating machines, explanations of graphs or tables of data, and proposed modification of organizational procedures are examples of the types of written communication that flow horizontally among peers or within work teams.

WORKPLACE CONNECTIONS

Employees work with teams in today's workplace; they communicate horizontally with co-workers to solve problems.

Downward communication flows from the top level downward in the organization, and consists of messages from the officers, supervisors, or management to members or employees. Good communication from the top levels to organization members improves morale and job performance. Written communication that flows from the top of an organizational structure may include memos or reports with such specific purposes as informing employees of retirement benefits, health insurance, and vacation policies; documenting personnel evaluations; and notifying employees of changes in procedures.

Employees understand their jobs better when an organization has good communication from the top.

External Messages. **External communication** goes to people outside the organization. Successful businesses or other organizations must communicate effectively with customers, the general public, and potential customers or members. Examples of external writing for organizations include advertisements, approval of credit applications, responses to requests, congratulatory messages, and invitations.

Organizations need external communication.

CLASSIFYING TYPES OF WRITING

1. List three written messages that you sent or received in the last two weeks. Identify the type of message and its general goal using the codes below. In the last column, write an "I" if the message was for you as an individual or an "O" if the message was written for an organization that you represent.

   Types: (1) Personal Expressive Writing, (2) Literary Writing, (3) Transactive Writing

   General Goals: (A) To inquire, (B) To inform, (C) To influence, (D) To build goodwill, (E) To entertain, (F) To engage in personal reflection.

Description of Message	Type	Goal	"I" or "O"

2. For two of the messages above, identify one or more characteristics of the reader that could have influenced the response or reaction to the message.

   Message **Characteristic(s) of the Reader**

CHAPTER SUMMARY

- The importance of clear communication—especially as technology makes communication faster and more global—makes writing skills essential.
- Before writing, you should be able to state clearly the response or action you want from your reader. Messages are written to inquire, to inform, to influence, to build goodwill, to entertain, or to record your personal thoughts.
- An effective message addresses the needs and interests of the reader; relates to the reader's educational and cultural background; and is respectful, interesting, and understandable.
- Three categories of writing are reflection or expressive, literary, and transactive. Messages may also be classified as personal or organizational writing.

1. With the goal of learning from personal reflection, write a paragraph describing how you can benefit from improving your writing competency. If you have a computer available, use word processing software to compose the paragraph. If no computer is available, write the paragraph in the space provided below. Focus on expressing your thoughts rather than on style—this is just an unedited first draft.

2. Using the unedited first draft you wrote in the exercise above, rewrite the paragraph. This time, make sure that the paragraph is written using correct grammar, spelling, punctuation, and sentence structure. If you have a computer available, use word processing software to edit the paragraph. If no computer is available, write the paragraph in the space provided below.

3. Make a list of things that you can do to improve your writing skills. Use e-mail to share this list with two members of your class. Using the items that the three of you have listed, send an e-mail message to your instructor explaining how you will improve your writing skills. In this message, briefly develop the items on the list and show how you plan to refine your writing skills. Write the names of the two classmates with whom you shared your list below.

4. For each of the following messages, give the general goal (to inquire, to inform, to influence, to build goodwill, to entertain, or to engage in personal reflection) and the specific goal.

   a. A subpoena to testify in court about a traffic accident you witnessed.

      General Goal ____________________

      Specific Goal ____________________

   b. A novel received from a friend as a gift for your birthday.

      General Goal ____________________

      Specific Goal ____________________

   c. A request for directions to the home of a friend's parents.

      General Goal ____________________

      Specific Goal ____________________

   d. A letter from a band booster club requesting your support for a fund-raising project.

      General Goal ____________________

      Specific Goal ____________________

   e. An e-mail message to a customer congratulating her on the birth of her son.

      General Goal ____________________

      Specific Goal ____________________

   f. A manual explaining the use of a computer software package.

      General Goal ____________________

      Specific Goal ____________________

5. You are planning a trip to a national park. Access *http://www.us-national-parks.net/* and review information on several national parks. Select one national park you would like to visit in the future. Write a paragraph explaining what points of interest led you to pick this national park. If you have a computer available, use word processing software to write the paragraph. If no computer is available, write the paragraph on the space provided below.

6. Indicate by writing in the blank whether the following business or organizational messages are upward, downward, or horizontal communication.

   a. Report to your supervisor ______________________

   b. Promotion acceptance message ______________________

   c. Policy statement from a manager ______________________

   d. Technical report from one branch manager to another ______________________

   e. Message from the advisor to club members about a dues increase ______________________

7. Write a paragraph explaining why it is important to identify writing goals when planning a message.

8. Write a paragraph about a topic that interests you. Before writing, indicate the general goal.

   Goal

   Paragraph

9. Your class is planning a group trip to a nearby city. You would like the chief administrator of the school to pay the costs of this trip. The administrator states that she needs a proposal to justify the trip. With a team of three other classmates, develop a short proposal for this grant.

10. Mary and Jane are good friends who live in the same city 50 miles from your residence. Jane is in a hospital 150 miles from home. Write to Mary asking for information on Jane's health condition.

11. What is the difference between general goals and specific goals? Write a paragraph explaining this difference. Include examples of each type of general goal and an example of a specific goal.

12. After studying this chapter you are interested in determining if web sites satisfy the general needs of an Internet user. Access *http://www.nationalgeographic.com/* and give an example of how this site meets the three general needs of a reader.

Correct the grammar, spelling, capitalization, punctuation, sentence structure, and word choice errors in the following sentences. Write *Correct* for sentences containing no errors.

1. Why doesn't Bob and Teresa travel in the same car when they go to the conference next week.

2. Everyone ran for their car when the rain begun.

3. Yesterday the software company hire a new president to be their leader.

4. Sabrina plays basketball and runs track, works twenty hours a week, and is a member of the French Club, the National Honor Society, and FBLA.

5. Bennie deliver the annual report to the printer before he left on a one week vacation.

6. Competent workers no how to schedule time; budget funds; and assign staff.

7. Four businesses have went bankrupt in the past 3 months because of a declining economy.

8. The union will go on strike tomorrow if it does not except their contract.

9. A engineer will survey the landscape before designing buildings.

10. The total snow fall this year was 6 inches.

CHAPTER 2

APPLYING TECHNOLOGY TO WRITTEN COMMUNICATION

Imagine a nationwide delivery service that had only trucks. The company wouldn't be able to deliver goods as quickly or as far as a service with trucks and airplanes. In many ways, a writer using only pen, pencil, paper, and typewriter is working at a disadvantage similar to the delivery service with only trucks. Advances in computer technology and computer networking allow a rapid exchange of information and collaborative writing with individuals in other locations. Access to the Internet brings to the writer's desktop a vast array of information pertinent to topics of interest. Use of application software assists the writer with grammar, language usage, easy revisions, and merging of information. E-mail and worldwide Web addresses make written messages almost instantly accessible to one or to thousands of readers.

Learning Objectives

- Recognize the importance of technology as it relates to writing, especially in the workplace.
- Select computer hardware for electronic writing tasks.
- Recognize computer software features for composing and editing.
- Identify software features that enhance the appearance of written communication.
- Locate information using the Internet.
- Describe software features that assist collaborative writing.

COMMUNICATING WITH TECHNOLOGY

You are a writer. You are refining your writing skills. Chapter 1 helped you clarify message goals and tailor the message content to the reader's needs and interests. In this chapter, you will examine features of electronic writing that can simplify the writing process, improve the appearance of the message, and assure prompt transmission to the reader. The purpose of this chapter is not to teach you how to use specific software or the Internet but to provide information that will help you select appropriate tools to use for a variety of writing applications. Checkpoints and End-of-Chapter Activities help you practice applying electronic writing.

Technology in the Workplace

A report commissioned by the U.S. Department of Labor titled *What Work Requires of Schools* describes changes in the workplace and the know-how necessary for workers to succeed on the job. This report is often referred to as the SCANS report, because the content was developed by the Secretary's Commission on Achieving Necessary Skills. It lists the ability to select technology (including computers and computer-related technologies) and to apply technology to specific tasks as one of five essential competencies. Work-

“Computers are unreliable, but humans are even more unreliable.”

—Gilb

ing with a variety of technologies is essential for efficiently managing personal daily living skills and working in all types of jobs at all levels of an organization. Why has technology become so important? The major reason is that advances in computers and communications technology let you complete complicated tasks effectively and efficiently.

Goals for Computer Technology

Learning computer software takes determination and persistence. If you are unfamiliar with word processing, desktop publishing, desktop management, and database software, set some personal goals to enroll in computer software classes or take the time to work with the tutoring features of a variety of software packages. A lack of computer technology skills places you at a disadvantage in today's world and will become even more of a handicap in the future.

SELECTING COMPUTER HARDWARE

Workplace Connections

Selecting technology is an essential task in the workplace.

The term **computer hardware** refers to the computer and equipment that attaches to it. Examples of hardware are printers, monitors, scanners, and modems. Each type of hardware is used with a computer for specific tasks.

Desktop and Portable Computers

Microcomputers are compact computers such as desktop and notebook (portable laptop) computers. These computers have wide use in homes, schools, and businesses. Computer technology continues to decrease in cost and increase in the ability to handle large volumes of information quickly. Miniature computer chips make it possible for computers to take less space and to handle more complex tasks.

Computer Networks

A LAN consists of computers connected within an organization.

Businesses and schools often connect a number of microcomputers to form a network of electronic workstations. This network is connected to a high-capacity computer called a **host computer**. Electronic workstation networks vary from user to user, but often the **host computer** connects with one or more **file servers** that store large databases. Software programs can be placed on a server and licensed for use by all workstations. This connection of microcomputers can be called a local area network (LAN). A **local area network** consists of computer equipment in a room, building, or nearby site that can communicate and share the resources of an information storage center and connect with its printers.

Users of electronic workstations with a local area network system can share information and save money by reducing the need for duplicate software programs, files, and data. The microcomputers at each workstation can be less expensive models with less storage capacity because storage of data and software programs can be handled through the host computer.

Organizations whose writers do not key their own material into a computer can have each electronic workstation connected to a central dictation system so employees can dictate their messages for clerical personnel to key into computers. Electronic workstations allow quick, easy communication with others on the network. This brings together the best information possible for preparing reports or making decisions.

Printers

Printers produce printed copies of information prepared on the computer. Most printers on the market are laser printers or inkjet color printers. Laser printers produce a high-quality image similar to professionally printed copy. Moderately priced printers for small businesses and home use include laser printers that produce 6 to 8 pages per minute of monochrome (black) type and inkjet printers that print monochrome type from 5 to 8 pages per minute and color pages from 1 to 4 pages per minute. More expensive laser printers for large businesses produce high-quality monochrome or color print. These heavy-duty laser printers produce monochrome print at a rate of 12 to 34 pages per minute and color-printed pages at a speed of 3 to 4 pages per minute. Color print on laser printers does not require special paper for fast drying. Inkjet printers require time for the ink to dry. The quality of inkjet monochrome print compares favorably with the output of laser printers.

Color copies can be produced inexpensively on an inkjet printer.

Scanners

A **scanner** takes text, pictures, or drawings and converts them to a digital format that is readable by the computer. **Digital** format means that the information is translated into numeric language consisting of combinations of ones and zeros that can be processed by the computer. When a page is scanned, it is saved in a computer software file. This file can be modified and printed. Scanners input text into a microcomputer faster than an individual can enter it on a keyboard. Other advantages of using a scanner include decreasing the chance for errors that can occur when the material is keyed and the ability to reproduce high-quality drawings and pictures as illustrations.

Scanners allow you to input text or graphics quickly and accurately.

Display Units

A monitor or **display unit** has a screen that presents in visual format the digital text, pictures, objects, drawings, or data that are being entered or processed on the computer, as well as the symbols (icons) and words that represent the functions, tools, and software available on the computer. The point of data entry on the screen is controlled by a mouse and by arrow keys on the keyboard. A **mouse** is a small hand-operated device attached to the computer that is moved to control an arrow for moving the **cursor** (the point of data entry) and to activite a software feature. A **trackball** or a **touchpad** are variations of a mouse.

Modems

Web sites on the Internet can be accessed with a modem.

A **modem** (electronic communication unit) can be attached inside or outside the microcomputer to send and receive digital messages (text and images) over telephone lines. Communication software is used with the modem to send information to and receive information from other computers. A modem enables connection of a home or small business computer with the Internet.

WRITING WITH COMPUTER SOFTWARE

Uses of microcomputers include:

- *Word Processing*
- *Spreadsheets*
- *Databases*
- *Desktop Publishing*

Computer **software** is a package of programmed instructions that enable a computer to display and process information. A software program uses machine language (digital codes) to make the computer perform specific tasks or procedures in a sequence. Four major types of computer software are *word processing, spreadsheet, database,* and *desktop publishing software.*

Word Processing Software

Text material is prepared using word processing software.

Word processing software tells the computer to function like a typewriter—but with more capabilities and options. Using word processing software gives documents a professional appearance. Document layout features allow you to choose from a wide selection of type fonts, type sizes, and spacing variations. You can delete, add, change, and move text quickly and easily. Word processing reduces the time needed to produce written communications because changes can be made without rekeying pages. The most widely used word processing packages are Microsoft Word and WordPerfect.

Spreadsheets

Spreadsheets produce worksheets and charts.

Spreadsheet software functions as a columnar worksheet. Its primary use is to organize numeric data, perform calculations, and display the data in report format or as charts and graphs. Both text and numbers can be entered and arranged. Spreadsheet software has similar features to those of word processing packages in that items can be easily moved, changed, and displayed in a variety of type styles and sizes. Creating professional charts and graphs from worksheets is easy. You select text and numbers to display, choose from a variety of chart types, enter titles, and select backgrounds. The computer displays the results as a chart. Figure 2-1 illustrates a portion of a worksheet and a chart produced from the worksheet. A chart or a worksheet (or even portions of a worksheet) can be electronically copied and pasted into documents prepared with word processing software. The most widely used spreadsheet packages are Excel and Lotus 1-2-3.

Figure 2-1
Spreadsheet and Graph

Database Software

A **database** stores information. A database file (or table) looks like a worksheet in spreadsheet software. Related items of information are stored in columns (called fields) in the table. Each row on the table represents a separate record. Suppose you have a database for your holiday card list. Each row on the database table would be a record of information about one individual. The columns in that row would have items of information such as first name, last name, street, city, state, and zip code. Columns could be added for other items such as the date a card was mailed or received and pertinent notes about events related to the individual that you may want to include in a Christmas message. From the table, separate records can be created for each individual. These records can be easily located and displayed on the computer screen and printed. Reports can be created that arrange information from the database according to the fields you select. One type of report from a database prepares mailing labels based on your selection of name and address fields. Records can be sorted by last name or sorted by mailing date. A database can store and retrieve large volumes of information and arrange selected portions of that information in various formats and combinations. Figure 2-2 shows a report generated from a database record. Access, dBase, Paradox, and File Pro are database software packages.

Reports showing selected items of information can be produced using database software.

Figure 2-2
A Record and a Report Printed from a Book Collection Database

Desktop Publishing

Desktop publishing produces professionally designed publications.

Desktop publishing software is used to prepare layouts and designs for brochures and other publications. This type of software can be thought of as advanced word processing software. In fact, the more sophisticated word processing programs now perform almost all functions of desktop publishing packages. One function that is particularly useful with desktop publishing is the ability to work on facing pages in order to arrange elements, such as text and pictures, for fit and pleasing design. Desktop publishing software requires more microcomputer memory than word processing software does. **Memory** is the temporary storage space used by the computer to perform tasks. While the software is being used, the program giving instructions to the microcomputer must be held in the working memory along with other information being entered by the writer. The more complex the tasks performed by the software, the larger the microcomputer memory must be. Much of the material for a publication can be prepared in word processing and transferred to desktop publishing software for final arrangement and editing of layout. The main advantage of desktop publishing is its ability to produce high-quality material quickly at a low cost. Popular desktop publishing programs include Pagemaker, Quark, and In Design.

SELECTION OF WRITING OPTIONS

Match the hardware and software items in the first column to their uses as described in the second column by writing the appropriate letters in the blanks.

1. ________ Scanner
2. ________ Word processing
3. ________ File server
4. ________ LAN
5. ________ Database
6. ________ Modem
7. ________ Desktop publishing
8. ________ Electronic workstation
9. ________ Spreadsheet
10. ________ Mouse

(A) A system of connecting computer equipment in a room, building, or nearby site to share information and equipment.

(B) Computers that share files, storage, and equipment through a networked connection.

(C) Software to produce professional-quality publications.

(D) A means of connecting a home or small business computer with the Internet or of communicating with other computers.

(E) Software that stores information for locating and displaying specific items in records and reports.

(F) A computer part that moves the point of data entry on the display screen.

(G) High-capacity computer equipment used to store software and large data files as part of a computer network.

(H) Software that performs numerical calculations and displays data in graphic form on charts.

(I) Software that functions similar to a typewriter but with many more automatic features to change, correct, and enhance a document.

(J) Equipment that converts text, pictures, or drawings into a format readable by a computer.

COMPOSING AND EDITING WITH COMPUTERS

Word processing, spreadsheet, and database software have similar features for arranging information on a page (formatting) and selecting styles and sizes of fonts. The following paragraphs describe special features of computer software for composing and editing written communication.

Formatting

Different software packages have similar formatting features but can vary in menu locations and settings.

When you compose using a typewriter, you set margins, tab stops, and line spacing for your document. If you write a long manuscript, you can prepare a draft document with double spacing for ease of reviewing and editing. If you prepare a letter, you can follow an accepted letter layout, even for the initial draft. Similarly, on a computer, there are margin and tab setting, as well as other elements of document layout. All of these layout features have a **default** setting on the computer; these settings determine the layout for each document, unless you manually change the setting. Left and right margins, for instance, can have default settings of one inch. However, you can change default settings.

The specific software you use will determine how to set page-formatting features. However, there are certain features, or functions, common to these types of software. These common formatting features are described below. You can consult instructions for a specific software package by using the on-screen help features of the software. Usually, the help menu includes a choice for *Contents* and *Index*. When you make this choice on the menu, you get instructions for locating and using a specific function by keying in its name. For example, keying in the word *margins* or *tabs* would result in a display of information that would show how to use these features.

A printed page orientation can be:

- *Portrait—vertical*
- *Landscape—horizontal*

PAGE SETUP. A computer offers a number of page layout features that affect the appearance of printed communications. One of the first choices the writer has is to determine the page setup: will the final document be printed on a page with portrait or landscape orientation. A **portrait orientation** setting will print on a regular $8\frac{1}{2} \times 11$-inch letter-size sheet with the $8\frac{1}{2}$-inch width at the top. The **landscape orientation** places the paper horizontally with the 11-inch side across the top.

Headers or footers can show page numbers and document identification.

Using a menu similar to the one in Figure 2-3, you can set the page orientation, line spacing, and the top, bottom, left, and right margins. You set tab stops for indented material and *justify* the text. Justified text adjusts spacing so that both the right and the left margins are straight. Another page setup choice is selection of *page numbers* or *headers* (top of page) and *footers* (bottom of page). Inserting page numbers can be as simple as choosing the page numbers feature and selecting their placement on the page—top of the page, bottom of the page, at the left margin, at the right margin, or centered. The header and footer feature of word processing software permits information such as an abbreviated title, writer's name, and/or date with a page number to be printed on each page.

Figure 2-3
Page Setup Menu in MS Word

TYPE FONTS. Computer software gives writers a choice of a variety of type styles and type sizes. Type style is referred to on software menus as **font**. Traditional type fonts are Times New Roman, Courier, Bookman, CG Times, and Garamond. Commonly used fonts that are an open style without **serifs** (short lines at an angle to the upper and lower ends of a letter) include Ariel, Helvetica, and Universe. Type size is measured in **points**. The larger the point size, the larger the size of the type. Normal point size for most text is 12 pt. or 10 pt. Headlines are given prominence by increasing type size. Examples of some common type fonts and sizes are shown in Figure 2-4.

Helvetica	20 pt.
Times New Roman	16 pt.
Park Avenue	*24 pt.*
`Courier`	`12 pt.`

Figure 2-4
Type Font Styles and Sizes

PRINT PREVIEW. A **print preview** function in the software enables you to see the entire page layout before printing. Use of this feature saves paper that would be wasted by printing and reprinting pages in need of adjustment or change. Selecting print preview lets you see how the complete page looks before you print.

Editing Tools

In this section, you will learn the editing features common in software packages. These editing functions make editing easier and quicker.

Cut and paste moves the information from one place to another. Copy and paste duplicates the information.

The copy-and-paste function can be used to move information within a document or from file to file.

CUT, COPY, PASTE, AND UNDO. These features let you move words, sentences, and paragraphs from one place to another. Sections are moved by simply selecting and highlighting the part of the document to be moved and selecting *Cut*. The Cut function removes the selected section and places it in a special memory referred to as a **clipboard**. You can then move the cursor to where you want to insert the selected text and click on *Paste*, which takes the segment stored on the clipboard and puts it in the new location in the document. *Copy* works in a similar way as *Cut* except that the selected segment of the document that is copied to the clipboard also remains in the original location. This copied segment can be placed in more than one location in the document by moving the point of insertion and selecting Paste on the Edit menu for each insertion point. The copy-and-paste or cut-and-paste functions can be used to move sections of a document within a file or from one file to another.

Undo is another software feature. It allows you to go back to the last change made in your document. For example, if you have just inserted a drawing or picture and wish to remove it, just click on *Undo* to delete it. Also, if you accidentally delte a paragraph, undo will let you reverse that change, and brings back the deleted text.

FIND, GO TO, AND REPLACE. The *find* function gives you an opportunity to key in a word, phrase, or character and automatically go to the location where the item is found. *Replace* lets you change a word throughout the document. For example, if you have entered the abbreviation *Mrs.* in several places in the document and decide to change this to *Ms.*, the replace function will make these changes all at once. In a long document, using *go to* will let you key in the page you wish to work on and the computer will quickly show the selected page on the screen.

WORKPLACE CONNECTIONS

Spellcheck does not detect all errors—document accuracy requires careful proofreading.

SPELLCHECK AND GRAMMAR. When you have finished writing a document, you can click on the spellcheck grammar feature; and spelling and grammar will be checked and corrected throughout the document. **Spellcheck** is probably one of the most used software editing features. The spellcheck screen suggests correct spelling; you can choose to automatically change the word, ignore the suggestion, or make a manual change. Some word processing software automatically checks the spelling of all words as they are keyed into the computer and underlines words that don't match what is in the software dictionary (this does not always mean that the word is wrong). It is important to remember that you still must read the written material carefully to edit it. The software spellcheck function cannot catch all errors. For example, the software cannot distinguish between the proper use of to, two, or too. All three of these words are in its dictionary. You can add to the dictionary frequently used words that are not already in the software dictionary. Adding these words saves time because the software pauses at any word that does not match a word in the dictionary.

Word processing software can also include a **grammar check** or language feature that identifies common sentence construction errors. For example, lack of subject and verb agreement and exceptionally long sentences are marked. Remember, the spellcheck and the grammar or language features are helpers. You make the final decisions to change the text, and you need to do a final proofreading and editing. These features simply offer suggestions for part of the editing task.

THESAURUS. Writers often hunt for a word that says exactly what they mean, or they want a synonym to avoid too much repetition of the same word. By placing the cursor on a word in the document and selecting *thesaurus*, synonyms and related words will appear on the screen.

Finding the right word can be easier with a thesaurus.

WORD COUNT. Word processing software also has a feature that shows you how many words are in a document. This feature is particularly helpful when you write material that has a specified minimum or maximum number of words for the document.

SOFTWARE FEATURES FOR CHANGING AND EDITING A DOCUMENT

Key the following paragraph[1] in a computer exactly as shown using word processing software.

> The qualities of high performance that today characterize our most competative companies must become the standard for the vast majority of our companies, large and small, local and global. Buy "high performance" we mean work sittings relentlessly committed to excellence, product quality, and customer satisfaction. These goals are pursued by combining technology and people in new ways.

Make the following changes and corrections in the paragraph you just keyed in the computer.

1. Set the left and right margin for 1.2 inches.
2. Change the type size and font to 12 point CG Times or Courier.
3. Run spellcheck and proofread; then correct all errors.
4. Use the thesaurus to substitute another word for *qualities*.
5. Use Word Count to count the words in the paragraph. How many words are in the paragraph?
6. Save the paragraph in a file named SCANS.

[1] *What Work Requires of Schools: A SCANS Report for America 2000*, 1991, p. vi, The Secretary's Commission on Achieving Necessary Skills, U.S. Department of Labor. (Errors in the paragraph were added for the purposes of this Checkpoint.)

Files created with application software can be saved on a
- *hard disk drive*
- *removable diskette*
- *removable zip diskette*
- *CD optical disk*

STORING AND MANAGING INFORMATION

Having information readily available makes writing easier. The first chapter emphasized the importance of knowing your readers' characteristics and addressing their needs and interests. You can collect information for future reference or research topics of interest then save the notes from your research. You can save favorite recipes or an inventory of a stamp collection. Computer storage allows organization and ready access to information without paper clutter.

Storage Devices

Word processing, database, and spreadsheet software have saving and storage capabilities. Information can be saved in files on the computer's hard disk drive, a removable 3.5-inch diskette, a removable high capacity disk (Zip, Jazz, SyQuest), or a CD. Choosing the *save* function on your computer will let you use this storage capability and will let you choose where you want to save the data. Most computers have a disk drive that reads and writes to a 3.5-inch diskette, though some of the newer computers have drives only for the higher capacity media. All computers have an internal hard drive, though memory capacity varies widely. Newer microcomputers have memory that ranges from 4 to 8 gigabytes. A gigabyte is equal to one billion bytes. A byte represents one character (letter or number); therefore, an 8-gigabyte hard drive would store 8 billion characters or about 1.6 billion words. Remember, the hard disk drive, is used to store software programs as well as files you create. The software you install on your hard drive requires major storage space and reduces memory available for storing your data files. The 3.5-inch removable diskette holds up to 2 megabytes (or 2 million characters) and is a storage medium that can be carried from one place to another. For example, you can work on your home computer to start a writing project and then carry the disk to work or to school to finish your writing.

Graphics and photographs require much greater storage space than text does.

Photographs, pictures, graphics, and videoclips can be inserted and stored in a computer file. A document with color photographs, complicated graphics, or full-motion video requires a greater storage than a diskette has. Greater storage capacity is available on a CD optical disk or a laser videodisk. A CD is a compact disk that can store up to 650 megabytes. Many computers are equipped with a CD ROM drive—a disk drive that reads but cannot write (save) to a CD. CD ROM stands for "compact disk read only memory." A disk drive that reads and writes to an optical disk can be connected to a computer as an external device. The laser videodisk is one answer to high-storage capacity requirements for multimedia. A laser videodisk stores sound and visual images by using a laser to create billions of characters.

Data Management Devices

Personal Information Management *(PIM)* software is a tool that helps you store, organize, and retrieve personal data that you need to conduct business or your personal daily living tasks. Common items found in PIM software packages include a calendar for recording appointments or a list of jobs to be done, a journal, an address book, electronic clock, calculator, notepad, and world clock. Sidekick is an example of an inexpensive (less than $100) PIM software package that takes only about 6 megabytes of storage on your computer hard disk drive. Other examples of personal organizers are PalmPilot™, Lotus Organizer, and Schedule+. Packages such as Microsoft Outlook are part of a software suite that bundles together software for word processing, spreadsheets, and database. This package includes additional features for sending, receiving, and tracking electronic notes and messages.

PIM software organizes daily tasks.

Other electronic information management tools include a **Personal Digital Assistant** *(PDA)*, a hand-held computer that can accept handwritten commands and messages. A variety of hand-held personal computers are available. The smARTwriter® has handwriting recognition and voice recognition for certain computer commands. CrossPad XP is an electronic tablet with a paper notepad on top and a special pen with a radio transmitter. As you write notes on the paper, these notes are saved electronically and can be transferred to files in your desktop computer. These palm-size computers can also store addresses, phone numbers, and notes. In addition, they can use a phone line to connect with your e-mail and receive messages while you are traveling.

PDA's are hand-held limited-function computers.

Cassette recorders and dictation equipment can help writers capture their thoughts more quickly and more easily than doing it by hand. Recorder technology has improved in recent years with better sound quality and microphone sensitivity, lower cost, and smaller size. Portable recorders are small enough to fit into a pocket and can be used by the message originator while walking, driving, or riding in an automobile or airplane. Writers can dictate their thoughts into a portable recorder. Later they can listen to the recording and transcribe (key into the computer or write) the words. The primary disadvantage to this system is the long time it takes to replay the recording and convert the content into written form or key it into the computer. The Sony IC Chip Recorder is a palm-size device that saves voice recording in digital format. This feature lets the recorder link with your desktop or laptop computer to download and e-mail your messages and memos.

PRINTING MESSAGES

Information that is keyed into a computer is displayed on the monitor for editing and revisions. Print preview lets the writer see the layout of the information on the page. After the writer completes the document, the next step is to produce a printed copy.

Both expensive and inexpensive printers provide many options for printing.

Printing the Message

The *print* dialogue box for your software provides a number of options. You can choose which pages to print—all pages, the page on the screen, or multiple page numbers from the document. Depending on your printer, you may be able to select color or grayscale, or quality of printing, from low resolution to high. The other choice for printing is the number of copies to be printed.

To make a large number of copies, it is cheaper to use a copying machine or offset printer. Today, photocopiers can print on both sides of the paper, automatically feed original manuscript sheets into the machine, duplicate, collate the copies, staple the copies, and transmit documents to another copier via telephone lines. Photocopier capabilities include accurate reproduction of colors and enlargement or reduction of reproduced images.

Word processing and database software format addresses from a mailing list for printing on a variety of mailing label sizes or envelopes. Merge capabilities can be used to prepare a form letter and insert addresses and information from a database file.

SENDING THE MESSAGE

The primary choices for sending written messages are traditional mail, e-mail, fax, or Internet Web page. The audience receiving the message and the purpose of the message are primary considerations when choosing which way to send written communication.

Traditional mail is best for formal communication or when original documents must be sent.

Traditional Mail

Compared to e-mail and fax, traditional mail is slow. In the world of e-mail users, traditional mail is sometimes called "snail mail." However, mail services have the advantage of sending an original copy. If an original signature is required, this is your only option. Another factor in your consideration is purpose—traditional mail is a more formal way of presenting your message than e-mail is. Within the U.S., First-class or Priority Mail reaches its destination in about three days. Express Mail, Federal Express, or United Parcel Service are mail delivery services that can get the message to the recipient anywhere in the U.S. overnight or anywhere in the world in 2 or 3 days.

Fax

"Fax" is a shortened form of "facsimile," which means "an exact copy." when you need to send an exact copy—for example, to show a map, a sketch, or formatting that would not work via e-mail—you can "fax" an exact copy of the document quickly and easily to anyone else who has fax equipment. The image arrives at the receiving fax machine almost the same instant you are sending it.

There are two ways to send a fax: using a stand-alone fax machine or using a computer with a modem and fax software. The computer option can only send documents actually on the computer, though it can receive faxes from either a computer or a fax machine. The stand-alone fax machine can scan any sheet of printed material, convert the printed images into electronic impulses, and transmit the impulses over telephone lines or via satellite to another fax machine, or to a computer with fax software.

The fax machine or computer at the receiving end converts the electronic impulses back into the original images. In the case of the fax machine, it creates a printed copy of the original. With the computer, an electronic file of the original is created, which can be stored or printed. Stand-alone fax equipment does not require a computer to operate—just a phone line.

Electronic Mail

E-mail is ideal for informal communication; formal documents are often attached to e-mail messages.

Mail sent from computer to computer, either via the Internet or another, possibly local network, is referred to as **electronic mail** or **e-mail**. E-mail software gives a writer the capability to key a message at one location and send it electronically to another location. People in different time zones can send messages via computer and leave them in the "mailbox" of the receiver. E-mail allows recipients to read the message on the screen at their convenience and print it, file it electronically, or delete it. The recipient can also send a return message via e-mail. E-mail addresses are becoming almost as common as phone numbers. E-mail systems are used extensively by businesses to communicate with employees, as well as with people outside the organization. Widespread use of the Internet has made e-mail popular with people worldwide, speeding messages around the world.

REFINING THE APPEARANCE OF THE MESSAGE

When written communication is prepared on a computer, a large number of options are available for adding special features to the final copy. Word processing generally includes features for drawing an image, adding special characters, inserting photographs or pictures, and creating tables.

Shapes, Symbols, and Special Characters

Most word processing software offers a variety of shapes and lines, as well as borders and shading that are easy to add to your written document. Squares, rectangles, circles, octagons, ovals, arrows, and other shapes can be selected and inserted on the page. Once these items are added to the page, they can be moved around and enlarged or reduced. Special symbols or diacritical markings for phonetic characters can be added to words. For example, the marking over the "o" in "Björk" can be added, or the symbol ©, to indicate copyrighted material, can be added. Figure 2-5 shows examples of shapes, symbols, and special characters.

Figure 2-5
Example of Shapes, Symbols, and Special Characters

Data Tables and Columns

Word processing software can use tables to organize and present data.

You can create tables to help your reader see relationships among data items. The *table* function in word processing software gives the writer a choice of the number of columns and rows for entering data. Items in each column can be centered, begin at the left margin, or end flush with the right margin of the column. You can use software features such as shading, bold or italic type, different fonts, lines, and blocks to enhance the appearance of the table. The table separates rows and columns with gridlines—you can select an option to show these lines or remove them.

Another feature for special formatting of documents is the *column* function. Selecting columns gives you options for the number, width, and spacing of columns. This feature is useful for newsletters and brochures. You can have vertical lines separating columns or have them separated only by the space between columns. You can insert pictures and scanned photographs in the newsletter and have the type flow around them.

Style Templates

Templates are formats of frequently used documents like memos, newsletters, manuscripts, and faxes. Templates save the setup time you would spend setting margins, tabular stops, and type styles and sizes. You can create these templates and save them to use when you need them. Software packages include a number of pre-designed templates.

Templates save time for page setup of frequently used documents.

Objects and Pictures

Earlier in this chapter you learned how the functions *copy* and *paste* transfer portions of one file to another. The portion of the original document you select to move is called an object. Using *copy* and *paste* transfers the object just as it was in the original document. Later changes to this section of the original document will not change the object in its destination document. Some software allows you to copy and use a *paste special* function on the edit menu to link the copied object with the original document, so that any changes made to this part of the original document file will also change the object (transferred section) in the second document. If you do not want to link documents, *paste special* can be used to copy an object or embed an object in the new file. An *embedded object* can be selected at any time and edited in the new file. For example, you could move, size, revise, or make other changes to the copied object at any time in the new file by clicking with the mouse on the portion of the object you want to change.

Alterations in linked objects automatically change in both the original and destination documents, but alterations in embedded objects do not.

Most word processing software packages include Clip Art and WordArt. **Clip Art** is a file of simple cartoon-like pictures and drawings. Any clip art selections can be inserted into a document. **WordArt** offers special designs and spacing for the words in your text. (See Figure 2-6 for samples of WordArt and Clip Art.)

Figure 2-6
Word Art and Clip Art

Photographs can be inserted into a document using a scanner and scanning software or using a digital camera that takes pictures and stores them on a disk in digital format. Photographs or graphics such as WordArt and Clip Art, however, require much more computer memory and storage than regular text material.

Color

Computer software allows you to choose color for type, lines and boxes, clip art, and photographs. Selective use of color can attract attention to your message or emphasize important points but be careful not to overwhelm the reader by using too much color. To produce documents with color requires a printer capable of printing colors.

SOFTWARE FEATURES TO ENHANCE AND PRINT DOCUMENTS

1. Go to a computer and do the following tasks:
   a. Open a new document page in word processing.
   b. Use *WordArt* to add a centered heading COMPUTER ART in 14 pt. font of your choice.
   c. Triple space after the heading.
   d. Select a picture from *Clip Art* and insert it on the page.
   e. Size and move the picture so that it fits at the right margin.
   f. Print the page.
2. Use the table feature to create a table with three rows and two columns. Select three software features described in this chapter. Key these terms in column one of the table. In column two describe how these features can be used. Adjust the column width for the best fit.
3. Key the following sentences directly below the paragraph entered in the previous exercise. Use symbol and special character features. Print the page.
   a. Microsoft Office® 97 is a software package that includes programs for word processing,
   b. The copyright symbol © is used with printed material to indicate that unauthorized copying is illegal.
   c. The temperature yesterday was recorded at the airport as 75° F.

USING THE INTERNET AND THE WORLDWIDE WEB

The Internet is a world-wide digital network that links computers and other, smaller networks, creating a vast, accessible resource that combines communication, research, commerce and entertainment. About 50 million people use the Internet though the number increases daily. The Worldwide Web (www) is an array of *hypertext*-linked pages, databases, and files that can be accessed through an Internet connection. Hypertext is a system that organizes text pages through links. Clicking on a link takes you to another page, another file, or another database. Individuals, organizations, schools, and businesses have Web pages on the Internet.

Internet Service Providers

Individuals or companies can access the Internet by paying a monthly fee to a Internet Service Provider (ISP) who establishes and maintains the electronic connection of their computers to the Internet system. Service providers can be local companies or large communications organizations such as America Online, Microsoft Networks, General Telephone Exchange (GTE), and American Telephone and Telegraph (AT&T).

Information Searches and Web Sites

Your service provider determines the software needed to connect your computer with the Internet. Software for accessing the Internet is called a *browser*. Netscape and Microsoft Explorer are examples of browsers. Through the Internet it is possible to send and receive e-mail, enter discussion groups, talk with others on a videophone, search for information, or go to specific Web pages.

Browsers provide the user with a way to access the Internet.

You can research information on the Web by keying in a location address called a URL which stands for Uniform Resource Locator. URLs identify a specific location on the Web (e.g., *http://www.census. gov* or *http://www.irs.ustreas.gov*). Keying in a web address and pressing ENTER on the keyboard or clicking the START or GO button on the screen will take you to the Web page you selected. For example, the first URL above takes you to the U.S. Government census home Web page. The ending of the URL is the domain field and represents the type of site. Government addresses end with *gov*; universities and other educational institutions end with *edu*; and commercial and industrial organizations end with *com*. Nonprofit organizations end with *org*. Web pages have an outline of resource items that serve as hypertext links to other information. Clicking on a link with the mouse takes you to another page of information. These hypertext links are shown in color and underlined.

URLs are a quick way to research information on the Internet.

Browser software conducts searches based on areas of interest and specific topics. You can choose from a number of search engines such as Alta Vista, Yahoo, Web Crawler, and Lycos. After you select a search engine, you are given a list of categories to search. You can choose from listings such as *education and reference*, *health*, *business*, *home and family*, *sports*, or *computers and technology*. The choice you make will bring a list of types of information. You can make an additional selection from this list or you can key in a word or words in the blank shown by the word *Search* and click on the word *Go*. For example, to find information on real estate, you could select Alta Visa, select *business*, key in the words *real estate*, and you will get 20 real estate sites from which to select.

COLLABORATING WITH OTHER WRITERS

WORKPLACE CONNECTIONS

Most jobs require employees to work as team members, working cooperatively with others. Each person contributes to the group with ideas, suggestions, and effort.

Computer technology lets workers in different locations communicate and work cooperatively. You have probably heard the saying "Two heads are better than one." Employers encourage cooperation and collaboration in completing tasks and solving problems. Writing tasks can be developed jointly with two or more people. Teams at work or committees in organizations often work together to analyze problems, brainstorm, and draft reports. Two or more people can draft a letter, write an article, complete a cooperative project, or help improve one another's writing by reading it and making suggestions. E-mail, special features of the Internet, and word processing software features help writers collaborate to edit, add notes, and share files.

"Team spirit is what gives so many companies an edge over their competitors."

—George L. Clements.

E-mail lets team members work collaboratively from different locations.

E-Mail for Collaboration

Use e-mail to send documents to colleagues for review and suggestions. The e-mail addresses can be entered in the e-mail address book on your computer. The address book lets you send messages to all members by selecting the group name. A short document for review can be keyed in the e-mail message block. Your recipients can use the *reply* function to answer you. When *reply* is used, the original sender's e-mail address is automatically entered and the previous message is shown in the message block. Each person receiving the message could make changes in the document and return it to the sender. If the message is a long document and has been prepared using word processing or other software program that all recipients have, you can send the document as an attachment to your e-mail. Recipients of your attachment simply click on the *attachment* icon to open it, add notes, edit, and send it back with the reply. When you work in an organization with networked computers, a *public file* can be set up in e-mail that all people on the organization's e-mail system can access. If changes are made, the file can be saved under a new name that identifies the employee who reviewed it. Setting up electronic *mailboxes* or *folders* for major projects allows all e-mail received for these projects to be transferred to the appropriate mailbox or folder.

Another e-mail feature is a *listserv*. Everyone who signs on the listserv receives all of the messages sent to the listserv address. Using the Reply function with an e-mail listserv sends the reply to everyone on the listserv. If you want to send a message only to one individual on the listserv, you can do so by entering that individual's e-mail address rather than the listserv address.

Software Features for Collaboration

Word Processing software has features designed to help people who are working together. These features include *Versions*, *File Sharing*, *Notes*, and Web pages. Microsoft Word includes a save option called *Versions* under the file menu. This option lets you save the same file after review and changes by other people. Each version is identified with date and time, who saved it, and comments. Different individuals in an organization with a networked system and shared files on a server can work on the same document saved under different versions and review each other's changes. Without the *Versions* feature, individuals working in the same file could save the document with a name that identified the author and send it to other members of the writing team as an attachment to e-mail. Some software allows notes to be attached within the document by a co-author or writing team member by clicking *Comments* under *Insert* on the menu. The point where the note was entered will be highlighted in the document. When the cursor is held over the highlighting, the note appears. In effect, these notes are electronic "post-it notes." Another way responses to a document can be solicited from various people is by creating a Web page with links that allow comments or responses to be recorded.

Application software offers special features that help team collaboration.

THE INTERNET AND WEB PAGES

Use a computer connected to the Internet to complete the following tasks:

1. Key in this URL: *http://www.lib.byu.edu/byline.html*
   a. Select Database and Periodical Indexes.
   b. Select Subject List.
   c. Select General, Multi-Discipline & News.
   d. Select Writing Style Manuals.
   e. Select APA Format.
   f. Select typical Book Entry and print this page.
2. Use a search engine such as Yahoo or Alta Vista to locate an art museum. With the browser you are using, if Yahoo does not appear as a search engine choice, you can key in this URL: *http://www.yahoo.com* to retrieve it for use. Read any legal or copyright information on the museum home page to be sure you do not violate copyright law if you print a picture. Take a virtual tour. Select a picture that you like and print it if there was no legal restriction on copying.

CHAPTER SUMMARY

- Technology is an essential workplace competency. Complicated tasks can be completed effectively and efficiently through the use of technology.
- Computer hardware that is available includes:

  —Computers—file server, desktop, notebook, and handheld

  —Printers—laser and ink jet

  —Mouse—hand operated, track ball, and touch pad

  —Modem—internal and external

  —Scanner
- Computer software allows the writer to select formatting features such as page setup and typeface. Other features such as copy and paste, find and replace, spellcheck, and thesaurus help to edit documents.
- Document appearance can be enhanced by using special software features such as symbols, characters, tables, columns, graphs, templates, pictures, and color.
- Information from Web sites worldwide can be accessed through Internet Uniform Resource Locators (URLs) or by search engines such as Yahoo or Alta Vista.
- Electronic transmission of messages and special software features let work teams develop written documents.

1. In the following situations, imagine that all software and hardware tools discussed in this chapter are available. Which would be the best choice in each situation and why?

   a. Alex and Matthew are working together on an article for the school newspaper that is due in ten days. Alex will have two days to put together some rough notes in outline form; then, Matthew will have four days to develop the first draft. After Alex has had a day to read the material, they will work together on the final draft, which they expect to be about 1,000 words.

      Suggested technology

      Advantages

   b. A department in a large company wants to set up individual computer workstations for office workers and a network to let them use the same computer software and share centrally stored information.

      Suggested technology

      Advantages

   c. Desiree is a busy executive who makes frequent business trips. She needs equipment to take with her so that she can write letters and reports on the trip. She wants this equipment to send documents to her secretary so final documents can be on her desk when she returns to the office.

      Suggested technology

      Advantages

   d. Karen has organized a white elephant sale to raise money for her soccer team. She wants to distribute flyers around campus to let everyone know when and where the sale will be held and also to create interest in it.

      Suggested technology

      Advantages

e. Greg has been given the job of updating an employee handbook. Even though the handbook is a year old, most policies are still in effect, and only minor revisions are needed. The current handbook was prepared by a local print shop that is now out of business.

   Suggested technology

   Advantages

2. You are interested in purchasing a Fax machine. Access the Web to gather information about the features of different models of Fax machines. Write an e-mail to your instructor, based on the information, recommending purchase of a model for a small, low-budget office that has infrequent need for sending and receiving faxed messages. Give facts needed to support your recommendation.

3. You are working for a small family-owned business that has no modern technology. You feel that the purchase of computer hardware and software would be a good investment for this business. Outline points that you would use to convince the owner of the importance of technology in the workplace.

4. Using a computer, key the following paragraph exactly as shown.

   Americans' economic well-being and quality of life have become dependent on technology. The SCANS definition of technological competence requires workers to have the abillity to understand computers, machines, and other tools; to use them to solve problems; to select computers, machines, and tools; and to maintain them through troubleshooting skills. Selecting appropriate technology to fit the sitaution is a form of problem solving, because the desired outcomes and constraints define the problem, while the solution is the procedure, technilogy, or tool chosen to get the job done. Applying technology implies an understanding of the overall intent and purpose of the technology.*

   Use the appropriate software features and visually proofread the results to make these changes and corrections:

   —Set the left margin for 1.5 inches and the right margin for 2.0 inches.

   —Change the font to 14 point Arial.

   —Use the thesaurus to substitute another word for *workers.*

   —Run spellcheck and proofread; then correct all errors.

   —Save the paragraph in a file named TECHNOLOGY.

   —Print the paragraph.

5. Go to a computer and open the file TECHNOLOGY which was created above and do the following tasks:

   —Center heading IMPORTANCE OF TECHNOLOGY in 18 pt. font of your choice.

   —Double space after the heading.

   —Italicize and bold the word SCANS.

   —Select an image from Clip Art and insert it on the page.

   —Size the image to approximately two inches and center it under the text.

   —Insert a footer with your name flush with the right margin.

*This paragraph came from page 5 in Donna R. Everett's article "Teaching the SCANS Competencies in Business Education," Delta Pi Epsilon Instructional Strategies—An Applied Research Series, Volume 11, Number 3, September 1995. Errors in this paragraph were not in this publication but were added for the purposes of this exercise.

6. For the following situations, choose the electronic technology that would provide better results and make the task easier. Explain how your choice is better and easier.

   a. Martin plans to design a sheet to post on the employee bulletin board asking that people interested in carpooling to contact him. He wants to put a picture of a car on the sheet and use an attention-getting headline.

      Technology to use

      How quality will be improved

      How preparation will be easier

   b. Susan is revising a 12-page booklet that was not previously stored on a computer disk. Changes will not be major—most of the original text and pictures will be used in the revision.

      Technology to use

      How quality will be improved

      How preparation will be easier

7. Edit the following paragraph. Circle misspelled words. Above the misspelled words, write the correct spelling. Explain how using a computer with word processing software would simplify editing this paragraph.

   Good writrs are made not born. Adults have practised writing in one form or another since childhood. In kindergarten and first grade, children begin to make crudely printed leters. Later, they begin cursive writing. In elementery school, students can begin to use the computer to write stories and essays.

   How computer software can help in editing

8. Match the collaborative writing software features in the first column to the descriptions listed in the second column by writing the appropriate letters in the blanks.

   1. ________ Public file
   2. ________ Message block
   3. ________ Folders
   4. ________ Reply
   5. ________ Attachment
   6. ________ Address book
   7. ________ Versions
   8. ________ Comments

   (A) Permits recipients of a message to respond to sender, making changes or comments as necessary.

   (B) Method to send a message via e-mail that was prepared with word processing software.

   (C) Can be referred to as electronic "post-it notes."

   (D) An e-mail feature where a short document can be keyed in.

   (E) Permits committee members to review each other's changes to a message.

   (F) Used in an organization with networked computers so all persons on the e-mail system can access easily.

   (G) Permits you to send a message to everyone on the listserv.

   (H) Permits e-mail messages to be grouped according to projects.

Correct the grammar, spelling, capitalization, punctuation, sentence structure, and word choice errors in the following sentences. Write *Correct* for sentences containing no errors.

1. Sara won the senior citizen of the year award for her Community Service work.

2. The Telephone Company replaced their coaxial cable with fiber optics.

3. Our population consist of people from many different countries, therefore workers need interpersonal skills that enable him or her to work comfortably with colleagues from deverse backgrounds.

4. When Felix completes the tax return, he will make copies before mailing it.

5. Do you think that being a rail-road enginear shall be a good paying job?

6. On July 2, 2001 the band booster club will host a car show featureing both new and old-fashioned cars at the local high school cafeteria.

7. Simon do not know nobody at the university registrars' office who can help him with his transcript.

8. The computer programmer is a real smart person that can make a computer do almost anything.

9. We will drive to Norfolk, Virginia next Wendsday if the ice is melted off.

10. Molly is a very dishonest person whose been hired as a bankteller.

ANALYZING WRITING PRINCIPLES

CHAPTER 3

It was said that W.C. Fields, the comedian, found cause to deplore the lack of an adequate bookstore near his California residence. He approached a leading community member and gave a high-powered sales talk on the advantages of opening such a store for the local trade. "Thirty thousand will do it," said Fields with conviction. Surely you can raise such an insignificant sum at the drop of a hat." The young man allowed that it was a fine idea and that he would like nothing better than to open a well-stocked bookstore. "I think I can get my hands on about $20,000," he told Fields. "As for that remaining $10,000, how about your putting it up for me?" "Under ordinary circumstances," Fields assured him, "nothing would give me greater pleasure. At the moment, however, I find myself in rather a strange predicament. All of my available funds are completely tied up in ready cash."

—from Cerf, B. (1956). *Bennett Cerf's Bumper Crop*, Garden City, NY: Garden City Books, p. 454–455

APPLY THE WRITING Cs—NOT Zzzz

Use the 4 Cs of writing to get the reader interested—not bored! Write clear, concrete, concise, and complete messages. A clear message is expressed in words that are easily understood. *Concrete* words are exact—they attract and keep the reader's attention. A *concise* message eliminates unnecessary words. A *complete* message has just enough information to express your thoughts.

LEARNING OBJECTIVES

- Write clear, concrete, concise, and complete messages.
- Use unbiased language.
- Organize message components for thought flow and unity.
- Develop an effective writing style.

Clear Messages and Concrete Words

Clear writing comes from clear thinking. Keep asking yourself two questions: "What am I trying to say?" and "Did I say it?" Consult a dictionary or thesaurus for words that precisely express your meaning. Most word processing software has a dictionary and thesaurus. Use these resources for word choice. In addition, clear messages are accurate. An accurate message reflects careful editing to correct errors that detract from the message. Accuracy depends not only on word choice but also on correct information.

Clear writing comes from clear thinking.

A dictionary and a thesaurus are basic references for writing.

Specific, simple words send a clear message.

Concrete words help readers form an exact reflection of what the writer intends to convey. For example, the words *four men* are more descriptive than the words *several people*. The word *roses* is more specific than *flowers*. *Dancing* is more specific than *moving*. Concrete words appeal to the senses—sight, smell, hearing, taste, or touch. *Table* is a concrete word because you can see and touch a table. Concrete words will not always be appropriate. *Idea* is abstract because it cannot be experienced directly through one of the five senses, but it has meaning in your mind. However, use concrete words instead of abstract words whenever you can. Avoid vague terms that mean different things to different people. General terms such as *very*, *most*, *some*, *little*, *practically all*, and *few* are vague because they have many different interpretations. How many items is a *few*—a dozen or a hundred? The meaning depends on whether you mean 12 out of 14 or 12 out of 1,000; 100 out of 150 or 100 out of 10,000.

You convey a clearer message by using simple, everyday language—not long, obscure words. For example, use *end* rather than *terminate*; *distribute* or *send* rather than *disseminate*; and *think* rather than *ratiocinate*. Do not try to impress your reader with your vocabulary. Be sure the language of the message fits the reader's knowledge and background. Write in a conversational (not slangy) manner that is easily understood by your reader.

Concise and Complete Messages

A message is complete when just enough information is given to make the meaning clear.

Make the message concise, but complete. Say what needs to be said and no more. When you write, use only words that contribute to the meaning of the message. Be sparing with words; develop your sentences and paragraphs carefully. Practice word economy—if you don't need it, don't use it. If one word conveys the meaning, do not use two. The following expressions illustrate redundant words—words that repeat the meaning. Unnecessary words are in italics.

"Brevity is the soul of wit."

—Shakespeare

consensus *of opinion*	8 p.m. *in the evening*
every word *used* in a message	Both *of the two* boys
all *of the* facts	palette *of many colors*

Eliminate unnecessary adjectives and adverbs. Avoid trite expressions such as *trendsetter*, *hard facts*, *point in time*, and *timely fashion*. Also, forming verbs from nouns (such as *impact* and *prioritize*) is not a good practice. You will find that removing these terms makes your writing more powerful.

Check for completeness by asking "Have I answered the reader's questions?"

Test the completeness of the message by asking, "Did I say what I meant to say? Have I answered the reader's questions?"

WORD CHOICE

1. Keep in mind the need for clearness, concreteness, and simplicity. From the word choices shown in parentheses, circle the best word or words for the sentences below and write the reason for your choice.
   a. The shadows (moved, fluttered) along the wall.

   b. Interpersonal competence (minimizes, reduces) friction between workers and makes working together more pleasant.

   c. The lack of funds may be (seen, perceived) as lack of interest.

   d. He tripped and (fell, rolled) down the stairs.

   e. The (older, silver-haired) woman left the room quickly.

   f. The (lovely, pink fluorescent) sunset gradually faded into darkness.

   g. When she became angry, she (left, stamped out of) the room.

   h. The robber (waved, brandished) a gun.

   i. We took (a trip, an excursion) down the Mississippi River on a houseboat.

   j. The (shining, glistening) stars were like diamonds in the steel-gray sky.

(continued on next page)

(continued)

2. Rewrite the following sentences to eliminate unnecessary words, avoid trite expressions, and correct errors.

   a. The news came as sort of a surprise to us.

   b. Tell me just exactly what you mean by that statement.

   c. Try to maximize the impact of your writing by careful word choice.

   d. She owns her own home.

   e. I am very excited about the new job.

   f. Tell me a little bit more about yourself.

   g. Come by to see the paintings in the art museum.

   h. Nothing is so unpleasant to a person as to see some other person behave in a rude manner toward someone else.

   i. Can you eliminate the use of a large number of words with no use in the sentence by carefully selecting the words to be used and by cutting unnecessary words out of the sentence?

   j. Job performance that is based on basic skills and personal qualities that are essential preparation for all students should many times be taught in all of our schools.

USING UNBIASED LANGUAGE

Use terms and expressions that do not stereotype people. Stereotyping disregards individual capabilities and assumes that everyone in a group fits the same pattern and has the same abilities. Think of *people first* and avoid gender-specific pronouns in most cases when referring to people in general.

Think of people as individuals, equal but different.

Gender References

Masculine and feminine pronouns often imply stereotypical thinking—men are leaders or women are homemakers. Content can be biased, too. For example, token opinions can be expressed as universal or an issue can be presented without giving all of the facts.

Do not use stereotyped language.

NOUN AND PRONOUN CHOICES. Avoid using a male pronoun for unspecified gender by eliminating the pronoun, repeating the noun, using a plural noun and pronoun, changing from active to passive voice, using proper nouns, or including both masculine and feminine pronouns.

Reword sentences to avoid he or she.

Eliminate the Pronoun. Change the pronoun to one of the articles *a*, *an*, or *the*.

Biased: A student should determine *his* college major during his freshman year.

Unbiased: A student should determine *a* college major during *the* freshman year.

The pronoun can be omitted without substituting another word.

Biased: If a taxpayer pays *his* taxes by April 15, the late payment penalty is avoided.

Unbiased: If a taxpayer pays taxes by April 15, the late payment penalty is avoided.

An unbiased pronoun can be substituted for *he* in some sentences.

Biased: Anyone having *his* name called must report at once.

Unbiased: Anyone *whose* name is called must report at once.

Reword the sentence to eliminate the need for a pronoun.

Biased: The teacher who has pride in *his* profession keeps *his* teaching skills updated.

Unbiased: The teacher with professional pride keeps updated in teaching skills.

Repeat the Noun. The best alternative to the use of *he* may be to repeat the noun.

Biased:	If the juror does not get all facts, *he* cannot make a fair decision.
Unbiased:	If the juror does not get all facts, *the juror* cannot make a fair decision.

Plural pronouns must refer to plural nouns.

Use a Plural Noun and Pronoun. Changing a singular antecedent noun and pronoun to the plural form avoids the use of *he*. Be careful to maintain agreement in number with the antecedent and verbs. A singular pronoun refers to a singular noun and requires a singular verb; a plural antecedent requires a plural pronoun and a plural verb.

Biased:	An *individual* leaving home for the first time has *his* lonely moments.
Incorrect Pronoun:	An *individual* leaving home for the first time has *their* lonely moments.
Unbiased:	*Individuals* leaving home for the first time have *their* lonely moments.

Passive voice or proper nouns are ways to avoid gender pronouns.

Change from Active to the Passive Voice. Although the active voice is generally preferred, the passive voice can be the best solution in some sentences to avoid use of a gender-biased pronoun.

Biased:	The manager called *his* employees to *his* office.
Unbiased:	The employees were called to the manager's office.

Use Proper Nouns. As shown above, special care must be taken with general statements; however, factual statements may indicate gender without being considered biased.

John Wiggins called his employees to his office.
Reiko Umeki called her employees to her office.

Use Masculine and Feminine Pronouns. If rewording the sentence causes awkward phrasing, include the feminine pronoun.

Biased:	A surviving spouse with a personal annuity may designate *his* child as beneficiary.
Unbiased:	A surviving spouse with a personal annuity may designate *his* or *her* child as beneficiary.

APPROPRIATE GROUP REFERENCES. In writing which refers to all people, regardless of gender, avoid the use of *man*, *men*, and *mankind*. Acceptable substitutes are *human*, *person*, *people*, *human race*, *women and men*, *men and women*, *individuals*, and *humanity*.

Biased: *Mankind* has progressed significantly in the last decade.

Unbiased: *The human race* has progressed . . . or *Humanity* has progressed. . . .

A genderless term for specific groups of people should be substituted for words such as *man* and *mankind* when the sentence pertains to one group of people more than to others. Using a specific people word appropriate to the sentence meaning may add concrete language and clarity, as well as, avoid gender-bias.

Biased: Man seeks to understand theories of the formation of the Earth.

Unbiased: Scientists seek to understand theories of the formation of the Earth.
(*Scientists* refers to a specific group of people without gender reference and is appropriate for the sentence content.)

Avoid the words that stereotype any group of people, whether you are referring to individuals or to groups of individuals. This applies for age classifications, disabilities, and other cultures or religions. Avoid group-specific references unless this characteristic is germane to what is being said. Examples of age specific terms to avoid are *senior citizens*, *teeny boppers*, and *yuppies*. If an age reference is important to the meaning, it is better to state a specific age or say "people over 65."

An individual should not be referred to by a disability: for example, "an epileptic." If the disability is important to what is being said, it is better to say "a person who has epilepsy." Use words that emphasize the individual, not the disability.

When references are made to people from other countries or cultures, the writer should determine the appropriate reference or individual's personal preferences. Also, avoid references to economic class, geographic region, and physical characteristics unless these characteristics are germane to the sentence.

Avoid masculine words to describe generic terms.

Unbiased References for All Individuals

Respect for all people implies more than gender. Our country is made up of people with different ages, cultures, and religions. In addition, international communication is a part of everyday business for large corporations. An awareness of differences is a part of understanding an audience. Learning about other cultures will improve your ability to communicate effectively with a diverse population.

WORKPLACE CONNECTIONS

Employees should understand their own work in the context of the diverse work audience around them.

Words may have different meanings in different countries. Even the way parts of speech are used vary culturally. Japanese place the verb at the end of a sentence. First names are used in Germany only by close friends and relatives. If you are writing to an audience that includes other cultures, learning about these cultures becomes essential to knowing how to address the reader. Learning about the people with whom you communicate shows respect for them. Respect for all people is the basis of unbiased communication. The content of the message reflects the terminology, and the sentence structure should reflect this respect. In spite of differences, avoid making assumptions about the capabilities of specific groups of people. Base your message on knowledge and respect for the reader.

USING UNBIASED LANGUAGE

Rewrite the following sentences to avoid biased language:

1. A nurse must give good bedside care to her patients.

2. A student may have all A's, but he may not have gained the skills needed to perform on a job.

3. Man has advanced technology rapidly in the twentieth century.

4. A scientist spends long hours in his laboratory.

5. A doctor earns the respect of his patients by his caring attitude.

6. A parent must help his children to follow rules but still feel his love.

7. Any lawyer worthy of her training must follow a code of ethics with her clients.

8. The task of a teacher is not easy, but she can be rewarded by sharing in the success of her students.

9. Now is the time for all good men to come to the aid of their country.

10. If anyone thinks he can pass the course without studying, he will be disappointed.

ORGANIZING A UNIFIED MESSAGE

Good writing offers a smooth flow of ideas. The reader can move easily through the message if ideas connect in a logical sequence. Message unity and thought flow are achieved through planning. Organization is the key.

WORKPLACE CONNECTIONS

Organizing ideas is a basic skill that is important in the workplace.

Organizing and Planning

Well-organized writing reflects an outline with logical topics and subtopics.

Examine letters, news items, and other writing you enjoy. Notice the sequence of the ideas and how they are linked. If the message is well-organized, you should be able to prepare an outline of the major ideas as you read the material. As you read each document, you should find a logical progression of major topics. Following each major topic you will probably find two or more subtopics. These subtopics describe details about the major topics. If you are reading a story or an article, you may note that the main headings and paragraph headings form an outline.

Before you begin to write a message, make a tentative outline and choose the major topics to cover. These major topics are the basic skeleton of your message. What they are and how they are sequenced depends on the contents of the message, your purpose for writing the message, and the intended audience. Imagine you are writing a letter to your city council representative explaining a problem that you want resolved by the council. Your outline could have these major topics:

1. The problem to be resolved
2. Why the problem is important
3. A brief history of the problem
4. An appeal for help in solving the problem

Preparing a tentative outline helps organize a message.

Each of these topics could be subdivided. The number and content of topics and subtopics should be limited with in-depth coverage of an area included only if it serves a purpose in persuading the council to respond positively. Items can be changed, deleted, or placed in a different order if you see a more effective structure when you begin to write. Outlining will be addressed further in Chapter 4.

Message Structure

The basic structure of a message consists of three parts: a beginning, a middle, and an ending. Think of the beginning as a first impression and the ending as a last impression. The middle, usually called the body of the message, provides the important details. Your message will be stronger with proper use of these structural elements.

A unified message has a unified beginning, body, and end.

Understanding the purpose played by each basic part helps you to write a unified message. The reader looks quickly for the main point of the message. A good rule of thumb is to start the message with a clear, brief statement of the main point. The body of the message presents ideas related to the main point. The ending states or restates the action the reader should take or presents a conclusion or solution you want the reader to remember. The beginning and ending are critical parts of any writing. The beginning must attract the interest of the reader, and the ending should relate the message to the reader (what should the reader do or think) or reinforce the main point.

Writing the beginning with a you viewpoint helps include information about what the reader wants to know.

MESSAGE BEGINNING. A good beginning to a message states the main point in terms of benefit to the reader. Using the you viewpoint emphasizes the importance of the reader and helps the writer make decisions about what the reader wants to know. Below are examples of effective and ineffective beginnings:

A good beginning states the benefit to the reader and the main idea of the message.

Ineffective: We are starting a Health Walk program for our employees. After an employee has registered for the program, a Walk Log will be sent for recording the weekly mileage.

Effective: You can improve your fitness and become eligible for a $1,000 travel certificate by joining the Health Walk program for employees.

Ineffective: On the average, research shows that people are inefficient listeners and remember only about 10 percent of what they hear. We have some simple techniques to improve listening skills.

Effective: Are you a good listener? According to research, people remember only about 10 percent of what they hear. A few simple techniques can help you improve your listening skill.

Ineffective: We have received the request for replacement of defective parts in your washing machine. We are now processing the claim through our claims department, and you should receive a check for $255 within ten days.

Effective: You will receive a check for $255 to cover the replacement parts for your washing machine. Your request is being processed under the five-year warranty. The check should be in your hands within ten days.

Notice that the effective beginning relates the message directly to the reader. All three openings draw the reader in, but two show how effective beginning can be when the good news is given in the first sentence.

BODY OF THE MESSAGE. The content between the beginning and ending of the message adds important information to answer reader questions. These paragraphs may also cover subtopics and use examples to support conclusions. Deciding what to include goes back to two primary questions: What does the reader want to know? What information is necessary to get the intended reader response?

The body of the message adds the information to answer the reader's questions and leads to the ending conclusion.

MESSAGE ENDING. End the message with a strong conclusion, an action that you want the reader to take, or a solution to problems posed by the main point of the message. Effective and ineffective endings are illustrated below:

A strong ending should make the reader respond the way the writer intended.

Ineffective: We hope that you will consider this request to contribute to our local Habitat project to build homes for the needy. People in our community need our help. We are enclosing a return envelope for the donation. Please make your check payable to Community Habitat.

Effective: Your contribution to the local Habitat project will help build homes for the needy in your community. You can help by sending your donation by July 1. Please make your check payable to Community Habitat and return it in the enclosed envelope.

Ineffective: Remember, using word processing is much easier than typing a message. With typed messages, changes are a major ordeal. We believe computer and word processing software should be everyone's writing tool.

Effective: You will enjoy the ease of making changes with computer word processing software. Your writing will become easier and better when you begin to use this writing tool.

Ineffective: We hope to see you at the meeting. Notice should be sent to us by October 1 if you cannot attend.

Effective: Your attendance at the meeting is important. Please call by October 1 if you cannot attend. We look forward to having you participate.

MESSAGE STRUCTURE

1. Rewrite these two beginning paragraphs for messages to emphasize benefits to the reader. If you have access to a computer, use the computer to complete these exercises. If not, you may use the space provided below each exercise.

   a. Our policy is to make funds deposited in our bank available to the customer on the first business day after we receive the deposit. We are able to assure the accuracy of each day's transactions by following this policy. We know you appreciate having an accurate record of your funds.

   b. Seventy-five percent of the workforce will need retraining before the year 2010. We are presenting a conference in Miami on October 15 to deal with this issue. Attendance at this conference will help participants avoid problems with being employable.

2. Rewrite the following ending paragraphs to make them more effective:

   a. I am looking for a prompt response. Thanking you in advance for sending information on health care insurance, I remain

   b. To become more familiar with opportunities for computer programmers, you should, we believe, talk to people in the field. We suggest you find out more about this field by doing just that.

Consistent Verb Tense

Consistent verb tense contributes to message unity. Remember, **tense** refers to the time the verb action takes place. Shifting from one tense to another in the same time frame confuses the reader.

Shifting verb tense confuses the reader.

future past
George *will read* every book he *found* about flying anytime.

past present
Flight *fascinated* him, and he *likes* to find new flight stories.

future present
He *will read* anything that *has* the word "Fly" in the title. This

future present
habit *could lead* to interesting results because even "flies" *fly*!

present present
Revised: George *reads* every book he *finds* about flying. Flight always

present present
fascinates him, and he *likes* to find new stories about it.

present present
He *reads* anything that *has* the word "Fly" in the title. This

present present
habit *leads* to interesting results because even "flies" *fly*!

If the message relates to ongoing events, the present tense gives more force. For example, *the research says* implies current thinking, whereas *the research said* might seem to imply that the information is outdated.

Transitional words help the reader move smoothly from one thought to another.

Transitional Words and Phrases

Transitional words and phrases help unify messages. When the thought shifts, a transitional term such as *however*, *nevertheless*, *therefore*, *since*, *while*, or *but* ties thoughts together and helps move the reader from one idea to the next. Transitional terms such as *now*, *today*, *later*, and *meanwhile* alert the reader to a shift in time.

"If you have made mistakes, there is always another chance for you . . . you may have a fresh start any moment you choose, for this thing we call "failure" is not the falling down, but the staying down."

—Mary Pickford, American actress

DEVELOPING AN EFFECTIVE WRITING STYLE

Writing is a skill built on certain techniques. Practicing these techniques improves basic writing skills. Style shows the individuality of the writer. A forceful, effective writing style depends on the use of action verbs; the active rather than the passive voice; and a positive, natural tone.

Action Verbs and Active Voice

Verbs express action or a state of being. **Action verbs** express physical or mental actions (*learned*, *wrote*, *marched*, *walk*). Verbs that express state of being are often called **linking verbs** (primarily forms of the verb *to be*—such as, *is*, *was*, *be*, *am*).

Action verbs and active voice make a message forceful and concise.

Action verbs are stronger than linking verbs. Aim for having no more than two linking verbs per page. This will be difficult, but will force you to search for action verbs to express your thoughts. Figure 3-1 shows examples of action verbs in the present tense.

Action Verbs		Linking Verbs	
analyze	find	is	should be
apply	give	are	has
compare	learn	was	have
create	operate	were	has been
edit	purchase	am	have been
explain	write	will be	seem

Figure 3-1
Examples of Action Verbs and Linking Verbs

Active verbs describe action taken by the subject.

Verbs can be active or passive. **Active verbs** (also termed **active voice**) express action that the subject is taking, has taken, or will take. **Passive verbs** or verbs in **passive voice** reflect the subject of the sentence as the receiver of action—not the actor. The active voice is vigorous and direct while the passive voice is reflexive and inactive. The following examples show the difference between active and passive voices.

Passive: The recital **was attended** by Mary.
Active: Maria **attended** the recital.

Passive: Harry **was given** the prize by the class.
Active: The class **gave** the prize to Harry.

Passive: Muscles **are relaxed** by a steady, rocking motion.
Active: A steady, rocking motion **relaxes** muscles.

Natural Word Choice

Write in a natural, conversational style.

Write naturally, as you would speak. Avoid awkward words and phrases. As you read what you have written, ask yourself, "If I were speaking to the reader, would these words sound natural?"

Awkward: In receipt of your January 1 order, we are most appreciative of your order, which will be promptly shipped.

Natural: Your January 1 order will be shipped promptly. We appreciate your business.

When writing in the first person, use *I* or *we* as little as possible. It is difficult to project the *you* attitude in first-person writing.

Positive Tone

Positive tone means looking at what can be done and what is good rather than what cannot be done or what is bad. Words such as *hopefully*, *maybe*, *possibly*, and *perhaps* convey uncertainty and do not contribute to a positive tone. Figure 3-2 illustrates words that express a positive or negative feeling.

Positive words and expressions promote positive tone.

Positive Words		Negative Words	
good	joy	bad	despair
success	beautiful	failure	ugly
win	love	lose	hate
glad	can	sad, angry	cannot
happy	gain	fright	error
courage	integrity	fear	weak

Figure 3-2
Examples of Positive and Negative Words

Finally, in developing a natural, readable style, remember that using a variety of sentence and paragraph lengths gives your writing the greatest impact. Short sentences and paragraphs are stronger than long ones. However, they achieve more force when mixed with longer sentences and paragraphs.

VERB USAGE FOR MESSAGE UNITY AND STRENGTH

Complete the following exercises using action verbs and the active voice.

1. Circle the action verbs in the following paragraph:

   Expressive writing exhibits fluency, creativity, and logical organization. These qualities come from application of basic writing principles. If your writing is dull and disorganized, you can improve it through practice, practice, practice.

2. Rewrite the following sentences using the active voice:

   a. The beef industry is caused to suffer by a surplus of fish and poultry.

   b. Leaders are viewed as ineffective by employees who seldom see them.

   c. Writer's block is caused by fear of mistakes.

   d. The emblem was sewn on the jacket by Jamie.

(Continued on next page)

(continued)

3. Use the space below to rewrite the following paragraph to achieve a more natural, positive tone:

   You cannot be a good listener if you do not relax and concentrate. Your faulty listening habits come from your lack of interest and bad attitude. Negligence in directing your attention and making the other person the central focus can keep you from career advancement. Overcoming these bad habits should be a priority on your self-improvement list.

4. Rewrite the following paragraph to promote unity by using consistent verb tense throughout the paragraph.

   Competent workers will be skilled team members. They negotiate with others to solve problems. They have worked comfortably with colleagues from diverse backgrounds. They challenge existing procedures and policies.

CHAPTER SUMMARY

- Effective writing is concise, complete, and uses clear, concrete language.
- Written communication recognizes and respects diversity and avoids stereotypes.
- Message structure contributes to message unity. The beginning and ending create the first and last impression with the reader. The body of the message supplies details.
- An effective writing style is individual but should have a natural, positive tone.

1. In the sentences below, select the best word choice from those words in parentheses. Consider clarity, concreteness, and simple expression. Write your choices in the blanks.

   ______ a. The (thick, two-inch) ribeye was the best thing on the menu at Brian's Bar and Grill.

   ______ b. You should complete the investigation (quickly, expeditiously).

   ______ c. The additional homework was (a nuisance, an annoyance) to the students.

   ______ d. The (dark, black) sky gave no light for the travelers.

   ______ e. The home-run ball (accelerated, rocketed) toward the upper deck in center field.

   ______ f. Amy (ended, terminated) the agreement.

   ______ g. The flag (flew, fluttered) in the breeze.

   ______ h. The (wild, ticker-tape) parade welcomed the astronauts home from their flight to the moon.

   ______ i. Your (letter, communication) arrived in the mail today.

   ______ j. Place the box on the shelf (over there, in the corner).

2. Change the language in the following sentences so the message content is free of bias.

   a. An administrative assistant should determine which scheduling problem gives her the most difficulty and then ask her boss for assistance.

   b. Each senator should contact his constituents before he votes on the proposed bill.

   c. The stewardess told the blonde that she was sitting in the wrong seat.

   d. Babysitting is obviously a job for high school girls.

   e. The old man was very sick so the ambulance took him to the hospital.

   f. Rebekka is a female Indian physician who specializes in micro-surgery.

3. Rewrite the following message to have effective beginning and ending paragraphs.

    There are a number of *if, maybe*, and *probably* statements about pesticides. After careful review of all known factors about a substance, the best that can be said may be that given amounts of the substance will probably not hurt anyone.

    If you have a problem with pesticides, you need information, and you need it fast. A call to the
    ABC Pesticides Laboratory at 1-800-555-9400 may be the best call you have ever made.

    Pesticides can be a hazard to your health. Although all the answers may not be known, responsible scientists can give expert advice on precautions and safety hazards for commonly used home and garden pesticides.

4. Rewrite the following paragraph to maintain consistency of verb tense and make effective use of transitional words. Also, make the message clear, concise, and more appealing to the reader.

    Conservation of the Earth's resources has been recognized as critical not only to future generations. It is important to our generation, too, and is not something we can put off until tomorrow. Recycling can be the contribution of an individual to saving our natural resources. If you saved your newspapers, brown paper bags, and aluminum cans, you could take an important step toward conservation. A recycling truck will come to your neighborhood to pick up items twice a week to go to recycling centers. A recycling bin can be placed at your home by calling 1-800-555-6578. Pickup service is on Tuesdays and Thursdays.

5. Rewrite the following sentences to change from the passive to the active voice.
   a. The horse was hit on the freeway by a speeding motorist.

   b. The pizza was delivered at 6:30 p.m. by Vick's Pizza Service.

   c. The beneficiary of the will was notified by the estate lawyer of a meeting at 10 a.m. the next day.

   d. A decrease in her weekly salary occurred as a result of the strike.

   e. The championship game was won by the Forney Jackrabbits.

6. Rewrite the following sentences to achieve a more positive or natural tone:
   a. I hope that the operating instructions for the computer will be useful to you.

   b. Failure to respond to the survey may result in an insurance plan that is not well suited for you.

   c. Possibly you will be interested in purchasing season tickets for the fall series of plays at the Art Center.

   d. We are in receipt of your check for an August Caribbean cruise.

   e. Your remittance for the previous order experienced a mail delay; therefore, payment was 30 days late.

7. Write a paragraph describing your favorite hobby. Apply the four Cs of writing. Vary your sentence length and make use of transitional words, active voice, action verbs, and a positive tone. Use the most interesting point about your hobby in the first sentence. E-mail this paragraph to your instructor.

Correct the grammar, spelling, capitalization, punctuation, sentence structure, and word choice errors in the following sentences. Write *Correct* for sentences containing no errors.

1. One of the local architect's will be hired to build the new ymca sports center.

2. Sierra said, "that she hadn't never gone to a fashion show."

3. Jill has gave 8 presentations to the rotary club before last Friday.

4. We live in a information age, we must have the ability to organize, evaluate, and interpet information.

5. Its real difficult to correct all of the errors that the arthur made in his novel.

6. A child was injured at Southeast School when a garbage truck had gone out-of-control.

7. Ramon is looking forward to becoming the State's fortieth treasurer.

8. The President will arrive for the fund raiser at 7:30 p.m. o'clock.

9. The black limousine drove slow on it's approach to the bridge.

10. Tom and Margo are each members of the American bar association.

CHAPTER 4

APPLYING THE WRITING PROCESS

Writing is a process that can be practiced and learned. It is a tool for thinking, learning, and sharing information with others. Now more than ever, clear written communication is important in everything we do. Improving your writing skills takes work, but it is worth it!

You may find ideas for your writing by being an observant reader. When you read something that appeals to you, think about how the ideas are structured. How does it begin—what caught your attention? Sometimes lead-in sentences become so memorable and are repeated so often that they become worn-out and trite. How many times have you heard these beginnings? "Yes, Virginia. . .," "It was the best of times, it was the worst of times. . .," or "First the good news, then the bad news. . . ." Can you think of other well-known beginnings?

LEARNING OBJECTIVES

- Prepare to write by generating ideas.
- Research your topic.
- Overcome writer's block.
- Draft, revise, and refine written communication.
- Edit and proofread your writing.
- Prepare and analyze your final copy.

PREPARING TO WRITE

To write well, don't begin with writing—begin with thinking. Once you have a purpose for writing, the first step in the process consists of generating strong, clear ideas, putting the ideas in order in an outline, and researching the topic to develop the ideas.

Generating Ideas

After deciding on a topic and the purpose of your message, jot down ideas related to it. These ideas can come from reviewing printed materials, talking with individuals knowledgeable about the topic, free writing, or brainstorming.

Clarify the message purpose before writing.

The first step in generating ideas for a topic is to gain background knowledge of the subject. This step precedes selection of major points or subtopics for your writing and may be termed **preliminary research**. At this point in the writing process, you are identifying important areas to be covered. These areas serve as a skeleton outline and are the ideas that will be researched in further detail as you develop your paper.

Prepare to write by gaining knowledge of your topic.

One way to get ideas in written form is to set a time limit of five or ten minutes and begin writing on the topic. Write continuously until time is up without changing or

Free writing is a way to generate ideas by writing your initial thoughts about a topic without trying to evaluate these thoughts.

Brainstorming is generating ideas with others or by yourself by free thinking.

editing or even stopping to think of a particular word. When you cannot think of the right word, draw a line or write the first word that comes to mind. This method of getting ideas on paper is called **free writing**. The purpose of free writing is to generate ideas that can be used later in developing a draft for your written communication.

Another means of generating ideas is **brainstorming**. Brainstorming is free thinking: Any ideas that come to mind are noted, with no attempt to evaluate the quality of the ideas. The purpose of brainstorming is to generate possible thoughts on the topic. Although brainstorming with others may be the most productive method, it is also possible to brainstorm by yourself. Sometimes it is more comfortable to brainstorm by yourself because there is no fear of peer rejection. Before you begin brainstorming, you should prepare yourself by reviewing materials on the topic. Then, select a quiet place and keep track of your ideas by jotting them down on paper, speaking into a tape recorder, or keying them into a computer. At this point, complete sentences or correctness is not important. Remember, the purpose of brainstorming is to collect a variety of thoughts for possible inclusion in your writing.

Making an Outline

After generating ideas, the writer selects the main ideas and organizes them in order of importance or by other relationship to each other. This grouping generally takes the form of an outline. The outline may be as informal as jotting a few key points on a sheet of paper or as sophisticated as using the outlining feature of a word processing program, which automatically numbers and letters the subtopics and divisions.

WORKPLACE CONNECTIONS

Organizing and communicating information is an essential workplace competency.

Once the main ideas are organized, the outline provides structure but is not complete. Determine the subtopics you need to include by considering what you need to say to accomplish your purpose and what the reader needs to know to respond favorably. Each subtopic and subsection represents a specific point to be made in the written draft.

Now you are ready to begin researching your topic. While researching, you may find additional items of information that need to be added to the preliminary outline. The length of the document or paper you are creating determines the length and sophistication of the outline. The completed outline is a guide for the development of the written message.

Outlining gives structure for your writing.

In a formal outline, major divisions or subtopics of the main idea are numbered in Roman numerals. The subdivisions under these subtopics have capital letters. The next level of subdivision uses Arabic numbers; and if another subdivision is used, small alphabetic letters denote this level. Any subdivided topic must have at least two divisions, or the subtopic should not be divided.

Outlining involves thinking your story through. An outline gives organization to what you write. It forces you to break the message into component parts and put them in order. An outline is a roadmap of ideas put together in a logical manner that gives your message unity.

Figure 4-1 gives an example of a formal outline, as well as an informal outline that simply lists topics to be covered. Use the outline form that works best for you.

Formal Outline

I. Posture and Eye Movements
  A. Changes in Posture
    1. Indication of Emotion
      a. Body Language Plus Spoken Language
      b. The Head Movement and the Message
    2. Inclusion or Exclusion of Others
  B. Eye Messages
    1. The Stare and Nonperson Status
    2. A Limited Look for Privacy
    3. Length and Direction of Glances
II. Body Language Use and Abuse
  A. Mental Healing
  B. Fake Body Language

Informal Outline

Posture and eye movements
Changes in posture
Emotional indicators
Body language and speaking
Head movement
The message of the eyes
The stare and nonperson status
A limited look
Using and abusing body language
Mental healing
Fake body language

Figure 4-1
Outlining Parts of a Manuscript about Body Language

> **"The beginning is the most important part of the work."**
> Plato, *The Republic*

There are a number of ways to organize an outline. All of these organizational patterns give you a logical structure, but each is best suited to a different type of topic. Some topics lend themselves to dividing the subject by problem and solution—stating the problem, discussing the background of the problem, proposing solutions, and stating a solution with its rationale. See Figure 4-2 for an example of this organization. Another organizational method is chronological, organized by dates or sequentially from present to past. Some topics lend themselves to organization by location; for example, a discussion of weather patterns may be organized

Topical organization of a message groups related topics together.

by geographic parts of the country. Probably one of the most common organizational patterns is topical. Topical organization shows points arranged in a construction with related topics grouped together. The formal outline shown in Figure 4-1 follows a topical organizational pattern.

SELECTING COMPUTER HARDWARE

I. Compatibility Issues
   A. What Is Compatibility?
   B. Why Is It Important?
II. Past Problems with Hardware Compatibility
   A. Memory Requirements
   B. Operating Systems
   C. Operating Speed
III. Solutions to Compatibility Problems
   A. Know Your System Requirements
   B. Rely on Manufacturers
   C. Hire a Consultant
IV. Knowledge about System Requirements
   A. What You Need to Know
   B. How You Can Learn about Your System

Figure 4-2
Problem and Solution Organization

GENERATING IDEAS AND OUTLINING

1. Complete the exercise below to practice generating ideas and gathering data for writing.

   a. Select one of the following topics: Goal Setting, Heroes of Today, Computer Technology, or Basic Career Skills. Meet with three or four classmates and brainstorm to accumulate ideas for your selected topic. Generate a minimum of 12 different thoughts on the topic. On the following lines, list the ideas from this brainstorming session:

______________________	______________________
______________________	______________________
______________________	______________________
______________________	______________________
______________________	______________________
______________________	______________________

   b. Use a computer or a sheet of paper to brainstorm by free writing. Choose one of the following topics and free write for five minutes, putting down your thoughts without considering word choice or correct

(continued)

(continued)

mechanics: Peer Pressure and Its Effect on Teenagers, My First-Grade Teacher, Happiness: A State of Mind, or My Favorite Hobby.

2. Use the ideas generated in 1.a and 1.b above, select subtopics for each subject and develop them into outlines.

   a. Use the topic selected from 1.a above and select ideas from the brainstorming session for development of a formal outline. Your outline may include additional points not mentioned in the brainstorming session.

   b. Use ideas generated by free writing on the topic selected in 1.b above to develop an informal outline. Your outline may include subpoints other than those taken directly from your free writing.

RESEARCHING THE TOPIC

Preliminary research gathers information about the topic before drafting the message. After identifying the main ideas to be covered in the message, the writer researches information related to these ideas. Collecting and organizing information for the message makes writing the first draft easier.

Gather information on the topic before drafting a message.

Information sources for the topic include library research, Internet resources, observation of specific events, interviews, surveys, and questionnaires. Using your preliminary outline of topics and subtopics as a guide, determine what you need to know and locate resources that can provide this information.

WORKPLACE CONNECTIONS

Today's workers must know how to locate appropriate information sources.

Libraries are a reliable source for many kinds of information. They have collections of books; periodicals (magazines); newspapers; government documents; and microfiche of conference presentations, papers, and reports. In most libraries, you will be able to do an electronic topical search to locate appropriate books or periodicals. Libraries provide access to a variety of computerized electronic databases such as InfoTrac and FirstSearch. To locate information in these databases, enter a key word or words related to your topic to generate a list of possible sources. If you are unfamiliar with using electronic database searches or other library resources, ask the librarian to help you begin your search.

WORKPLACE CONNECTIONS

Using technology to research is a competency that will help you advance on the job.

When using the Internet for research, school and government sites are often the most reliable and accurate. Not all information on the Internet is factual and reliable. Be sure that the resources used are fair and balanced and come from an authority on the topic. The quickest and most direct way of accessing information on the Internet is to know the location address or **Uniform Resource Locator (URL)**. As described in Chapter 2, you may key in this address at the Location or Address blank found at the top of the page on browser software such as Netscape or Microsoft Explorer (See Figure 4-3).

Figure 4-3
Keying in the Locator Address on the Internet

Figure 4-4 gives examples of locator addresses. Remember that location addresses for government sites (other than military) end with **.gov**, university and other educational institutions end with **.edu**, not-for-profit organizations end with **.org**, and commercial and industrial organizations end with **.com**. If you do not know a specific locator address or if you wish to obtain a list of multiple sites on a topic, you may use a search

http://www.howstuffworks.com

http://www.homeworkcentral.com

http://www.gsn.org

http://www.ed.gov/free/subject.html

http://metalab.unc.edu/wm/

http://www.kansascity.com

http://www.bsu.edu/careers/

Figure 4-4
Examples of Internet Uniform Resource Locator (URL) Addresses

engine such as Alta Vista, Yahoo, Lycos, or Infoseek. Search engines provide a blank for you to key in a topic or key words. In addition, they provide categories such as Business, Entertainment, Sports, Lifestyles, and Hobbies to help narrow the search.

When you research your topic by interviewing or doing a survey, carefully word the questions you plan to ask so that you get the information you need. Have someone review your questions to make suggestions on content and clarity. An interview with someone knowledgeable about your topic can provide interesting information and quotes that give "reader appeal" to your message. Make an appointment for an interview. Even if the interview is to be conducted by telephone, the first call should be to gain permission for the interview and to arrange a time convenient for the person to be interviewed.

Plan what you need to know before beginning to research a topic.

As you complete your research, be sure that you record information about each source: the author(s), title of book or article, the publisher, date of publication, and page numbers. This information makes it possible for you to go back and check information and to give proper credit in your paper to the sources you use. If you are developing a formal paper on your topic, consult a style manual for the proper way to cite references.

Be sure to record author, title, publisher, date, and page numbers for all sources of information for your writing.

When you complete your research, look at your tentative outline. Make changes indicated by what you found and make notes on the outline to remind you where resource information fits. One author suggests numbering your pages of research notes and writing the page numbers on the outline in appropriate places. Another technique that can be used for a long paper and extensive research notes is to prepare a separate envelope for each section of the outline. Place the reference material for each section in its envelope. When you begin to write, you can work with one envelope at a time. Now you are ready to begin writing the first draft.

Organize your research notes before beginning to write.

OVERCOMING WRITER'S BLOCK

When you start to write, does a blank computer screen or sheet of paper cause your mind to go blank? Do you find other things to do when it is time to start writing? Do you wait for inspiration before you begin? If so, you have experienced **writer's block**—a feeling that you cannot start writing because the words will not come. What causes writer's block? How can you overcome it?

> "It is by will alone that I set my mind in motion."
>
> Mentat Prayer

Two things—discipline and routine—can cure writer's block. Set up a writing schedule. If you are a morning person, get up an hour earlier each morning and use the extra time to write. If evenings are better than mornings for you, spend an hour writing before you go to bed. Establishing a time to write and sticking with it takes self-discipline. Make writing routine and write on a regular schedule.

Organize your time, your tools, your notes, and your research materials. A work area that is comfortable and functional can help you become a more productive writer. To help you get started, research your topic and make an outline before you begin to write. Organize your notes and research in folders for each project. Keep those folders accessible while you write. You want to spend your time writing and keep your mind focused when you sit at the computer or writing desk.

Establish a routine schedule for writing.

After you establish a routine and organize your work area, you may have times when writing comes more easily than at other times. It is important to write no matter how you feel. Know that what you initially write is a draft, one that does not have to be perfect. Get the words on paper. Revising and refining are easier than writing the draft.

COMPOSING A DRAFT

Use your outline as the foundation for developing a rough draft. The first draft will not be flawless, but make it as good as possible. Do not try to polish every phrase, but keep in mind good writing principles as you write.

An outline is a guide for writing the first draft.

The purpose of the first draft is to put words on paper using your outline as a guide. When words, sentences, and paragraphs are on paper, they can be corrected, improved, and refined. Remember that the outline is a *guide* that can be changed if another idea or organization seems more logical as you write the draft.

Determining Content

The purpose of the first draft is to get your ideas on paper for content about the topic.

The first draft is the most difficult to write because you are getting ideas on paper in an organized way for the first time. The completed message will include an introduction that sparks interest, a closing that summarizes your arguments or presents conclusions and leaves a final thought with the reader, and paragraphs between the introduction and closing that develop the message.

Your main focus in the first draft is basic content. Add details and expand the main ideas of your outline. Often, it is easier to begin the first draft with the body of your message—the details and supporting material—then go back and write the introduction. Sometimes the closing is the easiest place to start. So don't let trouble with the introduction slow you down, because you can always go back to it.

Attracting Reader Interest

Whether you are writing a letter, a report, or an essay, the beginning should attract the reader's interest. Start by thinking about the most important points and most interesting material. You can use specific examples and link them to the larger message. Look over your notes for interesting examples, quotes, key facts, or human interest items that can be linked to the important points in your message.

As you construct the paragraphs that develop the major ideas, remember you have a plan; you know where you are going. Your outline is your guide. Write simply and directly, leave out unnecessary words, make nouns and verbs do the work, and use action verbs in the active voice.

The beginning should attract the reader's attention; the closing should leave the reader with final thoughts about the topic.

Write simply and directly.

RESEARCHING AND WRITING A FIRST DRAFT

1. Practice using the Internet for research by completing the following exercises.
    a. Use a search engine to locate information on the topic that you selected for your outline in Checkpoint 4-1, exercise 1.a. Print a copy of one or more sources, and highlight points that will fit your essay.
    b. Use the following location addresses or other Web site addresses to search for information related to your outline from Checkpoint 4-1, exercise 2.a. Print a copy of at least one resource that applies to your outline. Highlight points that can be used in your essay.

        http://www.freeality.com/encyclopt.htm

        http://www.ala.org/parentspage/greatsites/parent.html

        http://coe.ohio-state.edu/cete/ericacve/index.html

        http://www.aboutwork.com

        http://www.golden.net/~archeus/reswri.htm

        http://www.ed.gov

    c. Use the outline from Checkpoint 4-1, exercise 2.a, and your research from 1.b above to develop a first draft of an essay. If a computer is available, use word processing software to prepare your draft. If a computer is not available, write the draft on a separate sheet of paper.

The closing paragraph should be one that brings the main thoughts to a conclusion. Sometimes the story builds to a climax, and sometimes the closing paragraph goes back to the ideas expressed in the beginning paragraph.

REVISING AND REFINING THE DRAFT

Polish the first draft for smooth thought flow.

Now that you have developed your first draft, it is time to make it better. As you go back through the draft, you may find reorganizing or moving statements from one location to another makes thoughts flow more smoothly. Certain parts of the draft may need to be expanded, while others need to be deleted. After working on the draft, leave it for a short time before making final changes. When you return to it, you will bring a fresh perspective and can make other improvements.

Reading the Draft Aloud

Good writing can be heard! Read your draft aloud.

Good writing flows well when it is read aloud. Reading your draft aloud helps you check the sense and the sound of the message. Is there a logical flow of thoughts with a smooth transition from one topic to another? Figure 4-5 gives examples of transition words and phrases that help the reader move from one idea to another. As you read the draft, think of your readers. Will they understand your ideas? Have you answered questions they might have about the topic? Is the tone friendly, positive, and conversational?

however	in the meantime	as a result
therefore	in addition	at the same time
at the outset	similarly	on the other hand
thus	although	currently
secondly	consequently	on the contrary

Figure 4-5
Transition Words and Phrases

As you refine the draft, select synonyms when you find word repetitions. Consider word choice and use a thesaurus to find the best words as you read through the draft. Polish sentence and paragraph structure. Use your knowledge of writing principles to check the draft. Is it clear, concise, concrete, and complete? Write and rewrite until the message expresses your thoughts clearly and completely.

Collaborating with Others

Collaboration helps revisions. Having someone read your copy and make suggestions lets you see the message from the reader's viewpoint. Working with others in the writing process multiplies the ideas generated and generally results in a better final product.

Collaborating with others helps you see the message objectively.

EDITING AND PROOFREADING

Editing and proofreading comprise the final stage of refining your written document. Everyone makes errors in written drafts: The challenge is to find the errors and correct them.

Correcting Errors

Asking another person to proofread your writing helps catch errors that you missed. You are too close to your own composition to be objective. Because you know what you have written, the tendency is to skim through the pages without focusing on specific words. It is easier for someone else to find the errors. You should proofread your writing first, and then ask a friend to read it and note errors or suggest changes.

It is easier for someone other than the writer to find errors.

When editing, go through the written message to correct errors in spelling, punctuation, grammar, format, word choice, parallelism, subject-verb agreement, and pronoun-antecedent agreement. Look for one specific type of error each time you go through the draft. For example, read the complete message to check for correct punctuation; then read for grammar; and then read for word choice. A good way to check spelling is to read the text backwards so that you will not be distracted by context.

Read carefully once just to check for grammar and format errors.

The spell-check feature on word-processing software can find some errors, but not all. A spelling checker identifies words with spellings that are not in the software's dictionary. A spelling checker may question a

Computer features such as spell check and grammar check assist in making corrections but do not replace careful reading of the document.

legitimate word because you made it possessive. Also, it won't catch words that are spelled correctly but used improperly; for example, *to* used incorrectly for *too* or *two* would not be identified by a spelling checker, since all three spellings would be in its dictionary. Many proper nouns will be flagged whether or not they are misspelled unless you have added them to the spell-check dictionary. Spelling checkers do not find words that are left out. Some programs identify words that are repeated.

The grammar and language feature of word processing software assists with editing tasks such as locating subject-verb agreement, pronoun-antecedent agreement, sentences without a subject, and sentences that are too wordy. As with a spelling checker, grammar features have shortcomings, too. Do not assume that the computer is right. When in doubt, check a dictionary or grammar book. Always remember that use of these features cannot take the place of careful reading. They should be used in addition to your own proofreading.

Using Proofreading Marks

Proofreading marks help when you edit your draft. Figure 4-6 shows commonly used proofreading marks.

PROOFREADING MARKS

Mark	Example
Begin a new paragraph	When you are writing
Change to capital letters	now is the tme for
Change to lowercase letters	When the Maker of
Close up the space	The Pro- Am games are
Delete	When the the time is
Insert a letter, word, phrase, etc.	More thn you will
Insert a period	Mr and Mrs. Jones
Move down	Anyone in the play
Move to the left	Mark is going to
Move to the right	This is an incorrect
Move up	More persons will be
Transposition (switch positions)	When see you the end

Figure 4-6
Proofreading Marks

PREPARING THE FINAL COPY

After rewriting and correcting, you have reached the point when the message must be finalized. This point may be called **design freeze**. There is no end to the number of different ways that messages can be written. Revising and refining is essential; but to get the writing complete, you must decide when it is good enough for you to stop revising.

With an effectively written message, *communication* is achieved—that is, accurate transmission of the meaning of a message from writer to reader. Figure 4-7 summarizes the steps in the writing process.

An effective message transmits the writer's meaning and gets the intended reader's response.

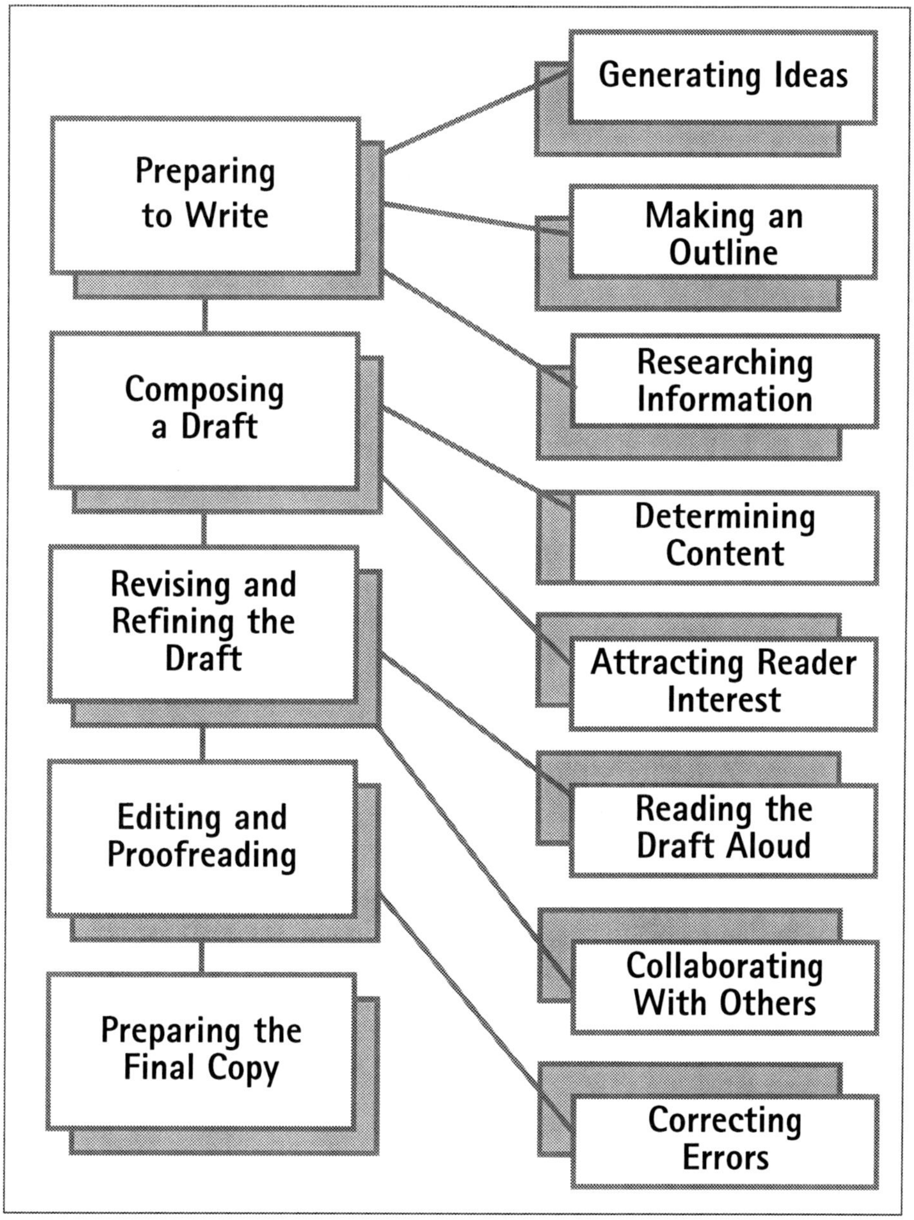

Figure 4-7
Steps in the Writing Process

REVISING AND EDITING YOUR WRITING

1. Use proofreading marks shown in Figure 4-6 to mark corrections in the following paragraph:

   references help writers write to correctly and are invaluable tools when editing and proof reading. For correct format or for a formal paper citing References, use a style manual such as the *Publication Manual of the American Psychological Association, A Manual for Writers of Term Papers, Theses, and Dissertations* by Kate Turabian, or the Modern Language Association *MLA Style Sheet.* Use of the dictionary thesaurus, and grammatical reference books help with word choice and cor rect usage of of words, phrases, and clauses.

2. Use a printout or your written first draft from Checkpoint 4-2 (1.a) and complete the following steps: (1) read aloud, (2) check for variety of sentence and paragraph length, (3) replace overused words, (4) remove unnecessary words, (5) replace vague words with more specific ones, and (6) make changes to improve readability. Mark these changes on your original draft. Use proofreading marks to indicate your changes.
3. Work with classmates to critique the first draft edited in checkpoint 2 above and go through proofreading steps 1–6 again.
4. Make all changes. Read through the entire document again making any additional changes that may be needed. Print.

ANALYZING YOUR WRITING

The ability to develop and refine your writing is a valuable communication skill for your personal life and career goals. Use the Writing Self-Analysis in Figure 4-8 to assess your strengths and set goals for refining your writing skills. At the end of this course, you will complete this analysis again to see how your writing has progressed and to set writing goals for further development.

Self-Analysis of Writing Skills

Directions: This checklist will help you analyze your writing skills. Read each statement and circle *yes* or *no*. Then, review each answer and circle the *plus* if you are satisfied with your level of skill and a *minus* if you wish to improve this skill.

1.	I clearly explain ideas.	yes	no	(+) (−)
2.	I can usually think of topics for writing.	yes	no	(+) (−)
3.	It is easy for me to organize my thoughts in outline form.	yes	no	(+) (−)
4.	I am a good proofreader; I usually catch my errors.	yes	no	(+) (−)
5.	Before writing, I always consider the purpose.	yes	no	(+) (−)
6.	I use a friendly, conversational tone in writing.	yes	no	(+) (−)
7.	When writing, I keep the reader's needs in mind.	yes	no	(+) (−)
8.	I feel confident writing for a variety of purposes.	yes	no	(+) (−)
9.	I can use computer word processing software.	yes	no	(+) (−)
10.	I am familiar with use of the Internet for research.	yes	no	(+) (−)
11.	I know how to send messages by e-mail.	yes	no	(+) (−)
12.	I know how to format different types of documents.	yes	no	(+) (−)
13.	I feel comfortable finding resources in a library.	yes	no	(+) (−)
14.	I know how to use most special features of word processing software.	yes	no	(+) (−)
15.	I write clearly and use words that are easily understood.	yes	no	(+) (−)
16.	I avoid vague terms and use concrete words.	yes	no	(+) (−)
17.	I omit unnecessary words when I edit my writing.	yes	no	(+) (−)
18.	I anticipate questions my reader may have and try to cover information the reader needs to know.	yes	no	(+) (−)
19.	I avoid stereotypes and sex-biased language.	yes	no	(+) (−)
20.	I can write beginning paragraphs that attract the reader's attention.	yes	no	(+ (−)
21.	I can write effective closing paragraphs.	yes	no	(+) (−)
22.	The body of my writing shows unity of thought and a smooth flow of ideas.	yes	no	(+) (−)
23.	I use mostly active voice and action verbs in my writing.	yes	no	(+) (−)
24.	I have a good command of punctuation rules.	yes	no	(+) (−)
25.	I am comfortable with my knowledge of grammar.	yes	no	(+) (−)

Figure 4-8
Self-Analysis of Writing Skills

CHAPTER SUMMARY

- Ideas for a writing topic may come from reading, talking with others, free writing, or brainstorming.
- Use an outline as a guide for researching information about your writing topic.
- Overcome writer's block with self-discipline.
- After composing a rough draft, edit, revise, and refine your writing.
- Software features help you edit compositions but do not replace careful proofreading.
- Follow the steps in the writing process: preparing to write, drafting, revising and refining, editing and proofreading, and preparing the final copy.

Note: If you have words@work, exercises from the section on "External Resources" can be used for student practice related to researching information.

Alfred Hitchcock (1889–1980)

Hitchcock had telephoned the prolific Belgian novelist Georges Simenon, who wrote his books at incredible speed, sometimes in as little as 10 days. Simenon's wife took the call. "I'm sorry," she said, "but Georges is writing and I can't disturb him."

"Let him finish his book," Hitchcock replied, "I'll hang on."

—Robert Hendrickson, *American Literary Anecdotes*
New York: Facts on File, 1990

1. Form teams of three to four classmates and brainstorm to accumulate ideas on one of the following topics: Outdoor Recreation, Entertainment, Sports Marketing, Music, or Historical Places. Generate a minimum of 12 different thoughts on the topic selected. List the ideas from the brainstorming session:

   Topic: ____________________

2. Interview a relative or friend who is at least 20 years older than you are. Ask this person to give an anecdotal record of his or her childhood. Record the information gained from the interview. Pretend you are going to write a biography of a small segment of this person's life. Use a computer or a sheet of paper to free write. Free write for five minutes about what you learned from the interview. Concentrate on ideas without considering word choice or correct mechanics.

3. Using the subject selected in Application 1 above, choose ideas from the brainstorming session to develop a formal outline. Your outline may include additional points not mentioned in the brainstorming session.

4. Using ideas generated by free writing on the topic of a friend's or relative's life in Application 2; develop an informal outline. Your outline may include subpoints other than those taken directly from your free writing.

5. Edit and correct the following message. The message needs reorganization into paragraphs centered around subtopics. Determine three or four major subtopics; prepare an outline grouping information under these subtopics. Use the outline as a guide to reorganize the content. Use a computer or a sheet of paper to rewrite the corrected message for better unity of thought.

EXPLORING THE SEA[1]

The sea can be both compeling and frightening. Early settlements developed around coastlines, but it is only in recent years that we have been able to explore the undersea world. The early use of water was for transportation and products from the ocean, not for adventure. People now swarm to seashores and islands during hollidays, and many people answer the "call of the sea" by bying diving outfits. Storms take a heavy toll on persons saihng the seas. Polynesian pearl divers and Greek sponge divers was the first underwater explorers. The first divers began his ritual with a prayer for protection from sharks and moray eels. A pearl diver averaged 40 or more dives a day, going 100 to 140 feet down into the ocean. The sponge divers provided a service for soldiers, who used the sponges to cushion heavy armor and as emergency wound dressings. Only in the last few decades have diving suits and br eathing apparatus made it possible for the ordinary person to enjoy exploration of the sea. In spite of the thrill of underwater exploration, however, the dangers remain. Compact diving machines with speed, maneuverability, and visibility were developed in the late 1960s. These submersible vehicles are our best hope to understand the deep-sea environment. Water is 800 times as dense as air. When a person descends in water below sea level, pressure increases rapidly. With the air cavities in the human body, pressure is a force to be dealt with when going beneath the sea. Our curiosity and spirit of adventure override our fear of the deep. Gases that are harmless at atmospheric pressure become toxic under high pressure, creating gas hazards under the sea. The "bends" and a euphoric stupor called *rapture of the deep* can incapacitate a diver. Use of the aqualung is popular for sports diving. Human intrusion into the sea is happening. Science fiction writers even dream of developing underwater cities. The mysteries of the sea continue to fascinate us.

Outline

[1] Information included in "Exploring the Sea" was taken from pages 26–29 in Cousteau, J. (1974). *The Ocean World of Jacques Cousteau: Man Re-enters the Sea.* New York: World Publishing. These passages were rewritten to provide for organization and editing.

6. Assume that you have been asked to write an essay on world cultures or business ethics in different countries. Use one of the two location addresses shown below or other Web addresses to search for information on these topics. Print a copy of at least one resource that applies to your topic. Highlight points that can be used in your essay.

   http://www.webofculture.com/

   http://www.pitt.edu/~ethics/countries

7. Use the research material gathered in Application 6 to develop an outline and first draft of an essay on this topic. If a computer is available, use word processing software to prepare your outline and draft. If not, write the outline and draft on separate sheets of paper.

8. Use proofreading marks to indicate errors in the following paragraph:

   Writing shouldbe used as a means of learning in all subject areas. A wide rnge of writing experiences provides practice you can improve your writing by practice, practice, practice. Good writing mechanics—command of English, spelling, grammar, and word usage—should be developed, Primarily by writing and secondarily through limited drills and exercises.

9. Interview five people about what is right and what is wrong with American education. Develop six to ten questions to ask, and write these questions on the lines below. From the information gathered, develop an outline. Use a computer or a sheet of paper to write a first draft; revise, refine, edit, and correct the draft; then write the final draft.

   Questions for the interview

10. Select one of the following topics for development as an essay. Follow all steps of the writing process, and use a computer to prepare the final essay. If a computer is not available, write your essay on a sheet of paper.

Topics: Reasons I Returned to School

How to Improve the Appearance of the Campus

Writing with the "You" Attitude

Pros and Cons of Dress Codes

11. Listed below are several items from the Self-Analysis of Writing Skills. Pretend that you need to improve the skills. Write in the space below each skill how you would improve that skill.

    a. I know how to format different types of documents.

    b. I write clearly and use words that are easily understood.

    c. I avoid vague terms and use concrete words.

    d. I anticipate questions my reader may have and try to cover answers the reader needs to know.

    e. The body of my writing shows unity in thought and a smooth flow of ideas.

Correct the grammar, spelling, capitalization, punctuation, sentence structure, and word choice errors in the following sentences. Write *Correct* below the sentences containing no errors.

1. The North West Territory is rich in wild life and vegetation.

2. Paul bought these items; snack crackers, bananas, an dog food.

3. An elderly man yelled, "Watch where your going." to a young man who nearly knocked him down with a bicycle.

4. Emily and her only cousin Andy will be in charge of organizing the volunteer fire departments dinner for next week.

5. People does not know nothing about the new field of alternative medicine.

6. Employers expects workers to have writing skills that clearly communicates information.

7. The short fat legs of the puppy kept it from being able to jump in to the arms of its owner!

8. After examining the accident victim the doctor pronounced that the victim was really dead.

9. Yesterday, Carol believes that Doug's plane would arrive before eleven-thirty p.m.

10. Miss Woo will accompany her husband next year for a well deserved vacation.

IMPROVING SENTENCE STRUCTURE

CHAPTER 5

Just as a house is made stronger by using high quality construction materials, so, too, written messages are made more powerful by using well-constructed sentences. Sentences and paragraphs are the building blocks of written messages. When you draft a message, concentrate at first on getting your thoughts keyed into the computer or written on a page. Then the next step is to revise, edit, and refine your writing so that it appeals to the reader and accomplishes your purpose. This writing revision improves sentence and paragraph structure. Carefully constructed sentences and paragraphs appeal to the reader and clearly communicate your thoughts.

Learning Objectives

- Identify sentence components.
- Write correct sentences.
- Write clear and direct sentences.
- Compose simple, compound, complex, and compound-complex sentences.
- Give emphasis to words and key ideas.
- Recognize and correct faulty sentences.

IDENTIFYING SENTENCE COMPONENTS

Every sentence must have a subject and a verb and must express a complete thought. The **subject** is a noun or pronoun that performs the action of the verb. The **complete subject** includes the noun or pronoun and its modifiers. A **verb** describes action or a state of being. When a verb or verb phrase tells something about the subject, it is called the **predicate** of a sentence. The **complete predicate** consists of the verb (the action word) and its modifiers (words that describe the action). In addition to having a subject and verb, a sentence must express a complete thought. For example, "When John left for the movie last night" does not express a complete thought. The reader is left wondering what happened. To express a complete thought, additional information can be added to the phrase. It would then read, "When John left for the movie last night, he took his umbrella with him."

The subject of a sentence performs the action of the verb.

Subject and Verb

It is essential to be able to identify the subject(s) and verb(s) in a sentence to be sure that all parts of the sentence are grammatically correct.

A verb describes action or state of being.

STATED SUBJECTS. Analyze a sentence by first locating the verb. Then look for the key word that performs the verb's action. The following examples show the subject in bold type and the verb as italicized:

Janet *runs*.

The **baby** *smiled* at her mother.

High winds *damaged* the building.

They *watch* television on Saturday morning.

In these examples all of the sentences have stated subjects. The word that represents the performer of the action is found in the sentence. Be careful not to confuse the subject that performs the action with the noun serving as the direct object.

UNDERSTOOD SUBJECTS. In sentences that do not have a stated subject, the subject "you" is understood. These sentences speak directly to the reader and are directives or commands. The reader is to perform or receive the action.
Examples:

Complete all exercises in Chapter 1 before tomorrow.
(**You** is understood as the subject of the verb *Complete*.)

Set the alarm clock for 5:30 a.m.
(It is understood that **You** *set* the alarm clock.)

Modifiers

Locating subject and verb modifiers helps check their correct use.

Modifiers of nouns are *adjectives* or *pronouns*. Adjectives describe a noun or pronoun; therefore, adjectives may describe a noun or pronoun serving as subject of a sentence. Adjectives make the meaning of the subject specific by answering questions such as *which one*, *how many*, and *what kind*. Adjectives can indicate comparisons; for example, *less*, *least*, *more*, or *most*. Some adjectives limit or restrict nouns; these are *limiting adjectives*. *A*, *an*, and *the* are limiting adjectives that call attention to the nouns.

While the primary job of pronouns is to substitute for nouns (for example, *he*, *she*, *I*, and *you* instead of people's names), pronouns can also be used as modifiers to indicate a specific person, place, or thing. Examples of these modifiers are *this*, *these*, *that*, *those who*, *whom*, *which*, and *what*. A pronoun clause may serve as a subject modifier; for example, **workers** *who can use computers*. *Who can use computers* tells which workers. The following sentences show the subject nouns in bold type, the verb italicized, and subject modifiers underlined:

The expert **worker** of tomorrow *needs* basic skills, thinking skills, and interpersonal skills. (*The* is a *limiting adjective* and calls attention to the noun **worker**. Expert is an adjective that tells what kind of **worker**.)

Skillful **employees** *can monitor* and *correct* performance of organizational systems. (Skillful is an adjective modifier.)

Time-management **leadership** by the company manager and employee **participation** in careful use of time *contribute* to an efficient workplace. (*Time-management* and *employee* are words that sometimes function as nouns but, in this example, are used as adjective modifiers of the nouns, *leadership* and *participation*, which are the subjects of the sentence.)

This **project** *will require* team participation. (*This* is a pronoun modifier that answers the question *which one*.)

Modifiers are words that describe other words.

Modifiers that describe verbs are called adverbs. Adverbs answer the questions *how*, *when*, *where*, *why*, *in what manner*, or *to what degree* about verbs. Adverbs often end in *ly* and are placed before or after the words they modify. As a general rule, place the adverb so that it does not break up two-word verbs, such as, *have been*. For example, it is better to write *have been slowly* or *slowly have been* rather than *have slowly been*. Adverbs shown in the following examples are underlined, and the verbs are italicized; the subject is in boldface:

All **employees** in the organization clearly *understand* how to apply technology in performance of their tasks.

The **ability** to demonstrate computer proficiency significantly *improves* employability.

Workers who *solve* problems creatively *can advance* rapidly on the job.

In the last example sentence, **workers** is a noun and the subject of the sentence that performs the action *can advance*. Rapidly is an adverb that describes the action of the verb *can advance*. Note the placement of rapidly avoids separating the two words of the verb *can advance*. What makes this sentence a little tricky is that an entire phrase, with a subject, verb, and adverb, is used as an adjective to modify "workers." In this phrase, the pronoun **who** is the subject of the verb *solve*. Creatively is an adverb that answers the question *how* about the verb *solve*.

Modifiers should be placed as close as possible to the words they modify so the word referred to by the modifier will be clear to the reader. So far, all examples have had the subject placed before the verb. When asking a question, place the verb before the subject. In the following examples, the subject is in bold type and the verb is italicized:

Is the hot air **balloon** red or yellow?

When *will* **Bob** and **Jenny** *repair* the oven?

Workplace Connections

Editing documents for appropriate emphasis, form, grammar, spelling, and punctuation is a basic foundation skill for employment.

@ % $!

Newspaper Headline Bloopers:

Grandmother of eight makes hole in one.

A quarter of a million Chinese live on water.

Dealers will hear car talk at noon.

Squad helps dog bite victim.

SUBJECTS, VERBS, AND MODIFIERS

1. Underline the subject(s), or note if the subject is an understood "you," and circle the verb(s) in the following sentences:
   a. She plays ball.
   b. The picture fell from the wall.
   c. The pizzas were carried in by Soolyn and John.
   d. Learn computer skills to prepare for the job market.
   e. An employer looks for people who can teach technical skills to others.
2. Underline the subject(s), circle the verb(s), and draw a box around modifiers of a subject or verb:
   a. Is that picture a recent one?
   b. Both Jane and Mary communicate well with clients and customers.
   c. Can she work well with people who have a variety of different ethnic, social, or educational backgrounds?
   d. Communication skills enable a person to share thoughts, feelings, and ideas.
   e. Improving the quality of goods or products may involve modifying or creating production systems.

WRITING CORRECT SENTENCES

Complete sentences and correct grammar help convey clear messages.

Correct sentences give the reader a positive image of the writer and help convey a clear message. This section teaches you to write correct sentences by making them complete, having subject and verb agreement and pronoun and antecedent agreement, and maintaining parallel structure.

Complete Sentences

Sentences are more than groups of words; they must also express a complete thought. Even with a subject and verb, a group of words may not be a sentence. The groups of words below are examples of incomplete sentences.

> If Jan goes to the movies
>
> All candidates in the race for treasurer
>
> Preventing, identifying or solving problems in maintaining and troubleshooting technological equipment

Incomplete sentences are called sentence fragments.

Incomplete sentences are called **sentence fragments.** In these examples, the first fragment has a subject and verb but left the reader "hanging" for meaning. The other examples of sentence fragments are not even clauses. They have no verb and no subject. Because of its length, a quick look makes the third appear to be a sentence.

As noted above, some sentence fragments have subjects and verbs. A group of words that includes a subject and verb is called a **clause**. Clauses beginning with words such as *if*, *when*, *because*, or *since* signal the reader that more information is coming and do not express a complete thought. Clauses that do not complete the thought are called **dependent clauses**. Dependent clauses appear to be a sentence because they have a subject and verb, but they cannot stand alone as a sentence; they must be connected to an independent clause to complete the meaning. *If Jan goes to the movies* . . . leaves the reader with the question, *then what*? To complete the thought, you could say, *If Jan goes to the movies, we will have dinner at 8 p.m.* The last clause, *we will have dinner at 8 p.m.*, can stand alone as a complete thought; it has a subject and verb, and is an **independent clause**. (Clauses will be covered in more detail later in the chapter.)

An independent clause has a subject and verb, expresses a complete thought, and can stand alone as a sentence.

To determine if your sentences are complete, see if they pass the test in Figure 5-1.

TEST YOUR SENTENCES.

A group of words must pass a three-point test to be a sentence:

1. Is there a verb?
2. Is there a subject?
3. Do the words express a complete thought?

Figure 5-1
Essential Parts of a Sentence

Subject and Verb Agreement

A subject and its verb must both be plural or singular. For instance, *The soccer player kicks* is singular. *The soccer players kick* is a sentence which uses a plural subject and verb. The following is an example of a more difficult sentence construction:

Both subject and verb must be singular or both must be plural.

> A **school** with a reputation for poor student achievement on tests *improves* its reputation by having recent **graduates** *perform* well on the job.

In this sentence **school** is separated from its verb *improves* by three prepositional phrases. One of these phrases contains a plural noun. Even though the plural noun is closer to the verb, the verb is singular because the action of the verb refers back to the singular subject, **school**. The verb *perform* is plural because of its plural subject, **graduates**. It's often easier to determine agreement if you keep the subject and verb close to one another in the sentence. However, this simple construction is not always possible, because sometimes prepositional phrases are needed to modify the subject. Because modifiers should be placed close to the words they modify, subject and verb often get separated.

Two or more singular subjects joined by* and *or* both/and *require a plural verb. Singular subjects joined by* or, neither/nor, either/or, *or* not only/but also *require a singular verb.

Make sure the subject and verb agree in a sentence with a compound subject. Singular subjects joined by the conjunctions *and* or *both/and* take a plural verb. Singular subjects joined by *or*, *neither/nor*, *either/or*, or *not only/but also* take a singular verb. The following examples illustrate compound subjects and the correct verbs. Subjects are in bold type, conjunctions are underlined, and verbs are italicized:

She and **Robert** *attend* the summer theater performances.

Both **Jill** and **Paul** *live* in Canterbury Estates.

Jim or **Therese** *plays* tennis at noon today.

Neither **Amy** nor **Brian** *takes* classes this semester.

Either **Joe** or **Jerry** *is* to pick up the ice for the party.

Not only **Steve** but also **Ginny** *is* to attend the conference.

Compound subjects with both singular and plural nouns joined by* or, neither/nor, either/or, *or* not only/but also *require a verb that agrees with the number of the subject closest to the verb.

Verbs that have compound subjects comprised of a singular noun and a plural noun joined by the connectives *or*, *neither/nor*, *either/or*, or *not only/but also* must agree in number with the subject closest to the verb.

Terry or his **parents** *plan* to buy the house next door.

Terry's **parents** or **Terry** *plans* to buy the house next door.

Neither **Daniel** nor his **friends** *have lost* a baseball game this season.

Collective nouns take a plural verb if they indicate separate actions by members of the group.

Collective nouns are usually singular, but they can be plural if they indicate separate actions by members of the group. Examples of collective nouns are *committee*, *board*, *staff*, *herd*, *pack*, and *family*.

The **board** *permits* the president to make daily decisions. (Collective noun used as a singular unit.)

The **board** *disagree* on the expansion project. (Plural collective noun representing individual actions.)

The indefinite pronouns *each*, *every*, *neither*, *anybody*, and *everybody* are singular. Indefinite pronouns make a general reference and do not refer to a specific person, place, or thing. Other examples of singular indefinite pronouns are *anyone*, *nobody*, *everything*, *neither*, *someone*, and *something*. Examples of plural indefinite pronouns are *several*, *many*, *both*, and *few*.

Each of the kittens *has* a white-tipped tail.

In this country **everybody** *has* the right to free speech.

Both of the students *attend* after-school classes.

Nobody *scores* as many free throws in basketball as Tom does.

Pronoun and Antecedent Agreement

A pronoun must agree in number and gender with its antecedent. An **antecedent** is a noun referred to by a pronoun. Good sentence construction makes the antecedent clear by location; it should be close to the pronoun. A sentence should be reconstructed if it is difficult to determine the antecedent; for example, *Johnny refused to consider the job offer from Mr. Ramirez because he lived outside the city limits.* The reader cannot determine whether *he* refers to Johnny or Mr. Ramirez and would not know which person lived outside the city limits. The sentence should be reworded: *Because Johnny lived outside the city limits, he refused to consider the job offer from Mr. Ramirez.*

An antecedent is a noun referred to by a pronoun.

Generally when a demonstrative pronoun such as *this* is used, you should restate the noun to which it refers; for example, avoid *Please send this immediately*. Use a noun after the word *this*, as in *Please send this book immediately*.

Be sure the reference noun is clear for each demonstrative pronoun.

In the following sentences, the pronoun is italicized; its antecedent is in boldface. The following sentences give examples of pronoun and antecedent agreement:

Antecedents and pronouns must agree in number.

People who play the stock market have gains and losses in *their* accounts. (*People* is a collective noun referring to people acting independently, not as a group, and requires a plural pronoun.)

Everybody should learn computer skills if *he* or *she* is not already computer literate. (*Everybody* is an indefinite singular pronoun and requires a singular pronoun reference.)

Isabel and **Carmen** left *their* homes to go to Spain. (Compound singular subjects joined by *and* require a plural pronoun.)

COMPLETE SENTENCES, VERB-SUBJECT AGREEMENT, AND PRONOUN-ANTECEDENT AGREEMENT

1. Rewrite the following sentences or sentence fragments making any corrections required for clear, grammatically-correct sentences. Rewrite the sentences using a computer or rewrite them in the space below. You may add or omit words to construct a correct sentence.

   a. Every little problem noticed by a skilled driver and considered to be important by the automobile makers.

   b. George and Tammy has moved their residence to New York.

   c. Some individuals with a small-town background has difficulty working for companies that are located in metropolitan areas.

2. Using a computer or using the space below, write sentences as instructed.

   a. Write a sentence using *either* and *or* to join a compound subject. Use *was selected* or *were selected* as the verb.

   b. Write a sentence using the indefinite pronoun *each* as the subject. Use the verb *play* or *plays.*

3. In this exercise it is not clear who thinks the policies are unfair. Rewrite the sentence to make it obvious that John thinks the policies are unfair; then write another sentence that clearly states that Jerry thinks the policies are unfair.

   When John became unhappy with the policies of his company, he talked with Jerry, and he thought that the policies were unfair.

Parallel Structure

Parallel structure in a sentence means using similar structure (words, phrases, or clauses) for equal or parallel ideas. Being consistent between or among parts of sentences that serve the same function achieves parallelism. The following examples illustrate incorrect and correct structure for parallel ideas. The parts of these examples that are not parallel are shown in bold font, and explanations are given of what is wrong in each case and one possible way to fix the problem.

Parallel ideas in a sentence should have parallel structure.

- Use either **infinitives** or **gerunds** in a series, but do not use both. An infinitive is a verb form, usually preceded by *to*, that is used as a noun, an adjective, or an adverb. A gerund is a verb form ending in *ing* that is used as a noun.

The word to plus a verb is an infinitive; a verb ending in -ing is a gerund.

His plans were to shop at the market, **going** to the ballgame, and then to attend evening classes.
(Incorrect: The sentence is not consistent in the use of infinitives.)

His plans were to shop at the market, to go to the ballgame, and then to attend evening classes.
(Correct: The change creates a parallel series using infinitives.)

Exercising regularly, reducing fat, and to eat nutritiously are primary concerns of the 1990s.
(Incorrect: The sentence is not consistent in the use of gerunds.)

Exercising regularly, reducing fat, and eating nutritiously are primary concerns of the 1990s.
(Correct: This parallel construction uses a gerund series.)

- Use parallel construction for a numbered series in an outline or a series in a sentence.

Items in an outline should have parallel structure.

1. **To create** an outline
2. **Writing** the story
3. The final product **is published.**
   (Incorrect: #1—infinitive phrase, #2—gerund phrase, and #3—sentence)

1. Creating an outline
2. Writing the story
3. Publishing the final product
   (Correct: all three items—gerund phrases)

- For sentence constructions using conjunctions such as *or*, *and*, *but*, *nor*, *for*, *than*, and *not only/but also*, parallel construction should be used since these expressions connect parallel ideas.

  Travel agents set priorities for tasks, make travel reservations, and **are contacting prospective customers.**
  (Incorrect: *Set* and *make* are active, present tense verbs; *are* is a linking verb—a form of *to be*.)

  Travel agents *set work priorities*, *make travel reservations*, and *contact prospective customers*.
  (Correct: All three have similar construction—active verbs followed by an adjective modifying a noun.)

  The medical assistant completed the report *quickly*, *correctly*, and *with thoroughness*.
  (Incorrect: Two items are adverbs; the third is a prepositional phrase.)

  The medical assistant completed the report *quickly*, *correctly*, and *thoroughly*.
  (Correct: A series of three adverbs is parallel construction.)

Sentence elements showing comparison or contrast should have parallel structure.

- Parts of a sentence that show comparison or contrast serve the same function and should be parallel in structure.

  Child-care aides work *as a team* in the classroom, not *individually making decisions*.
  (Incorrect: Two prepositional phrases contrast with an adverb, gerund, and noun.)

  Child-care aides work *as a team* in the classroom, not *as individuals* in decision making.
  (Correct: Similar prepositional phrases are contrasted.)

  Your computer skills are better than *he is* with computers.
  (Incorrect: The noun *skills* and modifiers are compared to a clause that has a subject noun, linking verb, and prepositional phrase.)

  Your computer skills are better than *his computer skills*.
  (Correct: Equal constructions are compared—possessive pronoun, adjective, and noun.)

PARALLELISM

1. Rewrite the following sentences to use parallel construction for parallel ideas:

   a. Someone cannot rescue you from a sinking ship, you cannot be carried from a burning building, or saved from an earthquake if you have never been in danger.

   b. Reading reports, writing memos, and to speak at conferences are primary functions of a manager.

   c. The organization needs to increase communication and to have its image improved.

2. Make an outline for the topic General Goals for Writing.

WRITING CLEAR AND DIRECT SENTENCES

Write to express; not to impress.

People sometimes try to impress others by using complex sentences, big words, and long messages. They miss the point because the purpose of writing is to communicate, not to impress. The best writing uses simple but specific language, a conversational tone, and understandable content. You do not communicate unless the reader understands the message. It is far more important to *express* than to *impress*.

Word Selection

Choose words that accurately reflect your meaning.

Expressing thoughts clearly in a sentence, paragraph, and message depends on word choice and arrangement of those words. A good writer differentiates between words and chooses ones that accurately express the intended meaning. Check a dictionary or thesaurus to select the right words.

Read this sentence and find a misused word:

> The speaker's comments about hostility peaked my interest in the topic.

Do you think the writer meant piqued? Check it out! How do the two meanings differ? Figure 5-2 displays examples of other words that are commonly misused.

An American businessman, addressing a Chinese audience, mentioned in his opening remarks that he was ". . .tickled to death to be in China." After his interpreter converted those words, there was a murmur from the audience. It seems his interpreter had explained, "The American gentleman says he scratched himself until he died in order to be here."

—Roger E. Axtell, *Do's and Taboos of Using English Around the World*, 1995, John Wiley, p. 123

Words used in a message must be understandable to the reader. Technical words should be used only if the reader is familiar with them. For example, it is appropriate to use terms like RAM or megahertz when you write a letter to a computer manufacturer. In a letter written to an audience that is unfamiliar with computer technology, these terms should be changed to non-technical, commonly used language such as working memory and operating speed, or should be defined in the letter.

Build your vocabulary; develop the dictionary habit!

Words are fascinating. There are always new ones to learn. Increasing your vocabulary will be valuable to you in many ways, especially in your writing. Using a dictionary and a thesaurus is helpful. Get into the habit! When you see an unfamiliar word, you can improve your vocabulary by checking its meaning in the dictionary. The word *thesaurus* means "treasure house" in Latin. For each word listed in the thesaurus, synonyms, or words with similar meanings, are given. Antonyms, words with

TERMS	DEFINITIONS
accept/except	Accept means to take; except means to leave out.
adapt/adept/adopt	Adapt means to adjust for use; adept means skilled; adopt means to use in its present form.
adverse/averse	Adverse means opposite or opposed to one's interest; averse means a feeling of distaste, disinclined.
advise/advice	Advise is a verb meaning to give advice; advice is a noun meaning counsel or suggestion.
affect/effect	Affect as a verb means to influence; effect as a verb means to bring about; effect as a noun means the result of influence or change.
among/between	Among compares more than two items; between compares two items.
compliment/complement	Compliment means praise (noun) or to praise (verb); complement means to add or complete (verb) or something that completes (noun).
farther/further	Farther refers to distance; further means to extend or advance.
precedent/precedence	Precedent means an example or established rule (noun) or prior in time, order, or significance (adjective); precedence (noun) means preceding in time or the right to formal preference.
principal/principle	Principal (noun or adjective) means the chief person, thing, or a capital sum of money; principle (noun) means a rule.
respectively/respectfully	Respectively means in the order given; respectfully means courteously or with respect.
their/there	Their means belonging to them; there refers to a location.

Figure 5-2
Words That Are Frequently Confused

the opposite meaning are also given. A thesaurus can be used to look for words with similar meanings when you need variety in your writing. You may also use the thesaurus to help you recall a word that you know but cannot remember. By checking another word with the same meaning, you can find the word you want. Word processing software has a thesaurus feature. However, it is always wise to look up any unfamiliar word you find in a thesaurus, to make sure it really means what you want to say. For example, enormity and immensity both mean very great, but enormity means great wickedness, immoderate, or outrageous while immensity means great size or degree.

Clear, Direct Writing

Eliminate unnecessary words; use only words that contribute to the meaning of the sentence.

Make every word add to the thought of a sentence. Clearly written sentences should state a complete thought in as few words as possible. Prune unnecessary verbiage. Which of the following sentences is easier to understand?

> The company manager said, by way of illustration, that the financial chart of overhead expenses had been contemplated for the preceding three months and that, without a doubt, expenditures were excessively higher than one would expect them to be.
>
> OR
>
> The company manager said, for example, that overhead expenses for the past three months were higher than expected.

The second sentence is clearer and more direct. The message comes through better using 18 carefully chosen words than it does with 39 words. Most of the 39 words were not essential to the meaning of the sentence. Eliminate every word that adds nothing to the meaning. Change terms such as "during the course of" to "during" and "few in number" to "few."

TYPES OF SENTENCE STRUCTURE

Sentences consist of one or more clauses. All clauses have a subject and verb but may or may not express a complete thought. There are two kinds of clauses—*independent* and *dependent clauses.*

A clause that expresses a complete thought could stand alone as a sentence. Because the clause can stand alone as a sentence, it is called an *independent clause*. In the following independent clause, the subject is *tiger*, the verb is *originated*, and the clause expresses a complete thought; therefore, it can stand alone as a sentence:

Sentences are made up of at least one independent clause and may have one or more dependent clauses.

The Siberian **tiger** *originated* in Eastern Asia.

A *dependent clause* has a subject and verb but cannot stand alone as a sentence because it does not express a complete thought. The following dependent clause has a subject, *tigers*, and a verb, *require*, but does not express a complete thought; therefore, it could not stand alone as a sentence:

Because Siberian **tigers** *require* large territories for hunting food

An independent clause or combinations of independent and/or dependent clauses create **simple**, **compound**, **complex**, or **compound-complex sentences.** The following paragraphs describe these four types of sentence structure.

Simple Sentences

Simple sentences have only one independent clause. This clause can have either one subject or a compound subject. A simple sentence has either one verb or a **compound verb** (more than one verb connected by a conjunction). The following independent clauses are examples of simple sentences:

A sentence with only one independent clause is called a **simple sentence.**

Martin left the stadium after the third inning.
(One subject: *Martin:* one verb: *left*)

Wanda enjoys genealogy and spends hours tracing her family tree.
(One subject: *Wanda;* compound verb: *enjoys* and *spends*)

Tom and Daniel smiled and giggled for the picture.
(Compound subject: *Tom* and *Daniel;* compound verb: *smiled* and *giggled*)

A* compound *sentence has two or more independent clauses.

Compound Sentences

Joining two or more independent clauses makes a **compound sentence**. Compound sentences are used to link closely related thoughts. The following are compound sentences:

> Janet caught the string of fish, and Bob cleaned them.
> (Two independent clauses)
>
> Milburn and Wendell played golf; Pat and Thomas played tennis.
> (Two independent clauses with compound subjects)
>
> We wrote the company and asked for information, but the response was late and failed to supply the necessary details.
> (Two independent clauses with compound verbs)
>
> Mr. Johnson's résumé was outstanding, the interview was successful, and he was employed.
> (A series of three independent clauses)

Complex sentences *have an independent clause and one or more dependent clauses.*

A restrictive clause is essential to the meaning of the sentence and is not set off by commas; a nonrestrictive clause adds information but could be omitted without changing the meaning of the sentence.

Complex Sentences

Complex sentences have an independent clause with one or more dependent clauses. Complex sentences can be used to place emphasis on ideas. A dependent clause de-emphasizes an idea, whereas an independent clause gives emphasis. A dependent clause that comes before an independent clause is separated from the independent clause by a comma. When a dependent clause follows an independent clause, commas are used if the dependent clause is nonrestrictive but not if it is restrictive.

A **restrictive clause** is essential to the meaning of the sentence. A **nonrestrictive clause** gives additional information but could be left out of the sentence without changing the basic meaning of the sentence. The examples below illustrate complex sentences; independent clauses are italicized; dependent clauses are in boldface.

> **While the movie was being filmed**, *the small town did an excellent tourist business.*
> (A dependent restrictive clause precedes an independent clause.)
>
> *The small town did an excellent tourist business* **while the movie was being filmed**.
> (A restrictive dependent clause follows an independent clause.)
>
> *Charlie ate the overripe banana*, **which was the only one left on the fruit bar**.
> (A nonrestrictive dependent clause follows an independent clause.)

Compound-Complex Sentences

Compound-complex sentences have two or more independent clauses and one or more dependent clauses. In the examples below, the independent clauses are italicized; the dependent clauses are in boldface:

> *The Indianapolis 500 will be run today*, and **if the weather is nice,** *record times may be set.*
> (A dependent restrictive clause precedes the second independent clause.)
>
> **Although the Statue of Liberty is in New York City,** *it belongs to every American*, and *I experience a feeling of pride and ownership* **when I see it.**
> (A dependent restrictive clause precedes the first independent clause; a dependent restrictive clause follows the second independent clause.)

The number and kind of clauses determine the type of sentence structure. Figure 5-3 summarizes types of sentence construction.

TYPES	CLAUSE(S)
Simple	One independent
Compound	Two (or more) independent
Complex	One independent and one (or more) dependent
Compound-Complex	Two (or more) independent and one (or more) dependent

Figure 5-3
Types of Sentences

WORD CHOICE AND SENTENCE STRUCTURE

1. Check your word knowledge by circling the correct words:
   a. What was the (principal, principle) idea of the book?
   b. Send your application to the (personal, personnel) manager.
   c. I traveled (fewer, less) miles this year than last year.
   d. Did Mr. Jones (except, accept) your proposal?
   e. The budget cut was (quiet, quite) significant.

(continued on next page)

(continued)

2. Write correct sentences using these words: respectively, effect, complements, cite, and stationary.

   a. (respectively)

   b. (effect)

   c. (complements)

   d. (cite)

   e. (stationary)

3. Write an example for each sentence type specified.

   a. Write a simple sentence with a compound subject.

   b. Write a compound sentence with two independent clauses.

   c. Write a complex sentence in which the dependent clause precedes the independent clause.

   d. Write a compound-complex sentence using two independent clauses and one dependent clause.

PROVIDING EMPHASIS TO IDEAS

Successful writers emphasize ideas that are important to the message. You can emphasize ideas by appropriate use of sentence structure (where the idea is positioned within a sentence), key words, sentence length, specific names, and active voice.

Sentence structure, key words, varied sentence length, specific names, and active voice emphasize ideas.

Sentence Structure

The location of specific ideas or words within a sentence affects their emphasis. Ideas placed at the beginning of a sentence attract the reader's attention and give the most prominence to the thoughts expressed. An idea or word placed in an independent clause has more emphasis than it does if placed in a dependent clause.

> Your credit rating suffers when you do not pay your bills.
> **(Damage to credit rating is emphasized.)**
>
> When you do not pay your bills, your credit rating suffers.
> **(Failure to pay bills is emphasized.)**

When writers want to develop the main point by discussing supporting details, the end of the sentence can be the proper place for emphasis. This type of sentence structure uses the end of the sentence as the climax.

> Simply turn on the computer, load the software, select the graphics, and you are ready to print an eye-catching banner!
> **(The ease of creating a banner is emphasized.)**

Key Words

Repetition of key words effectively emphasizes ideas. However, you need to be careful, because overuse of repetition leads to dull, stilted, or unintentionally comic writing. The key words for emphasis in this sentence are italicized:

If used sparingly, repetition of key words gives emphasis.

> Our computer has the *best* features—the *best* monitor, the *best* processor, and the *best* keyboard.
> **(Repetition of *best* emphasizes the idea that our computer is best.)**

Sentence Length

Good writing uses a variety of sentence lengths. The average length of a sentence is 15–20 words. A shorter than average sentence catches the attention of the reader and emphasizes an idea. If all sentences are short, however, emphasis is lost and the writing becomes choppy. Look at the following two sentences and decide which one most effectively emphasizes the role of government:

Short sentences give emphasis when used with longer sentences.

It is imperative that freedom, the protection of which is a primary responsibility of government, be guaranteed to all citizens in the United States.
(Weak emphasis)

Protecting our freedom is the primary responsibility of government.
(Strong emphasis)

Use of Names

Using a person's name instead of an indefinite pronoun emphasizes sentence content. This technique is effective because the statement is more specific. *Dorothy left the coffeepot on over the weekend* is a stronger sentence than *Someone left the coffeepot on over the weekend.*

Active Versus Passive Voice

WORKPLACE CONNECTIONS

Use active verbs such as *developed, supervised*, and *implemented* when describing your work experiences for a job application.

Verbs in active voice create a more direct and forceful sentence than either passive voice or state-of-being verbs. With active voice, the subject of the sentence is the actor, and the verb states the action of the subject. The verb is said to be passive if the subject is the receiver of the verb's action. Passive verbs are made from a form of *be* combined with the past participible of a transitive verb (an action verb that has an object named in the sentence). There are times when the passive voice is your best choice; for example, the Mona Lisa was painted by Leonardo daVinci. But for most writing, the active voice creates greater reader interest and a stronger message. Compare the strength of these two messages:

The 16-ounce **steak** *was eaten* by Paul.
(Passive voice—weak emphasis)

Paul *ate* the 16-ounce steak.
(Active voice—strong emphasis)

FAULTY SENTENCE CONSTRUCTION

Thoughts in a sentence should be closely related.

Well-constructed sentences build clear communication. Three errors to avoid in constructing sentences are *run-on sentences*, *comma splices* and *misplaced modifiers*.

Run-on Sentences

A run-on sentence is one that contains several unrelated or loosely related clauses. The following examples show a run-on sentence and how it can be corrected.

Correct spelling, grammar, and punctuation make it easier for the reader to understand your message, and proper sentence structure also affects the image that the reader builds of the writer, and the message may be sabotaged with poor mechanics. **(Run-on Sentence)**

Correct spelling, grammar, and punctuation make it easier for the reader to understand your message. Proper sentence structure affects the reader's image of the writer. Poor mechanics sabotage a message. **(Example of corrected sentence)**

Comma Splices

A comma placed between two independent clauses without a conjunction is a **comma splice**. To correct comma splices, the writer may add a conjunction, replace the comma with a semicolon, or replace the comma with a terminal punctuation (period, exclamation mark, or question mark) that makes the second independent clause a separate sentence.

Replacing the comma with a conjunction or creating two separate sentences are the most common ways to fix comma splices.

Information is important to individuals and organizations, to gain needed information, use a variety of communication media.
(Comma splice because of the comma between *organizations* and *to gain*)

Information is important to individuals and organizations. To gain needed information, use a variety of communication media.
(Correct)

Misplaced Modifiers

Modifiers are words, phrases, or clauses that describe other words. For clarity, place modifiers close to the words they modify. The sentence meaning can be changed if modifiers are misplaced. Consider these sentences (misplaced modifiers are italicized):

Misplaced modifiers create confused and sometimes silly meanings.

As a dog that had won a blue ribbon in the All-American Dog Show, I did not want JoJo to suffer any injuries.
(Incorrect: Am I a dog or is JoJo?)

I did not want JoJo, a dog that had won a blue ribbon in the All-American Dog Show, to suffer any injuries.
(Correct: The modifer clause is placed next to the reference word.)

The basketball hit the opponent's foot *which went flying out of bounds*.
(Incorrect: Did the foot fly out of bounds?)

The basketball, which went flying out of bounds, hit the opponent's foot.
(Correct: The modifer clause follows the reference word.)

EMPHASIZING IDEAS AND CORRECTING FAULTY SENTENCES

1. Rewrite these sentences to give more emphasis to the ideas.

   a. The team is the best in discipline and in training. (Repeat key words.)

   b. I will not buy a new car because of its high cost. (Emphasize the high cost of new cars.)

   c. The political candidate's hair was dyed by the hairdresser. (Use the active voice.)

2. Rewrite the following exercises, correcting faulty construction:

   a. Many college students do not have health insurance, but some colleges require it, and some people do not believe it is a necessary expense.

   b. Every little problem noticed by a skilled driver and considered to be important by the automobile makers

   c. Driving 1,500 miles over rugged mountain terrain, the scenery was beautiful.

CHAPTER SUMMARY

- Improving your writing begins by identifying the basic parts of a sentence.
- Good writing contains correct, clear, and direct sentences.
- Using a variety of sentence structures makes writing interesting. Sentences can be simple, compound, complex, and compound-complex.
- Effective writing emphasizes key ideas and words.
- Faulty sentence construction confuses meaning and creates awkward statements. Correcting faulty sentences improves written communications.

1. Underline the subject(s) and circle the correct verb(s) in the following sentences:
   a. Members of the baseball team (is, are) going to Europe on a tour.
   b. The artists at the university (creates, create) original designs for advertising brochures.
   c. The most famous athlete of the twentieth century (appears, appear) on the cover of seven magazines this week.
   d. The debate on the homeless (is, are) likely to continue as long as Americans (is, are) caught in the stranglehold of poverty.
   e. Neither the university president nor the teachers (attends, attend) the concerts.
   f. Either LaDonna or Chris (goes, go) to the movies.
   g. Each member of the chorus (practice, practices) three times a week.
2. Rewrite the following sentences or sentence fragments, making any corrections required for clear, grammatically correct sentences. Rewrite the sentences using a computer or rewrite them below. You may add or omit words to construct a correct sentence.
   a. The artifacts in the museum from Africa were stolen and then sold in pawn shops throughout the city.
   b. The football players particularly Troy was disappointed with losing the championship game.
   c. When the storm moves through the area and the flood waters recede.
   d. The goals of the club is to build goodwill, maintain self-esteem, and creating opportunities for disadvantaged teenagers.
   e. When still a new employee, my manager assigned me to an elite fact-finding task force.

3. Write a short paragraph using at least one of each of these types of sentences: simple, compound, complex, and compound-complex. Use a computer or write the paragraph below.

4. Rewrite these sentences to give more emphasis to ideas or change emphasis.

   a. (Change to emphasize other people's trust.)

      When you tell the truth, people always trust you.

   b. (Vary sentence lengths to strengthen this message.)

      Making your child feel unconditionally loved and valued is not easy, especially with teenagers, but it is important to say, "I will always love you, in good times and bad." When bad behavior causes problems, reassure your child that your disapproval is of the behavior and not of the child.

   c. (Change the indefinite pronoun to a proper noun to make the sentence stronger.)

      I saw someone leave the door open during the fire drill.

   d. (Change the verb voice to strengthen the sentence.)

      The trees were blown down by the strong winds.

5. Rewrite the following sentences, correcting the lack of parallelism. Use a computer or write the sentences on the lines below.

   a. Brian goes to school in the morning, worked as a cook in the afternoon, and will party in the evening.

   b. The exam was difficult, lengthy, and many questions were taken from material that was not to be covered at this time.

   c. The secretary has good phone skills, could type 50 words per minute, and we will use her as an auditor during the next tax season.

   d. We improved our office by painting the walls and we bought new furniture.

   e. You can buy your automobile in Paducah or when you go to Nashville.

   f. Catherine may go to school to be a musician, a veterinarian, or in engineering.

6. Correct the faulty sentences using a word processing program on the computer or rewrite them on the lines below.

   a. When the rain and wind stop we will resume playing golf, we can finish the round before sunset.

   b. The house on the hill at the end of the road and with a pond located in the back.

   c. The tour guide hesitated to explain the change in plans to the tourists, seemingly confused.

   d. The player must condition his or her body, before they began serious workouts at the beginning of the season.

   e. While Rosa was busy arranging the flowers for the evening banquet, and José was stringing lights on the patio.

   f. Wilson served two terms as city councilman, was defeated in a school board race, and then the position of mayor was his next defeat.

7. You are interested in emphasizing several ideas that are critical to the goals of your message. Briefly describe in an e-mail to your instructor the various ways that this may be accomplished. In the space below, organize your thoughts before sending the e-mail message.

8. Write a sentence for each of the following directions:

   a. (End a complex sentence with a dependent clause.)

   b. (Show emphasis through use of names.)

   c. (Use two independent clauses with compound subjects.)

   d. (Repeat key words for emphasis.)

   e. (Use a complex sentence with a compound subject in the independent clause.)

Correct the grammar, spelling, capitalization, punctuation, sentence structure, and word choice errors in the following sentences. Write *Correct* for sentences containing no errors.

1. Businesses operates in a global marketplace to compete in this world market requires new ways of organizing and preparing workers.

2. New flight attendents must learn to manage her emotions in stressful situations.

3. The young married couple were sitting by the window; staring into the fire; and dreaming about there future.

4. The newly opened sports store were looking for well built young men to be members of its sales force.

5. "Are you sure that I can believe you?" the lawyer asked the prospective witness.

6. I planned to visit the History Museum yesterday but then it rained.

7. The fisherman casted his rod and real with his left-hand.

8. The sick child wined to his mother that he did not feel good enough to finish his assay.

9. Emily had already went to the movies afore her mother arrived home.

10. An alert school crossing guard can ensure that neither child or parent will be injured.

CHAPTER 6

WRITING EFFECTIVE PARAGRAPHS

"The agony was not John F. Kennedy's. It was Jacqueline Bouvier Kennedy's. He was serene in the cool darkness of death. She, the least prepared for violence, sat with it, prayed over it, crooned at it on her lap. Agent Hill, off the edge of the back seat, could not help her. He hung on, the gun in his right hand, and he saw the knots of people on the street corners; the joyriders pulled to one side and parked with people leaning out. The faces were beaming; the people waved; they saw the pink of Mrs. Kennedy, and they yelled greetings."[1]

The above description of the presidential motorcade in Dallas immediately after the assassination of John F. Kennedy shows how a well-constructed paragraph conveys the author's message. The author creates for the reader a vivid mental image of the scene.

LEARNING OBJECTIVES

- Group thoughts into unified paragraphs.
- Analyze paragraph structure.
- Develop paragraphs for different purposes.
- Write effective opening and closing paragraphs.
- Edit and refine paragraphs.

ARRANGING IDEAS IN PARAGRAPHS

Effective paragraphs accomplish the writer's intended purpose. They are more than well-constructed sentences. The way sentences are arranged in a paragraph and their connection to one main idea contribute to message clarity.

Message Organization

Paragraphs organize information for the reader. They group thoughts related to the main ideas in a message. Each paragraph consists of one or more sentences that develop a single idea. In other words, it includes one main idea and information directly related to that idea. It is a unit of thought. Beginning a new paragraph for each different idea alerts the reader to a shift in thought.

A paragraph consists of one or more sentences that develop a single idea.

Can you identify the thought shift in the following message?

> MasterWorks, Inc., wants employees who have technical competence, show maturity, can accept responsibility, and who communicate effectively. They consider work habits and attitudes as important as knowledge and skills; therefore, their recruitment and hiring processes for

[1]Bishop, J. (1968). *The day Kennedy was shot.* New York: Funk & Wagnalls, p. 145.

new employees target these characteristics. The rate of employee turnover at MasterWorks is less than one percent a year. Employees receive competitive salaries, insurance benefits, liberal vacation time, and education leave. In addition, the company offers opportunities for promotion and advancement. These employee benefits promote a stable and competent work force.

A new paragraph alerts the reader to a shift in thought.

The previous paragraph shifted from the first main thought about employee attributes desired by MasterWorks to information about employee benefits. See how separating these two ideas into the following two paragraphs alerts the reader to a shift in thought:

MasterWorks, Inc., wants employees who have technical competence, show maturity, can accept responsibility, and communicate effectively. They consider work habits and attitudes as important as knowledge and skills; therefore, their recruitment and hiring processes for new employees target these characteristics.

The rate of employee turnover at MasterWorks is less than one percent a year. Employees receive competitive salaries, insurance benefits, liberal vacation time, and education leave. In addition, the company offers opportunities for promotion and advancement. These employee benefits promote a stable and competent work force.

Paragraph Unity

Unified paragraphs come from linking ideas to show the connections from one thought to the next. Transition words or phrases, key word repetition, and parallelism are devices for making these connections.

Transitional words or phrases unify a paragraph.

TRANSITIONAL WORDS OR PHRASES. Expressions such as *moreover*, *first*, *then*, *meanwhile*, *for example*, *therefore*, *as a result*, *in addition*, *again*, *further*, *nevertheless*, *however*, *but*, *yet*, *thus*, *as a result*, *similarly*, *previously*, *later*, and *in fact* connect related ideas. These expressions are examples of transitional words or phrases that can be used to unify related ideas in a paragraph. Use of transitions helps the reader move easily from one thought to the next. A smooth thought flow is an essential characteristic of good writing. In the following paragraph, notice how the italicized transitional words help unify the paragraph and link ideas for the reader.

"This week the company has a sale on laptop computers. *Moreover*, each member of the sales force who sells 10 or more laptops will receive one free for his or her own use. Mickey [the salesperson] goes to the database he maintains on his computer to search his customer records for promising purchasers. He *first* lists owners of laptops from the same manufacturer, *then* owners of other laptops, and begins placing calls."[2]

[2]The Secretary's Commission on Achieving Necessary Skills. (1991). What work requires of schools: A SCANS report for America 2000. Washington, DC: U.S. Department of Labor, p. 9.

Key Word Repetition and Parallelism. Other devices for paragraph unity are repetition of key words or phrases and use of parallel form. Both of these devices, mentioned in Chapter 5 for sentence construction, can be used to strengthen paragraph unity, as shown in the following examples:

Repetition of key words contributes to paragraph unity and gives emphasis to ideas.

Word Repetition

E-mail *saves time*. Easy access and rapid transmission *saves time* for the message sender, and easy reply *saves time* for the message receiver. With inefficient use, however, this *time saver* can become a *time waster*.

Parallel Construction

"*To give* the important parts of your speech more emphasis, remind yourself of when *to do* it by ***taking*** a green highlighter and ***marking*** those places you want *to emphasize*; now, photocopy your speech. Why? Green highlighters reproduce as a distinctive grey, and you'll be able *to read* your copy clearly and easily."

—The speechhelper. *The Working Communicator*, 212 W. Superior St., Suite 200, Chicago, IL 60610

ORGANIZING IDEAS INTO PARAGRAPHS AND USING TRANSITIONS FOR UNITY

Mark a "P" where a new paragraph is needed to indicate a change in thought in the following excerpt. Circle transition words and underline examples of parallel structure or repetition of words and phrases.

The frontier forts of Texas were spearheads of civilization in a primitive land. As settlers poured West—ever eager for new fields to break and sow and new pastures to produce beef—lines of forts were established to secure and protect the far-flung frontier. The passions of that era were often volatile: frontiersmen on one side, tough and self-reliant, accustomed to taking what they wanted; Indians on the other side, resentful of intruders in a land they had once roamed at will. Often in between was the frontier soldier. His hardships were many and his dangers real. Usually it was the soldier who built the fort, felled trees and shaped crude timbers, quarried stone and heaved both into place with pure muscle. Then when it was finished—by the time frayed tents gave way to rude barracks—he looked around to find the nucleus of a town. Farmers were plowing new ground; stores and saloons were being built. Civilization had arrived, and the frontier had moved. But the frontier's edge was still bloody, and the soldier moved with it.

Connection Devices

Reference pronouns, perspective, adverbial clauses, and tie-in sentences unify ideas in a paragraph.

Construction of a paragraph affects the smooth flow of ideas from one detail to another. Using reference pronouns, writing a message from only one perspective, using adverbial clauses, and linking ideas with a tie-in sentence are devices that connect ideas for the reader.

REFERENCE PRONOUNS. The use of pronouns increases paragraph unity. Instead of repeating nouns in a paragraph, you can use pronouns for variety. Be sure, however, that the noun referenced by the pronoun is clear to the reader. In the paragraph that follows, see how cumbersome it would be if you replaced all of the pronouns with the character's name:

Using pronouns keeps a paragraph from being cumbersome while adding variety.

> Marty ran *her* fingers through *her* thick, red hair as *she* saw *her* image in the mirror. *Her* thoughts wandered to the past six weeks and how discouraged *she* was when nothing came from *her* first three interviews. *She* remembered the pain of rejection and the sense of fear that no job offer would ever come. But here *she* was preparing for *her* first day as copy editor for Markswell Publishing.

In most cases, a demonstrative pronoun such as *these*, *those*, or *that* should be followed by the noun to which it refers. An exception would be acceptable if the sentence construction makes clear the noun to which the pronoun refers. To check, ask yourself *those what*? *that what*? If the noun is not close to the demonstrative pronoun and is not immediately clear, add the noun or its synonym after the pronoun.

Changing perspective within a paragraph confuses the reader.

PERSPECTIVE. Writing from a consistent perspective improves unity of thought. Shifting viewpoints in the middle of a paragraph is confusing. Consider the following example. Who is speaking in the last sentence?

> Jane wanted to slip quietly into the house to avoid disturbing her mother. Much to her chagrin, the door closed with a loud thud. She called out in a trembling voice "Is anyone there?"

We cannot be sure whether the person speaking is Jane or her mother. If it is her mother, the paragraph has shifted perspective. To clarify the meaning, make the last sentence read, "Jane heard her mother call out in a trembling voice, 'Is anyone there?'" This change maintains a consistent perspective. The reader then sees the situation through the eyes of one person—Jane.

An introductory dependent clause that acts as an adverb is an adverbial clause.

ADVERBIAL CLAUSE. Another type of transition that unifies a paragraph is an introductory adverbial clause. An **adverbial clause** is a dependent clause that acts as an adverb and comes before an independent clause in a sentence. This clause answers questions such as *how, when, where, why, in what manner*, or *to what degree*. A beginning adverbial clause may be setting the stage or the condition for the main thought; therefore, it plays a supporting role and should not contain the main idea of a sentence.

When you walked into the room, people stopped talking. (The introductory adverbial clause is shown in italics. This clause answers the question *when* about the verb *stopped*.)

TIE-IN SENTENCES. A complete sentence may come between two sentences to help the reader move smoothly from the idea expressed in the first sentence to the next different but related idea. The following paragraph illustrates a tie-in sentence that makes the thought transition between two sentences. The tie-in sentence is italicized.

Visuals enhance communication. Communication takes place by sending a message from the sender to the receiver. The reader interprets the message through one of the five senses: sight, hearing, touch, taste, or smell. *Consider this fact.* Sight is the most powerful of the senses. Research from the University of Minnesota indicates that using visuals with oral presentations increases retention by ten percent.

CONSTRUCTING SENTENCES FOR SMOOTH FLOW OF IDEAS

1. Circle the reference pronouns and underline the adverbial clause in the following paragraph:

When Milburn entered the house at 907 Whitehead Street, Key West, Florida, he had the sensation of stepping back in time—back to the time when this Spanish Colonial house was home to Ernest Hemingway. It was here that this great American author lived with his second wife, Pauline, and their two sons. It was here that he wrote *For Whom the Bell Tolls, Green Hills of Africa, A Farewell to Arms, The Fifth Column, The Snows of Kilimanjaro,* and *The Macomber Affair.*

2. In the following paragraph, underline transition words, tie-in sentences, or reference pronouns.

To live and make a living in these changing times will require continuous learning. Such is the wave of the future. Today's middle and high school students will have to be life-long learners. They can expect to attend at least two years of post-high school education at a college, university, or technical school. Even then, their education will not be complete. They will be likely to change jobs at least five times during their careers. Each work role will call for new learning. With global interaction via the Internet (and communication advances yet to come), people will be learning as long as they live.

ANALYZING PARAGRAPH STRUCTURE

A paragraph has a topic sentence, supporting sentences, and a concluding sentence.

Each paragraph is structured around one main idea. In this section of the chapter, you will examine the parts of a paragraph and their relationship to one another.

Paragraphs consist of the following parts:

- topic sentence that tells the theme or idea of the paragraph
- sentences that give primary support to the main idea through further explanation
- sentences that support these explanations
- concluding sentence

Skillful construction and organization of topic sentences, descriptive details, connectives, and concluding sentences create structural paragraph patterns that attract readers' interest and aid their understanding of the message.

Topic Sentence

A topic sentence states the main idea of a paragraph.

The **topic sentence**, usually the first sentence in a paragraph, states the main idea of the paragraph. The topic sentence alerts the reader to the content or focus of the paragraph and, thereby, makes the rest of the paragraph easier to understand. The topic sentence in the following paragraph is italicized:

> *High-performance workers come from high-performance schools.* Fundamental changes in the nature of work are creating a demand for high-performance employees. To be competitive internationally, organizations must invest in workers who not only possess strong academic knowledge and skills but who also have problem-solving skills and can produce high-quality products or services. High performance schools require students to demonstrate critical thinking skills and high academic achievement. Therefore, their graduates have the necessary skills to meet the challenges of a changing workplace.

The first sentence in the paragraph above is a topic sentence that states the the main idea of the paragraph—that today's workplace requires workers with a high-quality education. The topic sentence placed at the beginning of a paragraph performs a dual function. It attracts the reader's interest as well as tells what the paragraph is about. Some writers call the first sentence a "hook" because it captures the interest of the reader.

Topic sentences are usually the first sentence but can be at the end of the paragraph.

Topic sentences that are placed at the end of a paragraph serve as a climax or summary. This type of paragraph would use another beginning sentence to serve as a hook that attracts the reader's interest. In this case, statements in the body of the paragraph contribute to the main idea stated at the end of the sentence. The hook in the paragraph that follows is underlined, and the topic sentence is italicized:

> Is privacy and security important to you? If it is, you may want privacy when you are home enjoying your own backyard. For pennies a day, you can install a fence around your yard that will limit access and make your backyard a retreat. *A Guardian cedar fence will give you privacy, security, and beauty.*

Concluding Sentence

The last sentence of a paragraph summarizes or restates the idea expressed by the topic sentence unless the last sentence is the topic sentence. This sentence also can bridge the thoughts expressed in this paragraph to the main idea discussed in the next paragraph. A good concluding sentence in a paragraph moves the reader's thoughts smoothly from one major idea to another. Consider the last sentence in the following paragraph:

The last sentence of a paragraph summarizes the idea of the message and can be a transition to the next paragraph.

> *The Internet connects people and ideas around the globe.* It is rapidly becoming one of the most comprehensive sources of information ever known. *Access to the Internet opens an exchange of ideas through e-mail, newsgroups, chat rooms, discussion groups, and web sites.*

The italicized topic sentence introduces the main thought about connections of people and ideas through the Internet. The last sentence restates this idea and mentions types of Internet resources that will be topics for the next paragraph or paragraphs.

Supporting Sentences

The other sentences in a paragraph relate in some way to the topic sentence. Some of these sentences give primary support to the main idea, and others give secondary support. The topic sentence presents the unifying idea for the paragraph; and supporting sentences provide data, definitions, examples, discussion, or other evidence that explains or supplements this idea. Consider the supporting sentences in the earlier example paragraph about high-performing work and schools.

Supporting sentences provide data, definitions, examples, discussion, or other evidence that supports the topic sentence.

Main idea: High-performance schools produce high-performance workers.

Primary support for main idea:

The changed nature of work creates a need for high-performance workers.

Secondary supporting thoughts:

Businesses compete internationally.

Academic knowledge and skills are important.

Organizations value problem-solving skills, high productivity, and high quality work.

Primary support for main idea:

Graduates of high-performance schools have the required work skills.

Conclusion: Graduates of high-performance schools are prepared for the challenges of a changing workplace.

Vary the length of sentences and paragraphs.

Paragraph Length

Using sentences and paragraphs of varying lengths strengthens a message. A paragraph with only short sentences is dull and choppy. A paragraph with only long sentences is difficult to read and understand. The average sentence length is from 10–20 words. Different sentence lengths help maintain reader interest. Good writers vary both sentence and paragraph lengths in their messages.

In novels, essays, and textbooks, you often find lengthy paragraphs that develop topics in depth. In technical and business writing, paragraphs are generally short. In business writing it is not unusual to have important information in a paragraph with only one or two sentences. It is uncommon to find business paragraphs longer than five to eight sentences. Business writing often places important ideas in bulleted or numbered lists rather than in paragraph form.

Workplace Connections

"Too many employees try to impress with complex sentences, big words, and lengthy memos, forgetting that communication is the name of the game."
—Hulbert

PARAGRAPH COMPONENTS

1. In the following paragraph, the topic sentence should be at the beginning of this message, but it is not. Underline the topic sentence that ties together related ideas in the paragraph. Draw a line through any inappropriate sentence that is unrelated to the main idea of the paragraph.

   Schools throughout the United States spend millions each year for computer equipment. Higher productivity and improved communication are the key benefits of communications technology—both in the work world and in education. It is not uncommon for managers to spend up to six hours per day video-conferencing with colleagues. Many businesses today have cafeterias for their employees. Technology can cut travel costs by 30 percent. Technology can easily get people involved to resolve issues and problems.

2. In the space below, write a sentence that could be used as the last sentence for the paragraph above.

3. Rewrite the complete paragraph so that it includes one or more transitions to bridge supporting sentences and the main idea in the paragraph. Leave out any sentence that cannot be linked easily to the topic sentence and add other sentences, if needed. You can compose the paragraph on a computer or write your paragraph on a separate piece of paper.

DEVELOPING PARAGRAPHS FOR DIFFERENT PURPOSES

Because there are different types of messages and different goals for those messages, there are a variety of ways to organize paragraphs. The general elements of paragraph construction are, as previously noted, a topic sentence, primary and secondary supporting sentences, and a concluding statement. Using these basic elements, there are a variety of patterns and combinations of patterns that can be used with these basic elements for organizing written material.

Depending on your purpose, organization might be chronological, spatial, or order of importance, or might show cause and effect.

The two primary patterns are called direct organization and indirect organization. **Direct organization** first presents the main idea and then gives details, examples, and supporting ideas. **Indirect organization** presents the details first and leads up to a concluding main idea. (These patterns are illustrated below in Figure 6-1.)

With either direct or indirect organizational patterns, ideas may be sequenced chronologically, by spatial order, or by cause and effect. The purpose of writing helps determine how to sequence content. **Chronological** organization arranges details in order by time. This pattern is used most often in *narrative* or in *descriptive process* paragraphs. Sequencing ideas by **spatial order** organizes details in a consistent direction: near to far, left to right, front to back, or top to bottom. Other patterns of organizing ideas are by *order of importance* or by *cause and effect.*

Narrative Paragraphs

A narrative tells a story by presenting a series of events that have a particular beginning and ending. Organizing events chronologically helps the

A narrative tells a story and often organizes events in chronological order.

Figure 6-1
Direct and Indirect Organization

reader understand the development of the narration and creates a sense of time. An indirect approach to chronological order would present events from the beginning of the story to a conclusion or climax; whereas, a direct approach would begin with the climax and then add details of events that led to it.

> "A crisis was imminent. It was the moment for drama. And it was furnished, obligingly enough, by the opening of the door to admit the two whom Magnolia Ravenal loved in all the world. There came first the handsome, haggard Gaylord Ravenal, actually managing, in some incredible way, to appear elegant, well-dressed, dapper, at a time, under circumstances, and in a costume which would have rendered most men unsightly, if not repulsive. But his gifts were many, and not the least of them was the trick of appearing sartorially and tonsorially flawless when dishevelment and a stubble were inevitable in any other male. Close behind him trotted Andy Hawks, just as he had been twenty-four hours before—wrinkled linen pants, double-breasted blue coat, oversize visored cap, mutton-chop whiskers and all. Together he and Ma Hawks, in her blue brass-buttoned coat that was a twin of his, managed to give the gathering quite a military aspect. Certainly Mrs. Hawks' manner was martial enough at the moment. She raised her voice now in complaint."[3]

The direct approach to paragraph organization is deductive and moves from the main idea to supporting details.

This narrative paragraph from Edna Ferber's novel *Show Boat* uses direct development of details. The first sentence tells that a crisis is coming. She then builds the details in chronological order up to the point of complaint that begins the crisis. Characters are described in the order that they enter the room—first Mr. Ravenal and then Mr. and Mrs. Hawks.

Descriptive Paragraphs

Descriptive paragraphs inform or instruct the reader.

A descriptive paragraph informs or instructs the reader. It can be organized with a direct or an indirect approach. As shown in Figure 6-1 at the beginning of this section, direct organization presents the main points first, then gives details in the succeeding sentences. This is **deductive writing**—moving from the main idea to supporting information. The indirect approach, called **inductive writing**, presents details first and leads to a conclusion that contains the main idea.

A process paragraph gives directions and describes steps in chronological order.

PROCESS PARAGRAPHS. One type of descriptive paragraph explains a process or directions. It tells how to do something or how to get somewhere. Organization follows a step-by-step chronological sequence.

[3]Ferber, E. (1958). Show boat in *Three living novels of American life: Show boat, So big, Cimarron* (pp. 7-232). Garden City, NY: Doubleday, p. 19.

Imagine how confused you would be if you tried to follow a recipe that did not present the steps in the order to be completed! Paragraphs describing a process generally use a direct pattern of organization.

> To grow poppies in your flower bed, first work up the soil with a rake or hoe. Then scatter seeds on the surface and cover them very lightly with soil. You don't need fertilizer. Wet down the tiny, black seeds with a fine spray so that they won't wash away. Annual and perennial poppies start blooming in late May. Many continue through midsummer if you water in dry weather and remove spent flowers.
>
> —adapted from Your garden: Advice for better midwest gardening, *Midwest Living*, *13*(3), p. 62.

COMPARATIVE PARAGRAPHS. A descriptive paragraph may use comparison or contrast to describe or analyze more than one subject. A simple comparison paragraph begins by stating the two things being compared and the criteria for comparison. Next, you make the comparison by applying the criteria to the items, either one item or one criterion at a time. If more than three or four things are compared, you can make the comparison by organizing from best to worst. The closing statement might briefly conclude why you consider one item to be best.

A descriptive paragraph can compare more than one subject and conclude which is best.

OTHER DESCRIPTIVE PARAGRAPHS. Descriptive paragraphs can be used to present a word picture of people, places, or things. This type of writing uses sensory details or descriptive facts. Sensory details are ones that describe things you can see, touch, taste, hear, or smell. Consider what the reader needs to know to get an accurate mental picture.

Sensory details describe what you see, hear, touch, smell, or taste.

When the details you are using are factual and objective, rather than sensory or objective, you need to gather your information from reliable sources. References might include an encyclopedia, library resources, the Internet, or interviews with knowledgeable people. Be specific and accurate. It is better to say "salaries increased three percent over the last five years" than to say "salaries increased gradually over the last five years."

Be specific and accurate with factual details.

Remember that descriptive information that relates spatial details should move in a consistent direction, as if you were moving a camera in for a close up or moving back for a landscape view. This orderly movement helps the reader visualize what you are describing.

The introduction to this chapter began with a paragraph describing President Kennedy's motorcade scene immediately after he was shot. This paragraph follows a direct pattern. The opening sentence gives the climax followed by sensory details from an initial focus on individuals in the car and then moving the imaginary camera lens to the crowd.

The following paragraph from *Kidnapped* by Robert Louis Stevenson uses an indirect approach to describe a character. Notice how the details progress from the stature of the man, then to his face and to his eyes, and back to his total appearance and manners. The concluding sentence sums up the total impression of the man. It is as if a camera moves in for a close up and then moves back to long range.

> "He was smallish in stature, but well set and as nimble as a goat; his face was of good open expression, but sunburnt very dark, and heavily freckled and pitted with the smallpox; his eyes were unusually light and had a kind of dancing madness in them, that was both engaging and alarming; and when he took off his great-coat, he laid a pair of fine, silvermounted pistols on the table, and I saw that he was belted with a great sword. His manners, besides, were elegant, and he pledged the captain handsomely. Altogether I thought of him, at the first sight, that here was a man I would rather call my friend than my enemy."[4]

"If you cannot persuade your colleagues of the correctness of your decision, it is probably worthwhile to rethink your own."

—Alan Greenspan, Chairman, Federal Reserve Board

Persuasive Paragraphs

A persuasive message is written for two purposes:

- to change the opinion of the receiver
- to request action the reader may be unwilling to take

Examples of persuasive writing include attempts to persuade readers to respond to a questionnaire, donate to charity, or grant a job interview. Persuasive messages convince the readers to take action or to change their opinion about something. Persuasive messages must convince readers that the desired response is in their best interest. Think of the messages with which you are bombarded every day. Whether they are urging you to buy, vote, subscribe, recycle, or save wildlife, a very large percentage of the messages you receive are persuasive.

A persuasive message uses an indirect approach that gives details first and concludes with the main idea.

A persuasive paragraph or message uses an indirect approach. Benefits to the reader are presented before the request. This order puts the receiver in the right frame of mind to consider the request. If the request comes first, the rest of the message may go unread or be read with a negative attitude.

Writing a persuasive message from the reader's viewpoint is critical. To effectively persuade readers, consider what factors will motivate them. Figure 6-2 lists a sequence of points to include in a persuasive message.

[4]Stevenson, R. L. (1935). *Kidnapped.* Chicago: Goldsmith Publishing, p. 69.

INDIRECT PLAN FOR PERSUASION

1. **Attention**
   A. Attract reader's attention in the opening sentence.
   B. Entice the reader to read or to listen to rest of message.
   C. Be positive and brief.
2. **Interest**
   A. Build on attention gained in opening sentence.
   B. Show how your argument benefits the reader.
   C. Motivate the reader to continue reading.
3. **Desire**
   A. Build attention and interest by giving proof the benefits will be delivered.
   B. Re-emphasize benefits to the reader.
   C. Downplay any negative points.
4. **Action**
   A. Motivate the reader to take immediate action.
   B. Be positive.
   C. Make action easy.

From p. 247 in Kriszan, A. C., Merrier, P., Jones, C. L., and Harcourt, J. (1999). *Business communication* (4th ed.). Cincinnati, OH: South-Western College Publishing.

Figure 6-2
Persuasive Messages

ORGANIZING PARAGRAPH DETAILS

1. Read the paragraph below and check the items that best describe the paragraph.

"According to Peter Senge, systems thinking is a framework for seeing interrelationships rather than things, for seeing patterns of change rather than static 'snapshots.' It is a set of general principles—distilled over the course of the 20th century, spanning fields as diverse as the physical and social sciences, engineering, and management. It is also a set of specific tools and techniques, originating in two threads: in 'feedback' concepts of cybernetics and in 'servo-mechanisms' engineering theory dating back to the 19th century."

—Cited in Everett, D.R. (1995). Teaching SCANS competencies in business education. *Delta Pi Epsilon. Instructional strategies: An applied research series, 11*(3), p. 4.

Length of Sentences:	Varied	☐	Short	☐	Long	☐
Unity of Thought:	Unified	☐	Disconnected	☐		
Type of Structure:	Direct	☐	Indirect	☐		
Type of Paragraph:	Persuasive	☐	Descriptive	☐	Comparative	☐

(continued)

2. Write a persuasive paragraph that urges parents to get involved with their child's education. They can join the parent-teacher organization at the school, volunteer, or become a member of a school-based council or other committees. Include these facts: Research shows that parent involvement in a child's education improves student achievement. A personalized school setting where teachers know students as learners and as individuals promotes learning. Teacher awareness of students' family cultures and life outside school is an important key to student achievement.

3. Rewrite the fragment below to create a topic sentence. Develop a comparison paragraph from the topic sentence that compares this fear to the fear of going to the dentist to have a tooth extracted.

   The fear of standing before a crowd to give a presentation

OPENING AND CLOSING PARAGRAPHS

The two most important paragraphs in a multiple-paragraph message are the opening and closing paragraphs. Writing these paragraphs follows the same guidelines presented earlier in this chapter for first and last sentences of a paragraph. The first paragraph attracts the reader's attention and introduces the topic of the complete message. The last paragraph leaves the final impression and makes the final appeal for the reader's response to the message.

Appeal to the reader's interests in the introductory paragraph. Put your main idea in the first paragraph and in the first sentence. Your first paragraph clearly presents the scope of the subject, its value, and/or consequences. This paragraph sets the tone for the complete message. If you are not sure what you want to say in the opening paragraph, wait to write it until the rest of the message is written. You may find it easier to write the first paragraph last.

The closing paragraph summarizes the main points by using memorable statements, looking to the future, or calling for action. You may have some remark in your notes that adds an interesting detail or neatly sums up the main message. A snappy quotation can work well as the final sentence. This can be something said or written by a person mentioned in the message. Give special thought to the last paragraph just as you did with the first paragraph. These two paragraphs create the first and last impression of the message.

> **"Do you recognize these opening leads? 'A funny thing happened. . . .', 'Fasten your seatbelts. . .', 'There's good news and bad news. . .', 'It was the best of times; it was the worst of times. . .'"**

EDITING AND REFINING PARAGRAPHS

Paragraph construction follows steps in the writing process. Before beginning to write, brainstorm ideas on the topic. Next, gather information about the topic before you draft the ideas into one or more paragraphs. Editing and refining paragraphs require two or three readings. Read the paragraph aloud to listen for smooth flow, thought transitions, positive tone, and meaning.

Examine the paragraph for structure and unity. Ask yourself these questions: What is the main idea? Which sentence gives this information? Do the supporting sentences in each paragraph closely relate to the main idea and expand the thought with details and information? What sentence brings the ideas expressed in the paragraph to a conclusion? Are transitional words or phrases used appropriately to link ideas? When you are satisfied that the meaning is clear and that the writing helps the reader, you are ready to edit for correctness.

Read it again for structure and unnecessary words and phrases. In the final reading, edit grammar, punctuation, and word choice.

WRITING AND REFINING PARAGRAPHS

1. Use the Internet to research information about a topic that interests you. Use word processing software to develop an outline for a descriptive paper on this topic. Use a computer to write the opening and closing paragraphs.
2. Answer these questions about the opening and closing paragraphs that you have written:
   a. What is the main idea?

   b. What is the hook that will motivate the reader to read the message?

   c. What is the final message of the closing paragraph?

   d. What is the response you want from the reader?

3. Read your paragraphs to revise, edit, and refine. Rewrite the paragraphs making all changes that are needed. Add a footer to the page with your final copy of the paper. Have the footer show your name at the left margin, the date in the center, and the page number at the right margin. Print a copy to submit to your instructor.

CHAPTER SUMMARY

- Paragraphs have one main idea connected to supporting sentences by transition words or phrases, key word repetition, and parallel construction. Use of reference pronouns, a consistent perspective, adverbial clauses, and tie-in sentences help unify the paragraph.
- Paragraph components include a topic sentence, supporting sentences, descriptive details, and concluding sentence. Good writers vary the length of sentences and paragraphs.
- The type and purpose of paragraphs determine the organization and sequence of details. Messages that tell a story, describe, or persuade follow specific organizational patterns and use direct or indirect approaches to writing.
- Opening paragraphs attract the reader's interest; closing paragraphs use memorable statements, look to the future, or call for action. These two paragraphs create the first and the last impressions of the message.
- Writing paragraphs follows the basic steps in the writing process: brainstorming, researching, drafting, revising, editing, and refining.

1. Use the following paragraph to answer the questions below it.

   The telecommunications field is challenging and exciting. Students will learn how to connect leading-edge technologies like optic systems, satellites, telephony, and cable with computers to permit organizations and individuals to communicate instantaneously around the world. Mathematics is an important subject for students who study telecommunications. Moreover, a student graduating with a degree in telecommunications can expect many job opportunities. Market need exceeds the number of graduates in the field. Therefore, starting salaries in this field will be higher than in most other fields.

   a. What is the topic sentence?

   b. What sentence is inappropriate or unrelated to the main idea of the paragraph?

   c. What are the transition words or phrases?

2. Form a team of two to three students and use your creativity to write a paragraph on one of the topics listed below. Write the paragraph using the **direct** approach. If you have a computer, use word processing software to write the paragraph. If no computer is available, write the paragraph on a sheet of paper.

   a. Anyone can make money in the commodity market.
   b. Ethical individuals have a better chance for success than unethical ones.
   c. Hot weather is better than cold weather.
   d. Cold weather is better than hot weather.
   e. A cat is a better pet than a dog.
   f. A dog is a better pet than a cat.
   g. When obtaining a job, fringe benefits are as important as the salary.
   h. Walking is as good as jogging for exercise.
   i. Going to the movies relieves stress.
   j. Essay exams are more difficult than computational exams.

3. Using the same team as in Exercise 2 above, write a paragraph on one of the topics using the **indirect** approach. If you have a computer, use word processing software to write the paragraph. If no computer is available, write the paragraph on a separate sheet of paper.

4. The sentences below about purchasing an automobile, can be arranged into two paragraphs. Some of the sentences do not relate to the topic of the paragraphs. Fill in the blanks at the end of this exercise with the letters of the sentences in the order that they should appear in the two paragraphs. In the last two blanks, fill in the letters of the sentences that do not relate to the paragraphs.

Purchasing an Automobile

a. I have decided to keep some savings for security; therefore, I will check into interest rates on automobile loans.

b. Once I owned a car that was a real lemon.

c. Now that I know what I want and what it will cost, I begin thinking about finance options.

d. I decide to buy a car; the choices and excitement begin.

e. Currently, financial institutions are having a difficult time.

f. After selecting a financial institution and making a loan application, I feel the excitement build as I wait for my new car.

g. When I know what I can afford, I can choose the car's features—the fun part of buying a new car.

h. First, I get to select what I want—a Mercedes, a Cadillac, a Chrysler, a Mercury, a Honda, or a Yugo.

i. After comparing interest rates on my savings and on a loan, I choose to use money from my savings account to reduce the amount of the loan.

j. Which one can I afford?

k. A decision must be made whether to take money from savings or get a loan.

Sentence Order

First paragraph ______ ______ ______ ______ ______

Second paragraph ______ ______ ______ ______

Unrelated sentences ______ ______

5. Assume that you are writing a research report on any of the planets in the solar system. Access *www.anu.edu.au/Physics/nineplanets/nineplanets.html* and review the information on the various planets. Select one of the planets and use a computer to write the opening and closing paragraphs for the paper. Answer these questions about the opening and closing paragraphs that you have written:

   a. What is the main idea?

   b. What is the hook that will motivate the receiver to read the message?

   c. What is the final message of the closing paragraph?

   d. What is the response you want from the reader?

6. Write a descriptive paragraph about the program of study in which you are currently enrolled. Include specifics of the program that would interest high school students. Include the courses that must be completed for the program, length of time it normally takes to complete the program, and job opportunities that are available after completing the program. If you have a computer, use word processing software to write the paragraph. If no computer is available, write the paragraph on a separate piece of paper.

7. Write a paragraph comparing spring and autumn in your region, describing differences in the beauty of each season. Use sensory details. Conclude the paragraph by stating which season you think is the more beautiful of the two. If you have a computer, use word processing software to write the paragraph. If no computer is available, write the paragraph on a separate piece of paper.

Correct the grammar, spelling, capitalization, punctuation, sentence structure, and word choice errors in the following sentences. Write *Correct* below the sentences containing no errors.

1. Self esteem and sociability and self management and integrity are essential personal qualities for individuals whom succeed in the workplace.

2. 98% of the clients will have celebrated their 80th birthday when Mildred obtains that age.

3. Have your read Judy Hawk's new novel "The Blind and the Beautiful?"

4. Of the two billionaires living in Tulsa Jim is the wealthiest.

5. The almost perfect painting just completed by the author has only one blemish.

6. Brian has the higher SAT Score in his class of 400 students.

7. The doctor advised the young mother, "If I was you I would feed oatmeal to the baby."

8. Him and his family will move to Texas after he will retire next year.

9. After finishing the marathon Kelly was so tired that she couldn't hardly move a muscle.

10. Nancys pay check was for six-hundred eighty-five dollars and 67 cents.

WRITING ESSAYS

CHAPTER 7

Essays are a means of sharing ideas, points of view, and information with others. Christopher Morley said that an essay presents "a cross section of life as seen through the lens of self." More than any other type of writing, the essay reflects the personality of the writer. Writing essays helps you develop your own writing style. Through essay writing, you become a word artist—painting a picture with words for the reader. Just as an artist has a picture in mind before beginning to paint, an essay writer decides on one main idea before beginning to write.

How will you use essay writing? You may be asked for a writing sample when applying for a job or an educational program or preparing materials for an award nomination. It is not uncommon for applications to ask you to explain why you are applying, to describe past experiences relevant to the application, or to explain your goals and aspirations for the future. In addition, you may find that you enjoy expressing your ideas and feelings in written form and decide to keep a personal journal or to share your writing with others through organizational newsletters, newspaper columns, or other publications. Advertising, teaching, and writing for the news media are examples of careers that make daily use of writing skills. Regardless of how you use the essays you write, essay writing practice will improve your ability to express ideas.

ANALYZING ESSAYS

Chapter 1 explored writing goals and described how to analyze the needs of the reader. Chapter 4 focused on steps in the writing process. In Chapter 6, you practiced writing paragraphs for different purposes. In this chapter you will focus on essays: what they are, what their general purpose is, and how to write them. You will explore types of essays and different ways of expressing ideas. Examples from essays written by both early and modern authors illustrate important techniques and writing styles.

LEARNING OBJECTIVES

- Analyze techniques and writing styles for essays.
- Review purposes and audiences for essay writing.
- Examine descriptive, expository, narrative, and persuasive writing.
- Practice developing ideas into essays.
- Format essays following standardized style guidelines.

Nature of Essays

An **essay** is a literary form, a nonfiction composition generally written from a personal point of view. While essays are analytical or interpretive, they are usually less methodical than formal, structured, scholarly works. An essay addresses one subject and is usually shorter than literary forms (such as a play or a novel).

An essay discusses a single subject from a personal point of view.

The term *essay* originated over 400 years ago in France when a retired lawyer, Michel de Montaigne, began writing for his own amusement and referred to his writings as *essais*, a French word that translates to "attempts" or "tries." Since that time, authors have written essays on almost every subject imaginable and in a variety of forms.

Today essays include such diverse writings as personal reflections, biographical accounts, humorous pieces, critical reviews, historical reports, editorials, and magazine articles. Essays are sometimes published as collections in books. Examples of such books are *The Complete Essays of Mark Twain* edited by Charles Neider and *Profiles in Courage* written by the late President John F. Kennedy.

Types of Essays

Essays can be formal or informal writing.

Before you begin writing essays, you need to know something about the types and purposes of essays. Along with descriptions are examples from essays that demonstrate how the use of language and organization of ideas mirror the purpose. Essays can be categorized in a number of ways—for example, essays can be *formal* or *informal.*

FORMAL ESSAYS. Generally, a *formal essay* is referred to as *traditional writing*. It is associated with formal language and is serious in tone. **Formal language** does not include slang or "folksy" expressions or regional dialect. Formal writing reminds us of master writers of the past—writers such as Daniel Defoe and Ralph Waldo Emerson.

A paragraph from Daniel Defoe's essay "A Journal of the Plague Year" describes the despair of the people of London at the worst point of the Black Plague. He interprets the stages of this deadly epidemic as he sees them. The language is formal and somber, yet personal. The reader sees the events through the eyes and emotions of the author.

> It is here . . . to be observed that after the funerals became so many that people could not toll the bell, mourn or weep, or wear black for one another, as they did before; no, nor so much as make coffins for those that died; so after a while the fury of the infection appeared to be so increased that, in short, they shut up no houses at all. It seemed enough that all the remedies of that kind had been used till they were found fruitless, and that the plague spread itself with an irresistible fury, so that as the fire the succeeding year spread itself, and burned with such violence that the citizens, in despair, gave over their endeavors to extinguish it, so in the plague it came at last to such violence that people sat still looking at one another, and seemed quite abandoned to despair.

Emerson's essay from *Nature* uses an equally serious but less somber tone to express his relationship with the natural universe. Again, the language is formal, although the author conveys a personal message reflecting on how we take the wonders of nature for granted.

To go into solitude, a man needs to retire as much from his chamber as from society. I am not solitary while I read and write, though nobody is with me. But if a man would be alone, let him look at the stars. The rays that come from those heavenly worlds will separate between him and what he touches. One might think the atmosphere was made transparent with this design, to give man, in the heavenly bodies, the perpetual presence of the sublime. Seen in the streets of cities, how great they are! If the stars should appear one night in a thousand years, how would men believe and adore; and preserve for many generations the remembrance of the city of God which had been shown! But every night come out these envoys of beauty, and light the universe with their admonishing smile.

Emerson uses **paradox** (seemingly contradictory expressions) to make specific points. An example of paradox is the expression in the last line "admonishing smile." It is as if the stars, in all of their beauty shining upon us, scold us for our inattention and unconcern. Terms or phrases that express seemingly contradictory ideas are also called **oxymorons**.

Paradox mentions or describes two ideas or situations that appear contradictory.

INFORMAL ESSAYS. The *informal essay* is more personal than the formal essay. The author uses informal conversation that can be serious or humorous. It sounds as if the writer is speaking directly to the reader. Ellen Goodman uses an informal, humorously satirical tone in the following excerpt from her essay on "The Cult of Mid-Life Beauty:"[1]

Informal essays use conversational style.

For those of you who missed it, Sophia Loren turned fifty in 1984. We are told that she celebrated her birthday publicly in a shopping mall in Atlanta. What glamorous errand had brought the Italian movie star to the mall? Had she run out of candles or panty hose?

No, Sophia Loren had joined the bustling ranks of certifiably older women promoting beauty. By now it appears that nearly all the women who are pumping and primping, selling their shapes and their books on the circuit, are more than halfway through the average life expectancy.

Joan Collins, at fifty, wrapped her body in nothing but boas for *Playboy*. Before that Jane Fonda, forty-six began bumping and grunting on thousands of videotapes. Now we have Raquel Welch writing and posing as a forty-four-year-old pinup queen and Sophia Loren hustling for Coty and a book of beauty tips. Middle age is so popular that soon a younger woman may have to lie to get a publisher or endorse a face cream.

[1]Goodman, E. (1985). The cult of mid-life beauty. *Keeping in touch*. New York: Summit Books, p. 140.

Satire ridicules human vices and follies.

Satire holds up human vices and follies to ridicule using wit and sarcasm. Goodman's article ridicules our preoccupation with looks and youth. In the last sentence above she uses satire to overstate the facts to make her point in a humorous manner.

Dr. Joyce Brothers uses a different tone, nostalgic and even more personal, in writing about her adjustment to widowhood:[2]

> Milt and I even played Easter bunny to each other. This was a deep, deep secret between the two of us. How can you tell anyone that the Easter bunny brings you presents?
>
> That first Easter after his death, I went out and bought myself a present from the Easter bunny. It was a little ceramic jar with the Big Bad Wolf on the lid. The wolf is wearing granny glasses that are removable. It is perfectly sweet and ridiculous. I keep tea in it. But it did not really help. It was not really a present. It just accentuated the fact that Milt was not there to give me one; it made me feel even lonelier.
>
> The Fourth of July was even worse. It would have been our thirty-ninth wedding anniversary. I spent it alone in bed with a raging fever and a case of flu. I felt terrible and kept wishing I were dead. If I were dead, I thought feverishly, I would be with Milt. Or if that was not the way things worked in the hereafter, at least I would not be a widow, ill and alone in bed on my wedding anniversary. It did not seem fair that I should be so miserable. I truly was about ready to curl up my toes and die, but my body was not. In a couple of days my temperature was down and I was on the mend. I was a little wobbly and I looked terrible and I just could not see how I was going to live without Milt, but it was obvious that I was going to have to.

Sharpening your observation skills helps make you a good writer.

Writing about familiar things and people helps you to write freely and to express your thoughts and feelings. Become observant of details in the world around you and of your feelings and reactions to your experiences. Reflect on what you see so that you can write with understanding. The writer's personality is revealed when the reader clearly sees the world that the writer sees. The essay is your "talk on paper." Use it as a way to express yourself to others. Most essays today are written as informal essays in which writers speak directly to the readers in a conversational tone.

---

[2]Brothers, J. (1990). *Widowed.* New York: Simon and Schuster, pp. 120–121.

SELECTING AND DEVELOPING A TOPIC

1. List two familiar topics that are of interest to you. (example: your children or other family members, a vacation, or plans for your future).

2. For each of the topics selected above, indicate whether you would choose to develop it as a formal or informal essay if you wrote about it. Explain why you would make this choice.

3. Label the following writing example as satire or as paradox.

   Erma Bombeck described a broken handle on a refrigerator door to the repair company as: ". . . there was no way the handle could have come off by itself, as the three-inch pin in it was bent double. Now I ask you, who do you think did it? Certainly not my husband and I, who were watching "Dukes of Hazzard," and certainly not our four-year-old son, Budro, who was swinging from the spare tire in his bedroom at the time of this unfortunate event."[3]

   Satire or Paradox ______________________________

4. Label the following expression as satire or paradox: cruel kindness

   Satire or Paradox ______________________________

FICTIONAL ESSAYS. The word **fiction** means something created by the imagination, an invented story. Technically, there is no such thing as a fictional essay—in literature, a "fictional essay" is called a short story. Sometimes, parts of a story are based on facts, but some of the facts are altered to make a better story. This altering of reality blurs the line between short stories and essays. "Early Marriage" by Conrad Richter is an example of a "fictional essay." Richter begins his story with this paragraph:

> For two days the leathery face of Asa Putnam had been a document in cipher to anyone who could read the code. Since Saturday but one traveler had passed his solitary post, a speck of adobe and picket corrals lost on the vast, sandy stretch of the Santa Ana Plain. Far as the eye could see from his doorway, the rutted El Paso Trail, unfenced, gutterless, innocent of grading, gravel, culverts, or

Fiction is invented by imagination and alters facts.

[3]Bombeck, E. (1983). *Motherhood the second oldest profession*. New York: McGraw-Hill, pp. 59–60.

telephone poles, imprinted only by iron tires, the hoofs of horses and oxen, sheep and cattle, and the path of the loping lobo wolf lay with dust unraised.

Fiction or storytelling communicates an abstract truth in an effective and enjoyable way. Stories allow us to experience situations through the images painted by the author's words. From "Three Little Pigs" or "Red Riding Hood," which you read as a child, to more complex stories read as an adult, stories entertain.

Plot describes conflict or complications.

The basic part of a story is the *plot* or situation in which a character wants something or has a conflict and complications develop. The **climax** is the most exciting moment in the story when either the main character or the situation is changed. The plot ends with a resolution for all problems, either a happy or an unhappy solution.

Nonfiction relies on fact or opinion about facts.

NONFICTIONAL ESSAYS. Technically, all essays are, by definition, nonfictional. Sometimes, as mentioned above, the lines blur, but essays are generally classified as nonfiction. This chapter focuses on essays precisely because they are nonfictional and, therefore, apply to a greater variety of personal and career writing activities than fiction does. **Nonfiction** relies on fact rather than imagination, although these facts should be presented in creative, interesting ways. With the exception of "Early Marriage," above, where the lines between fiction and essay blur, and "The Emperor's New Clothes," later, which is used to demonstrate narrative technique, the excerpts used as writing examples in this chapter represent nonfictional essays.

Ideas for nonfictional essays may come from a variety of sources. A topic can be based on personal experiences, views of life, interviews, discussions, research, or observation. Whether your topic is then treated in a formal or an informal essay depends on your purpose for writing.

Purpose of Essays

The reader should be able to state the main idea of an essay after reading it.

The essay conveys a point of view to the reader and is built around a central idea or theme. However, before you communicate an idea clearly to others, you must be able to state it clearly and briefly. Your first step in writing an essay, therefore, is to choose a topic and decide precisely what major idea, principle, or mental picture your essay is to present to the reader. In other words, you must decide the specific purpose of the essay.

- Are you writing to express your opinion on a proposed new park for the community?
- Is your essay written to relate your memories of a favorite relative?
- Do you want to share an interesting experience?

Before beginning to write, be able to state the main idea, purpose, and audience.

The next step is to identify the audience and the general purpose. In the first example above, the audience could be the city council or the general public in the community. In either case, your purpose would be *to persuade*. However, the choice of audience would help you decide how to write the essay. For example, you might write a formal essay that identified the issue and stated your position to the city council. The next paragraphs would explain the rationale for your position. What are the benefits to the community? to the council members? If there are disadvantages to your position, explain how these can be overcome. If your audience is the general public, you could choose to write an informal essay using humor to make your point in a persuasive but entertaining way. It is less likely that you would choose a humorous way to appeal to the city council. When you have your audience in mind, this helps you decide the most effective writing approach as well as the information to include.

Essays in the late President John F. Kennedy's book *Profiles in Courage* illustrate both a general and specific purpose. With a general purpose *to inform*, the specific purpose of these essays is stated in the last sentence of the foreword by his brother Robert F. Kennedy, "What happens to the country, to the world, depends on what we do with what others have left us." Thus, the essays support the premise that courage to make the hard decisions based on beliefs and values is important to sustaining the ideals of our country.

To persuade and to inform are the two essay purposes you are most likely to use in business. Other possible purposes for essays are to entertain or for personal expression (such as a journal entry or the relating of personal feelings, as in the Joyce Brothers excerpt).

TYPE AND PURPOSE

1. Give an example of an essay that you have read. What was its main idea or specific purpose and what was its general purpose?

   Title:

   Main idea (specific purpose):

   General Purpose:

2. Review the topics you selected in Checkpoint 7-1. Choose one of the topics and complete or respond to the following items as if you were preparing to write an essay on this topic.

   a. Topic:

   b. Main idea (specific purpose):

   c. General Purpose:

   d. Would your essay be formal or informal if you wrote on this topic?

WRITING MODES

The four major modes of writing are *description*, *exposition*, *narration*, and *persuasion*. This section will briefly describe each of these modes as a technique for essay development. **Description** uses words to help the reader see things more clearly. **Expository** writing (exposition) explains, informs, defines, or clarifies information. **Narration** tells a series of events for the general purpose of informing or entertaining the reader. **Persuasive** writing is intended to cause the reader to think or act in a certain way.

Descriptive Writing

Descriptive writing uses sensory details to create an image for the reader.

Descriptive writing helps the reader see or experience what the writer describes; it appeals to the senses—*touch*, *hearing*, *taste*, *sight*, and *smell.* Think how adding sensory details to an essay could make it more appealing than simply including factual information. The following paragraph illustrates the imagery power of sensory words.

> "Words have a power beyond their meaning. I remember the stories of my childhood, but I remember the single words that shone out of fairy stories—milk and buns, a flask of wine, a cabbage cut fresh from the garden. I see the whiteness, feel the sticky brown, marvel at the beads of moisture on thin, cold glass, hear the knife click through the stem and touch the dew along the ribbed leaves. I would read again stories that frightened me, for the sake of such perceptions. They seem to echo an older life, beyond my knowing."
>
> —Pamela Brown (cited in *Book Lovers Quotations* by Helen Exley, 1990)

Which words used by Brown create sensory images?

- Sight: "whiteness" of milk; "brown" of buns; "beads of moisture" on the wine flask
- Touch: "sticky brown" of the buns; "thin, cold glass" of the wine flask; "touch the dew along the ribbed leaves" of the freshly cut cabbage
- Hearing: "knife click" as it cut the cabbage stem

Go back in the chapter under formal essays to the paragraph written by Defoe. What words are descriptive of one of the five senses?

- Sight: "wear black;" "sat still looking at one another, and seemed quite abandoned to despair"
- Hearing: "toll the bell"

Decide what feeling or emotion to convey before writing a description.

Description may create a mood or emotion. The descriptive writer's attitude toward the subject, characters, or audience creates a tone. Examples of tone are happy, critical, somber, or playful. What mood did Defoe create in the description of the plague? Sadness and despair are evident. The tone is somber.

Desciptive writing can be about people, places, objects, animals, or locations. It is used in fiction, nonfiction, and poetry. This excerpt from Erma Bombeck's essay "The First Day of School for 'The Baby'" expresses feelings and emotion with a humorous description of an event:

> What am I doing, sending this baby out into the world before the umbilical cord is healed? Where's all the relief and exhilaration I'm supposed to feel? If only I hadn't been so rotten to him all summer, "Go play! Get out of the house! Take a nap! Why don't you grow up?" I think I blew it. I talked too much and said too little. There are no second chances for me. It's all up to someone else now.
>
> —from *Motherhood The Second Oldest Profession*, p. 30

Descriptive writing frequently uses figures of speech such as *similes* and *metaphors*. These figures of speech are used to help us understand what is being described. Metaphors and similes compare things that are unrelated but that have some quality in common that helps us experience what the writer is trying to convey.

Similes and metaphors are used for comparisons.

A **simile** makes a comparison between two things using comparative words such as *like*, *as*, *resembles*, or *than*. We commonly use similes in speech—"she's as white as a sheet," "run quickly like a rabbit." Similes are common in literature.

"I wandered lonely as a cloud. . ." —Wordsworth, line 1 from *I Wandered Lonely as a Cloud*

". . .we live meanly, like ants. . . ." —Thoreau *Why I Went to the Woods*

Metaphors compare two things by stating or inferring that one is the other. Metaphors do not use the connecting words *like*, *as*, *than*, or *resembles*.

"The moon was a ghostly galleon. . ." —Alfred Noyes *The Highwayman*

"All mankind is of one author and is one volume, when one man dies, one chapter is not torn out of the book, but translated into a better language. . . ." —John Donne *Meditation 17*

Note that the second example states the metaphor somewhat less directly than the first example; however, the content says that all mankind is a book and that each man is one chapter. Another figure of speech often used in descriptive writing is *personification*. Describing something as if it has human qualities is called **personification**.

The trees waved their arms.

By now this door must recognize me.

DESCRIPTIVE WRITING

1. Circle the sensory words in the following paragraph:

    She felt the icy fingers of the wind on her back as she hurried home. The snowflakes were like fluffy cotton swirling and falling to the ground. Her thoughts jumped ahead to the roaring fire in her study at home that would quickly chase away the chill.

2. Find the figures of speech in the above paragraph and write them on the lines below.

    Simile ____________________ Metaphor ____________________

    Personification ____

3. Write a description of a pet that you have owned, a friend, or a favorite place. Use words that appeal to at least two of the senses and that use one or more similes or metaphors. If a computer is available, use it to write the description, or use a separate piece of paper.

Expository Writing

Expository writing explains and informs.

Expository writing has a main purpose of providing information. It explains something for the reader. News articles are an example of writing that is predominantly expository in nature. In stories, it is that part of the plot that gives information about the characters and their problems or conflicts.

The following examples of expository writing come from an essay "Straw into Gold: The Metamorphosis of the Everyday" by Sandra Cisneros, a Mexican-American writer. In the first paragraph shown below, she is explaining her feelings about being asked by friends to make tortillas.

> Why did I feel like the woman in the fairy tale who was locked in a room and ordered to spin straw into gold? I had the same sick feeling when I was required to write my critical essay for my MFA [Master of Fine Arts] exam—the only piece of noncreative writing necessary in order to get my graduate degree. How was I to start? There were rules involved here, unlike writing a poem or story, which I did intuitively. There was a step-by-step process needed and I had better know it. I felt as if making tortillas, or writing a critical paper for that matter, were tasks so impossible I wanted to break into tears.

In the next example, she begins an explanation of her background:

> I've managed to do a lot of things in my life I didn't think I was capable of and which many others didn't think me capable of either. Especially because I am a woman, a Latina, an only daughter in a family of six men. My father would've liked to have seen me married long ago. In our culture, men and women don't leave their father's house except by way of marriage. I crossed my father's threshold with nothing carrying me but my own two feet. A woman whom no one came for and no one chased away.

Narrative Writing

Narratives relate events over time.

Narrative writing relates a series of events—what happened over a period of time. Although commonly found in fiction, drama, or poetry such as ballads, narration is used widely in nonfiction as well. It may be a writing technique for personal experience, for an autobiography, or for other writing that tells about the occurrence of events (anything from a project report to a travel article). Narrative writing can tell a story to entertain as well as relate the events. *Plot*, *dialogue*, *suspense*, and *characterization* are devices for telling a story. Narratives often use chronological order; that is, they relate events in the order they occurred.

Omniscient point of view is "all knowing."

The writer tells the story from one of three possible *points of view*: omniscient, third-person limited, and first person. **Omniscient point of view** allows the writer to know everything there is to know about all characters—the past, the present, and the future. Omniscient means "all knowing." The narrator is not in the story but can relate the thoughts of characters and what is going on in different locations. A wide range of fictional tales use an omniscient narrator—from novels to short stories to fairy tales. For example, "The Emperor's New Clothes" by Hans Christian Andersen tells the story as if looking over the whole kingdom and describing what is taking place. Notice how the writer reads the thoughts and speaks for each of the characters:

> "Many years ago, there was an Emperor, who was so excessively fond of new clothes, that he spent all his money to dress. . . .Time passed merrily in the town which was his capital. . . .One day, two rogues. . .gave out that they knew how to weave stuffs of the most beautiful colors and elaborate patterns. . . .The two pretended weavers set up two looms, and affected to work very busily, though in reality they did nothing at all. . . . 'I will send my faithful old minister to the weavers,' said the Emperor . . . 'he will be able to see how the cloth looks. . . .' So the faithful old minister went into the hall, where the knaves were working with all their might, at their empty looms. 'What is the meaning of this?' thought the old man, opening his eyes very wide. 'I cannot discover the least bit of thread on the looms.' However, he did not express his thoughts aloud."

Third-person limited gives the impression the story is told from the point of view of one character.

A narrative told from **third-person limited point of view** gives us the impression that the story is told from the thoughts and feelings of one of the characters in the story. If the previous part of "The Emperor's New Clothes" is told from the point of view of the Emperor, the story might go like this (with apologies to Hans Christian Anderson):

> The Emperor wanted desperately to dress in the finest clothes in all of the Kingdom. He sent out the word that he was looking for weavers who could make clothes of the finest cloth and most elaborate patterns. When two persons new to town came to him and offered to make these clothes, he was excited and told them to go to work immediately. He sent his old minister to observe the work. He was pleased when his friend, the minister, came back and told him that the clothes were indeed beautiful.

First person tells a story from the "I" point of view of one character.

The third point of view for a narrative is the *first person*. In a **first-person narration**, one of the characters tells the story using the pronoun "I." Let's examine how shifting to first person changes the story of "The Emperor's New Clothes."

> I have been Emperor of the Kingdom for many years, and no one has dressed in clothes as fine as those I wear. Just recently I sent out the word that I wanted new weavers that could make clothes of the finest cloth and most elaborate patterns. When two new people in town came to see me and offered to make these clothes, I told them to go to work immediately. When I sent my old minister to observe their work, he came back and told me that the clothes were indeed beautiful. I was pleased to hear this.

These final two points of view would be the ones used in writing essays. Third-person limited might be used if you were writing based on an interview of someone else or relating observations of what others were doing (like news reporting). However, most essays are written from the first person point of view.

EXPOSITORY AND NARRATIVE WRITING

1. Identify the point of view used by the following authors of essays used as examples in this chapter.

    a. What point of view does Defoe use to tell about the plague?

    b. What point of view is used in Emerson's essay?

2. Write a short essay on your feelings about something that happened to you. Use the sample of Sandra Cisneros expository writing as a guide or use a narrative to tell about the event and your feelings. If a computer is available, use it for your writing; if not, use a separate sheet of paper.

Persuasive Writing

Persuasive writing uses language that appeals to reason and/or to the emotions for the purpose of getting the reader to think or act in a certain way. Newspaper editorials, advertisements, and political speeches make extensive use of persuasive writing. Persuasive writing is also a part of application letters and writing samples for entry into educational programs or nominations for recognition awards.

Persuasive writing appeals to reason and/or to emotion.

When persuasive writing appeals to reason, it is called **argument**. Use of facts from reliable sources is one means of making a persuasive argument. Opinion or interpretation of facts requires building a logical case that appeals both to reason and to the reader's emotions. This type of writing follows thought processes similar to one side of an oral debate. Consider the emotional appeals in this example:

> I'm writing today to ask for your immediate help as a loyal supporter of the March of Dimes. And as a token of my thanks, in advance of your support, I'm pleased to present you with this box of specially commissioned holiday cards. These beautiful cards were created exclusively for supporters like you who have demonstrated an active commitment to the fight to save babies from birth defects and infant mortality.

The first sentence creates a sense of urgency with the request for "immediate help." In addition, this statement refers to past support as a "loyal supporter' and "active commitment" to the cause. The cards sent as a gift appeal to your sense of obligation to reciprocate with gift giving. All of these are emotional appeals. A similar message could use a factual appeal: "Every $3\frac{1}{2}$ minutes, an infant is born with a serious birth defect. Please help. . . ." The facts themselves can have an emotional impact, such as the statement about birth defects.

Persuasive argument uses facts, opinion, and/or fact interpretation to build a logical case.

Samuel Clemons—better known as Mark Twain—is recognized universally as an outstanding essayist. His writing style reveals his personality, sharp wit, and ability to use humor and sarcasm (sharp, critical overstatement to make a point). In his essay "Is Shakespeare Dead?"[4] he uses persuasive writing as an appeal to reason through argument. The excerpts from this essay illustrate the logic sequence that he used to persuade the reader to accept his opinion that Shakespeare did not write works that have been attributed to him. Though most people believe that Shakespeare did, in fact, write the plays and sonnets that bear his name, Clemons does a good job of presenting facts, interpretations, and his own observations into an entertaining and masterful support of his opinion. Notice how he builds his persuasive argument to influence the reader.

---

[4]Clemons, S. (1963). Is Shakespeare dead? In C. Neider (Ed.), *The complete essays of Mark Twain* (pp. 407–454). Garden City, NY: Doubleday.

Argument	Quotes
1. He begins with the idea that people have always given attention to claims made publicly, no matter how unsubstantiated.	"Claimants, royal Claimants, pleb Claimants, showy Claimants, shabby Claimants, revered Claimants, despised Claimants, twinkle star-like here and there and yonder through the mists of history and legend and tradition—and, oh, all the darling tribe are clothed in mystery and romance, and we read about them with deep interest and discuss them with loving sympathy or with rancorous resentment, according to which side we hitch ourselves to. It has always been so with the human race. There was never a Claimant that couldn't get a hearing nor one that couldn't accumulate a rapturous following, no matter how flimsy and apparently unauthentic his claim might be. . . ." (pp. 407-408)
2. He describes how his interest in the topic developed.	"A friend has sent me a new book, from England—The Shakespeare Problem Restated—well restated and closely reasoned; and my fifty years' interest in that matter—asleep for the last three years—is excited once more. . . ." (p. 408)
3. He states the few substantiated facts about Shakespeare and then raises questions about the lack of facts supporting Shakespeare's authorship.	"His will mentioned not a play, not a poem, not an unfinished literary work, not a scrap of manuscript of any kind. Many poets have died poor, but this is the only one in history that has died this poor; the others all left literary remains behind. Also a book. Maybe two." (p. 417) "When Shakespeare died in Stratford it was not an event. . . .A striking contrast with what happened when Ben Jonson, and Francis Bacon, and Spenser, and Raleigh, and the other distinguished literary folk of Shakespeare's time passed from life. . . .So far as anybody actually knows and can prove, Shakespeare of Stratford-on-Avon never wrote a play in his life. " (p. 418)
4. He lists the suppositions or claims made about how Shakespeare got an education, his knowledge of law, and other details that would have given him the necessary skill for writings attributed to him. He then points out the implausibility of these claims.	"If he began to slaughter calves, and poach deer, and rollick around, and learn English, at the earliest likely moment—say at thirteen, when he was supposably [sic] wrenched from that school where he was supposably [sic] storing up Latin for future literary use—he had his youthful hands full, and much more than full. He must have had to put aside his Warwickshire dialect, which wouldn't be understood in London, and study English very hard. Very hard indeed; incredibly hard, almost, if the result of that labor was to be the smooth and rounded and flexible and letter-perfect English of the 'Venus and Adonis' in the space of ten years; and at the same time learn great and fine and unsurpassable literary form." (p. 420)
5. He uses documented activities to dispute the arguments of how Shakespeare had acquired his knowledge in a short period of time, although he was busy working in the theater and becoming a business man.	"Maybe he did all these things, but I would like to know who held the horses in the mean time, and who studied the books in the garret, and who frollicked in the law-courts for recreation. Also, . . . as early as '93 he became a 'vagabond'—the law's ungentle term for an unlisted actor, and in '94 a 'regular' and properly and officially listed member of that (in those days) lightly valued and not much respected profession. Right soon thereafter he became a stockholder in two theaters, and manager of them. Thenceforward he was a busy and flourishing business man, and was raking in money with both hands for twenty years." (p. 422)

continued

Argument	Quotes
6. His last argument is that Shakespeare was 52 when he died and had lived in his native village 26 years, yet when he died nobody took notice. For 60 years afterward no townsman remembered anything about him or his life in Stratford. He compares this to his own years in Hannibal, Missouri, and the people who told stories about him.	"Now then, I am away along in life—my seventy-third year being already well behind me—yet sixteen of my Hannibal schoolmates are still alive today, and can tell—and do tell—inquirers dozens and dozens of incidents of their young lives and mine together. . . ." (p. 427) "Isn't it odd, when you think of it that you may list all of the celebrated Englishmen, Irishmen, and Scotchmen of modern times, clear back to the first Tudors—a list containing five hundred names, shall we say?—and you can go to the histories, biographies, and 'cyclopedias and learn the particulars of the lives of every one of them. Every one of them except one—the most famous, the most renowned—by far the most illustrious of them all—Shakespeare!" (p. 452)
7. The closing paragraph of his essay uses this final appeal to reason.	"'Injun Joe,' 'Jimmy Finn,' and 'General Gaines' were prominent and very intemperate ne'er-do-weels in Hannibal two generations ago. Plenty of grayheads there remember them to this day, and can tell you about them. Isn't it curious that two 'town drunkards' and one half-breed loafer should leave behind them, in a remote Missourian village, a fame a hundred times greater and several hundred times more particularized in the matter of definite facts than Shakespeare left behind him in the village where he had lived the half of his lifetime?" (p. 454)

PERSUASIVE WRITING

1. Find an example of persuasive writing. Bring it to class and answer these questions about it.
   a. Does the writing appeal to reason, emotion, or both?

   b. If facts and/or logic are included that appeal to reason, list these facts below; if an emotional appeal is made, describe how the appeal is made:

PLANNING AN ESSAY

Now that you have looked at examples from essays and learned different writing tools to help you express your thoughts, you are ready to apply these skills by developing your own essay. This section gives ideas for planning and writing an essay.

Essay Topics

WORKPLACE CONNECTIONS

Creative thinking and communication are basic work skills in today's information age.

Think about topics that interest you and select a tentative working title for an essay. Don't worry too much about the working title, however. You can—in fact, are likely to—change the title as your ideas develop. Choose a limited topic that can be covered adequately. Essays can be written on a wide range of topics. Here are a few ideas to get you started thinking about a topic: changing a tire, a mountain vacation, grandmother or grandfather, a favorite place, career goals, the funniest person I know, a favorite sport, hometown, or reading a map.

The topic chosen for the essay should be one that affects you intensely. You cannot write an effective essay with a neutral attitude. You have something to say—a main idea or point that you care about and want to convey through your writing. You can write about people you know, places you have been, current issues, thoughts and feelings about the world around you, or lessons learned from experience.

Thesis and Subtopics

Next, consider the main idea that you wish to communicate. This is your *thesis statement*. Write one or two sentences to state your main idea. Narrow the topic if you have trouble doing this. The thesis for the essay can be an opinion, an interpretation, or a truth learned from an experience. A good statement is one that is not an obvious fact or aspect of the topic but one that is somewhat unusual or that reflects a very personal view. Review the section in Chapter 4 on "Generating Ideas." Jot down ideas about your thesis statement.

The main idea you wish to communicate is called a thesis statement. The main idea also represents the specific purpose of the message.

One way to develop subtopics that support your thesis or main idea is web clustering. This technique clusters ideas into a visual web-like structure that can serve as an organizer for the essay. As shown in Figure 7-1, the main idea is placed in the center. Subtopics extend from the center. Web clustering is a means of visual brainstorming, and from it you can develop an outline.

Visual clustering of the main idea and subtopics can help develop an essay topic.

The Outline

How much detail you work out in advance of writing is an individual matter. Some writers think through the complete manuscript and organization of detail before they write. Others begin drafting the manuscript after determining the main idea, the purpose, the audience, and major subtopics. An outline is a plan that keeps your writing on track and shows the relationships of essay components. It also serves as a guide for gathering information or organizing ideas for the essay. The outline in Figure 7-2 is a reminder of essay structure.

Figure 7-1
Web Clustering to Expand Ideas

INTRODUCTION

Attracts attention of the reader.

Tells what the essay will discuss.

Begins or ends with the thesis statement.

BODY

Develops the thesis or main idea.

Includes a topic sentence and supporting evidence for each paragraph.

Includes one or more paragraphs for each major subtopic.

CONCLUSION

Alerts the reader of the completion of the essay.

Restates, summarizes, or uses other techniques to emphasize the thesis statement and major subtopics.

Often includes a personal response.

Figure 7-2
An Informal Essay Outline

Add details to an essay that help the reader understand the main idea or thesis statement.

Supporting Details

Information for development of subtopics may come from direct experience, interviews or surveys, literature, research (Internet or library), discussion with knowledgeable individuals, or a combination of these. Make notes and record specific information about your sources so you can include this information as you need it. For personal interview information, make a note of the date, time, person's name, position, and area of expertise. For books, record the full name of the author(s), date of publication, title of publication, title of chapter or article, volume and number for journals, inclusive page numbers of the article, and specific page number for any quotes.

You can explore ideas for writing by keeping a personal journal of events that are meaningful to you: mental pictures of things you see, your thoughts and ideas, descriptions of interesting people, and reaction to experiences that affect you positively or negatively.

Another way to explore ideas for writing essays is to read and critique what others have written. What is their main point? How did they develop the main idea? Was it introduced in the first paragraph or did the paragraphs of supporting details lead to a climax at the end? Read essays aloud to get the sound of the word and thought flow. Are there smooth transitions from one idea to a related thought? How are these transitions formed? What details develop the main idea?

Writing essays is a blend of objective and subjective details. Facts, details, statistics that can be seen the same by everyone are objective, while details that have been interpreted by or filtered through your own thoughts and emotions are subjective. Interesting details may come from the time or location of events, your reactions or thoughts about something experienced, or the use of comparisons.

Comparisons and figures of speech are used frequently in conversation as a way to make our thoughts vivid and descriptive. You may be cold and say "This room is as cold as an iceberg." Good figures of speech and comparisons or contrasts make descriptions come alive.

"That is part of the beauty of all literature. You discover that your longings are universal longings, that you're not lonely and isolated from anyone. You belong."

—F. Scott Fitzgerald, cited in *Book Lovers Quotations*, Exley Publications Ltd., 16 Chalk Hill, 232 Madison Ave., Suite 1206, NY 10016

Don't tell everything you know about a subject. Instead, select those details that contribute best to the main point and present the idea in an interesting, powerful way. When you return from a trip and share experiences with someone, you do not give a complete chronological story of everything that happened. You select details that are most vivid from your experience and that best describe the important events of the trip. Writing an essay uses this same technique. Select details and descriptive words that convey to the reader the main idea about the topic. Your essay becomes powerful when your reader can mentally experience what you are saying and feeling. Sensory imaging and specific details give power to your writing. Consider these two ways of stating a similar detail. Which one creates a mental image?

Factual, general, and impersonal:

A storm moved in and the temperature fell to 30 degrees.

Specific, sensory details that convey the writer's attitude:

> I shivered as the gusting wind blew the loose leaves into tornado-like spirals. After two balmy, spring-like days, the plummeting temperature signaled a return—although hopefully a temporary one—to freezing temperatures.

Sensory details make a descriptive essay appealing to the reader.

The details included in the essay should represent your feelings, your ideas, and your point of view on the topic. Avoid generalizations that are an abstract of other authors' ideas. When using books as a writing resource, consider what you read in terms of your attitude and beliefs about the topic. Think about what you read and use only those ideas that best fit what you want to say and that effectively illustrate the main thought or purpose of your writing. Good writing is simple and concentrates on making the main idea of the essay clear to the reader.

Collaboration and Revision

After you have drafted the essay, the next step is revision. You may add ideas, delete unnecessary words and sections that don't contribute to what you are trying to say, fill in details, reorganize, and add transitions for smooth thought flow.

Collaborating with another writer to critique each other's work helps refine your writing.

Reread your draft at least twice, once for content and once for technical details. Collaborate with someone who is interested in writing, exchanging drafts and critiquing one another's work.

When you complete revisions, put the essay aside. Let some time, a day or several days, pass; then re-read what you have written.

PLANNING AN ESSAY

1. Use the essay topic selected in Checkpoint 7-2, No. 2, and complete the following steps:
   a. Use a separate sheet of paper to prepare a web cluster of the main thought and subtopics.
   b. Follow the steps in the writing process that you learned in Chapter 4 to develop a draft for an essay. Use a computer to write the draft.
   c. Ask another student to review the draft and offer suggestions.
   d. Edit for technical correctness and for wording changes. Save the essay on a computer disk for use in Checkpoint 7-7.
2. List the writing mode(s) that you used in the above essay and the point of view.

   Writing Mode(s)

   Point of View

FORMATTING AN ESSAY

Style manuals give standardized guidelines for preparing manuscripts.

Knowing how to format an essay gives it the finishing touch. The layout and appearance of the final draft influence the reader's impression of what you have written. Your written communication represents you. A style manual is a good formatting resource, as well as a guide for how to cite reference material that documents the resources used in the preparation of your essay.

Style manuals give standardized guidelines for preparing manuscripts, especially those written for publication. Publishers adopt and follow a standardized writing format as described in a particular style manual. The Web on the Internet presents publishing opportunities as well as resources for writing. Individuals, as well as organizations, develop Web pages on the Internet and attach articles on a wide range of topics to their Web pages. More and more professional journals are becoming Web-based for access through the Internet, at least for selected articles from back issues. Using a style manual gives you guidance in preparing an article for publication or formatting your essays for other public distribution.

WORKPLACE CONNECTIONS

Electronic commerce (e-commerce) includes the publication of journals on the Web. Internet research and resources are a part of most businesses today.

A well-prepared manuscript has a professional appearance and improves the likelihood of a publisher's or a reader's positive response. This section gives general formatting instructions for essays. Three commonly used style manuals are the *Publication Manual of the American Psychological Association* (APA style manual), *Chicago Manual of Style*, and the *MLA Handbook for Writers of Research Papers*. Reference citation formatting in this chapter and Chapter 8 is based on the APA style manual, with some adaptations made to locate resource information on the same page with the cited material.

Manuscript Fonts and Spacing

Essay manuscripts are double spaced with indented paragraphs.

The APA style manual recommends the use of fonts or typefaces similar to Times Roman, Courier, or other serif typeface in 12-point size. Refer to Chapter 2 in *Basics of Writing* for an illustration of typefaces or fonts.

Double-space all lines of the manuscript. Extra spacing is not used between double-spaced paragraphs. A paragraph indention of approximately $\frac{1}{2}$ inch indicates new paragraphs. Margins at the top, bottom, left, and right should be a minimum of one inch.

Use the word processing *header* function to number all pages. Set right justification on your software so that the header will be flush with the right margin. Key in two or three words from the manuscript heading with the page number directly below it or separated by about five spaces on the same line. Here is an example of a page header:

Writing Essays 2

Title and Headings

The title of the paper is centered at the beginning of the paper (using a mix of upper and lower-case or all upper-case letters.) For your essays, the "byline," that is, the word *by*, and your name, can be centered below the title. Essays submitted for publication usually are required to have no name on the first page of the manuscript. The author's name, title, affiliation, and date are on a separate title page. Within the essay, use headings and subheadings to help the reader follow the essay's organization, particularly if the paper is several pages long (8 pages or more). Short articles may require only one or two levels of headings. For one or two levels, use a centered heading as the first level and an underlined flush-left side heading for the second level. If a third level of heading is necessary, use an indented, underlined, lowercase paragraph heading with a period and one space separating this heading from the first word of the paragraph.

Headings and subheadings help the reader follow the organization of an essay.

MY VACATION (title)

by

Jane Washington (byline)

A Day to Remember (1st level heading centered)

The Setting (2nd level at left margin and underlined)

A peaceful day. (3rd level subheading is used at the beginning of the paragraph and is indented and underlined; only the first word is capitalized, and the phrase ends with a period.)

Publishers may follow a slightly different format from the above example. However, placement of headings would be the same regardless of formatting. Also, within your essay, headings remain consistent. That is, all first-level heading would be identical, all second-level headings would be the same, and so would all third-level headings.

Quotations

Quotations with fewer than 40 words are incorporated into the text and enclosed by double quotation marks. If the quotation has 40 or more words, indent the left margin of the quoted material five to seven spaces. An article being sent for publication would doublespace the indented quote. If an essay is prepared for purposes other than submission to a publisher, this long quote is sometimes single-spaced and indented from the left and right margins.

Quotations with 40 or more words are indented from the left margin.

Place double quotation marks around short direct quotes within a long indented quotation. The long, indented quotation does not have quotation marks placed at the beginning and end because the indented format indicates that it is a quote.

Short quotations, on the other hand, can remain in the body of the text. Short quotations are enclosed in double quotation marks. Use single quotation marks around a direct quote that comes within a short quotation.

A period or comma always comes before the quotation marks.

When a period or comma occurs with closing quotation marks, the period or comma comes before (inside) the quotation marks. Other punctuation with quotation marks comes outside the quotation marks unless it is part of the quoted material. An example of a short quote follows:

> Then I turned to him and said, "Remember that line you liked in the story—'You never know how things will turn out'?" He smiled and said he'd be back when he knew better how his own story would end.

Example of a longer, indented quote:

> I stared at the map in disbelief. I thought of all the stories I'd heard, the legends. The writing on the map made them all seem true. I read the old script slowly.
>
> > He who finds this map, if he be a true man and bold, can follow it to his heart's desire. They say that "dead men tell no tales," but if ye read this, then know ye that I am dead but my tale will still be told.
> >
> > Then I noticed smaller letters in the corner: "Acme Island Souvenirs—Printed in USA." So much for buried treasure. I didn't know whether I should laugh or cry.

Other Formatting

In addition to manuscript format and formatting of reference citations, style manuals have a wealth of information that is helpful to writers. Content includes designing and reporting research, writing style, grammar, punctuation, preferred spelling and hyphenation, capitalization, bias-free language, and abbreviations. How to cite and format references is a major part of style manual guidelines. More information on reference citations is included in Chapter 8.

Publishers use a style manual to keep layout consistent. This reference can be a valuable addition to your personal library, particularly if you plan to use your writing skills for publication. Even articles posted on the Web should follow an accepted format from a style manual.

USING A STYLE MANUAL TO FORMAT ESSAYS

1. Format the essay drafted, revised, and edited in Checkpoint 7-6, No. 1, following the instructions given in this chapter for spacing, headings, and quotations.
2. Copy the following headings or subheadings on the lines provided using the APA style manual format described in this chapter.

   1st level: Landscaping small gardens

   2nd level: Space considerations

   3rd level: Use and maintenance

3. Practice the use of single or double quotation marks by correctly placing them in the following short paragraph. Rewrite the quotation, placing the correct quotation marks in the text.

   According to Malen (1998), "Skilled writers meet certain performance standards. One of these standards is "Presents logical, coherent pattern to thought"s."

4. Write an essay describing your career goals. Use a computer and follow all steps in the writing process. Use the space below to develop an informal outline for the essay.

CHAPTER SUMMARY

- Essays reflect the writer's personality by sharing ideas, points of view, and information. They may be written using formal or informal style. Informal essays use conversational tone.
- Be sure that you have the main idea, general purpose, and audience in mind before you write an essay. Essays are nonfiction, personal, and have a purpose and a single, central idea or theme.
- Descriptive, expository, narrative, or persuasive writing can be used to develop essays. More than one of these writing modes can be applied to the same essay; however, the purpose of the essay influences which will be the primary mode.
- Choose essay topics that are familiar to you, and apply a variety of writing techniques to express your ideas.
- Using standardized format styles for layout, fonts, and spacing gives your manuscript a professional appearance. Style manuals provide writers and publishers with standard guidelines for layout, as well as grammatical construction, organization, style, and reference citations.

1. Brainstorm with others to identify a title, specific purpose (main idea), general purpose, and audience for the following types of essays:

a. Informal essay to express your ideas or feelings about writing.

Topic:

Main idea or thesis statement (specific purpose):

General purpose:

Audience:

b. An essay that uses descriptive writing—sensory details

Topic:

Main idea or thesis statement (specific purpose):

General purpose:

Audience:

2. Select one of the topics from Application No. 1. Free write on the topic to generate ideas. Review your thoughts on the topic and outline major areas for the essay. Using the Internet, gather information for topics under each of these areas. On the following line, write the topic that you selected and researched.

3. Select the other topic from Application No. 1. Draw a visual web cluster of your main idea and subtopics. Add as many subtopics as you wish. Save these ideas for further development in another application.

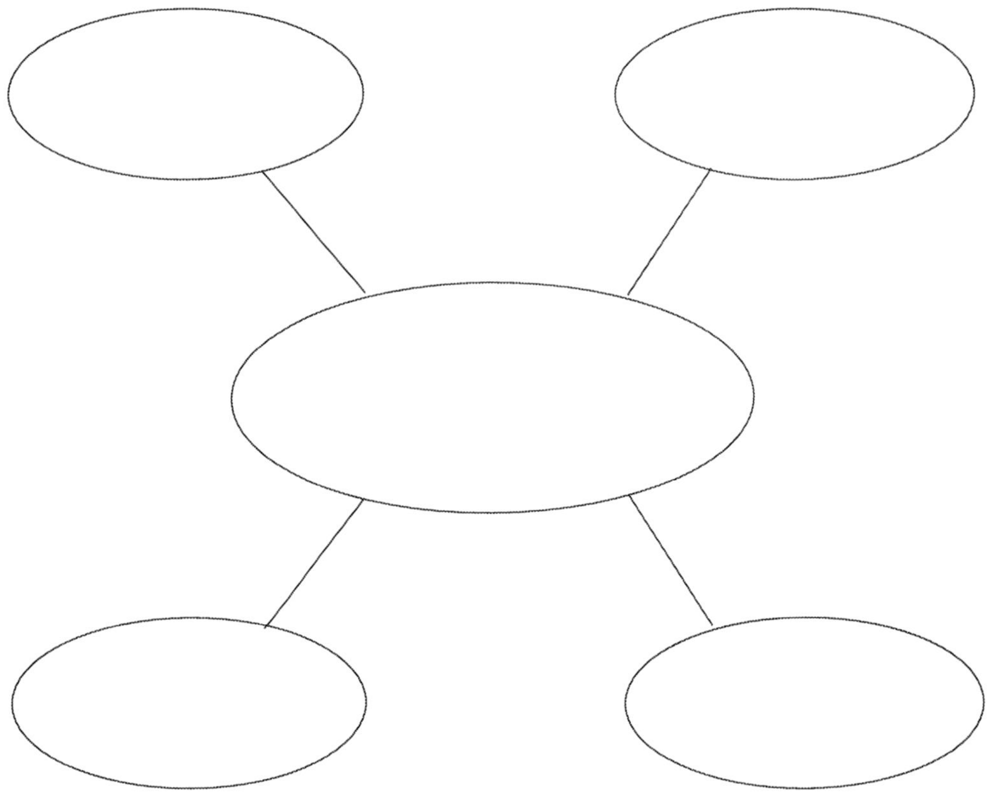

4. From Application No. 2 above, use the ideas to draft an essay on this topic. If a computer is available, use word processing software for this activity; print it, and save it on a disk. If no computer is available, write the draft on other paper.
5. Revise and edit the essay drafted for Application No. 4. Before revising, ask yourself these questions about your essay draft:
   a. Does the essay reflect your feelings or attitudes toward this topic?
   b. Do supporting ideas (subtopics) contribute to an understanding of the main idea of the essay?
   c. Is the essay written with general statements or did you include relevant examples, experiences, or comparisons to bring the topic to life for the reader?
   d. Did you add sensory details that add appeal to the factual information?
   e. Do the details that you added contribute in a meaningful way to the main idea of the topic or do they take your thoughts on wandering side trips?
   f. What organization pattern did you use? topical organization of subtopics, chronological order of events, or another logical construction?

6. Ask a colleague to read the essay that you revised and edited for Application 5. Ask your colleague to write in one or two sentences the main idea from the essay. Record this main idea on the line below. How closely does the colleague's statement match the main idea that you stated as a specific purpose for this topic when you listed it in Checkpoint 7-1? Explain any difference.

   Colleague's Statement:

   Difference between colleague's statement and the main idea you intended:

7. Practice using similes and metaphors to make comparisons by completing the following open-ended phrases or clauses. Avoid common cliches; strive for creativity.

   a. as hot as

   b. beautiful like a

   c. lazy as a

   d. graceful like a

   e. Write a statement or a phrase that expresses a paradox about a city.

8. Use the web cluster and topic from Application 3 to develop an essay on a computer. Follow all steps of the writing process described in Chapter 4. Format the essay using the guidelines given in Chapter 7. Print the essay.

9. Bring an editorial to class. Meet in a small group of colleagues to read the editorial. As a group, come to a consensus on the main idea (specific purpose) of the editorial and the major subtopics. As a group, work together to answer the following questions.

   a. Does the editorial appeal to emotion, reason, or both?

   b. What facts or arguments are used? List these.

   c. What ideas are used to persuade by appealing to emotions? List these.

10. From magazines, the Internet, or books, locate a paragraph that illustrates each of these writing modes: description, exposition, narration, and persuasion. Meet in small groups to share these illustrations and discuss them. As a group, select by consensus one illustration for each of the writing modes. Prepare a poster or bulletin board for the classroom that displays these writing mode examples. Use a separate sheet of paper to plan a layout for this display.

11. Identify an essay topic of interest to you. Use a separate sheet of paper to develop an informal outline. Complete the essay using all steps of the writing process. Use two or three levels of headings for the subtopics of the essay. Use at least one simile, metaphor, expression of satire, or sensory word description. Meet in a group of 2 or 3 other students. Exchange papers and provide feedback to one another on the essays. Did the intended main idea come across to the reader? Are all corrections made? Incorporate final revisions and format the manuscript according to directions in this chapter.

12. Select one of the following topics for development as an essay. E-mail the selected topic to your instructor. Use the space below to make notes for the e-mail message. Following all of the steps of the writing process, prepare the final product. Send the final essay to your instructor as an E-mail attachment.

Topics: Reasons I Returned to School

How to Improve the Appearance of the Campus

Writing with the You Attitude

Pros and Cons of Dress Codes

Why Car Manufacturers Use Animal Names for Car Models

13. Answer the following questions about the essay that you completed for Application No. 12.

a. What primary writing mode did you use: descriptive, expository, narrative, or persuasive? Explain why you used this mode.

b. Give examples of a simile, metaphor, personification, satire, or sensory word from the essay.

c. What point of view was used: third-person limited or first person? Explain why you used this point of view.

Correct the grammar, spelling, capitalization, punctuation, sentence structure, and word choice errors in the following sentences. Write *Correct* for sentences containing no errors.

1. The university basketball team have lost just one game during this perfect season.

2. An example of writing skills used by a retail worker is the ability to write product evaluation reports and to make recommendations to their employers.

3. The birdwatcher was watching at three birds that are almost extent

4. The community air show has more than 100 plains in it last Sunday.

5. The Chef baked 5 dozen cookies for the first-grade classes' party and shared the receipe with the mothers.

6. The instructor told the computor keyboarding class to double space they're compositions.

7. The receptionist answers the phone, and told the customers too call back later.

8. The perfect weight for healthful athletes is 155lbs.

9. Yestday the patrolman stationed behind the large green bush has clocked motorists who were speeding.

10. She has her fingers on the wrong keys and is making a mess of the manuscript.

CHAPTER 8

WRITING REPORTS AND PROPOSALS

A report provides information written in a logical, systematic manner that can help decision makers select a course of action on a problem or issue. As an employee, you may be asked by your employer to write a report about a subject related to your specific expertise or job assignment. Technical reports provide information for a specialized audience made up of an individual or group of people who have responsibility for addressing a problem or issue. At times, you may be asked to develop a proposal to solve a problem or to secure funding for a special project. This chapter will help you use your written communication skills to write both technical reports and proposals.

LEARNING OBJECTIVES

- Identify report characteristics.
- Determine content and organization.
- Cite and list references.
- Conduct research.
- Display data in a report.
- Write a proposal.

IDENTIFYING REPORT CHARACTERISTICS

Reports may be formal or informal. **Informal reports** use first and second person pronouns (*I*, *we*, and *you*) and generally do not contain charts or tables. Businesses frequently use informal reports that are written in letter or memorandum format to communicate routine information or information that can be described without extensive data. These reports relay facts and observations, make recommendations, or provide a written record of an incident or action. **Formal reports** are generally written in third person and convey facts and interpretations based on research and investigation of data pertinent to the issue or problem addressed. In addition, these reports tend to cover more complex issues and decisions than those addressed by informal reports, or cover the issues at greater depth and in more detail, thus requiring a more formal structure. The type of formal report discussed in this section is a technical report.

Informal reports can be letters or memos; formal reports are more complex and require a more formal structure.

Purpose and Audience

A technical report informs readers about a specific topic, and supplying information may be its only purpose or goal. However, technical reports also often reach conclusions based on the report's information and may offer recommendations based on those conclusions. These reports try to influence the reader's decisions or actions as well as provide

Technical reports explain a specific topic, reach conclusions, and make recommendations to address a problem or assist with decision making.

information. An example of a specific purpose might be to compare a product made by your company with similar products on the market. Other purposes might include identifying new markets, improving a process, or simply showing how something works. Identifying the intent of the report determines how you need to organize and communicate information to readers.

When you have a clear picture of the goal and purpose of your report, analyze the audience. Formal reports normally are prepared for individuals in top levels of management. In addition, these reports may be read by people outside the writer's organization. Determine as precisely as possible the needs of the audience: common needs and differences, technical expertise in the subject of the report, educational background, and professional position. Knowing the attitude of the audience toward the subject helps identify the concerns and questions the report is expected to answer.

The background and interests of the audience determine what you say and how you say it, as well as what technical details you need to include. In some cases, what you tell the reader may be all the audience knows about a particular topic. Try to show how the topic relates to work situations and how the knowledge can be helpful. Try to bridge the gap between your topic and what your audience needs and wants to know. You may be writing to colleagues within your area of specialization who share the vocabulary and basic knowledge of the discipline. In such a situation, you can present complex technical details and theory without having to supply definitions, background, or explanations. When writing to upper-level management, remember that they will look for what the report is about, the significance and logic of the information, and the conclusions that call for action. When your audience has different levels of technical expertise, the readers' needs might be addressed by placing information everyone understands at the beginning and then including specialized sections in the report.

WORKPLACE CONNECTIONS

Employers want employees who can acquire, evaluate, interpret, and communicate information.

Tone and Language

Technical reports use factual, concrete, and straightforward language. Creative descriptions and emotional language are not appropriate. Facts and conclusions are presented in an objective, rather than subjective, manner.

Technical reports present specialized information that has its own technical vocabulary and body of knowledge. The audience for the report dictates the degree to which technical terminology is appropriate for the report. When in doubt, define terms and explain essential background knowledge. The key to the tone and language of an effective report is knowing the audience and purpose of the report.

 # @ % $

A report fact blooper: "Our agency has been providing home health care to people in need for 125 years."

IDENTIFYING REPORT CHARACTERISTICS

1. For each of the following business situations, write a general purpose and one or more specific purposes for a formal report:

   a. A chef performed a cost analysis on menu items when the profits fell by 10 percent in the past six months.

   b. A cosmetologist attends fashion shows and keeps abreast of new hair styles and techniques when a competing beauty spa opens in the same neighborhood.

   c. A business manager performs analyses that compare current expenditures with next year's projected needs and revenues.

2. For each of the above situations, who is the audience and how does it determine the tone and language for the report?

   a.

   b.

   c.

DETERMINING CONTENT AND ORGANIZATION

A formal report has three major sections: Preliminary Section, Body of the Report, and Supplementary Section. Each section contains a different type of information, as outlined in Figure 8-1; however, all technical reports do not include all of the items listed under each section. The purpose of the report, audience, and directive from the person requesting the report will determine the components for a specific report. The following paragraphs describe the various contents of each section.

Preliminary Section

Preliminary pages vary from report to report. Formal reports have a title page and table of contents. Other items listed depend on the purpose, length, type, and detail of the report.

The report title should be descriptive of the purpose and content.

TITLE PAGE. The **title page** gives the title of the report, the name of the person and/or organization receiving the report, the name, title, and department of the writer(s), and the date of the report. The wording of the title should be descriptive of the purpose and content. If the organization has guidelines for the title page, they should be followed for format and content. If there are no specific guidelines, information on the title page should be centered horizontally, and the top and bottom

PRELIMINARY SECTION

Title page

Authorization or transmittal letter

Table of contents

List of illustrations

Executive summary

BODY

Introduction

  Related literature

  Definition of terms

Procedures or methodology

Findings/results

Analysis

CONCLUSIONS AND RECOMMENDATIONS

Supplementary section

Glossary

Appendix

Bibliography or reference list

Figure 8-1
Parts of a Formal Report

margin space should be equal. Titles of more than one line should be single spaced, and the title should be all capitals. A courtesy title precedes the name of the person receiving the report. The writer's name should not be preceded by a title.

AUTHORIZATION, TRANSMITTAL LETTER, OR MEMORANDUM. A letter or memorandum authorizing the study and giving relevant information such as the issue or problem, funding, and due date may be included as preliminary information for the report. In addition, the report writer may introduce the report to the reader with a letter or memorandum of transmittal. The writer may include opinions and comments, or suggest uses of the information in the transmittal. A preface or foreword may replace a letter of transmittal.

TABLE OF CONTENTS. The **table of contents** lets the reader locate specific information in the report. As a general guide, reports of five or more pages should have a table of contents. The heading TABLE OF

CONTENTS should be centered two inches from the top of the page. The word *Page* is aligned at the right margin a triple space below the heading. The major sections of the report are double-spaced with subsections single-spaced under each major heading. Section headings should be exactly as they appear in the body of the report. The section heading and page number should be connected by dot leaders (horizontally spaced periods). Page numbers may be included or may be omitted for subheadings. The table of contents is prepared after the report is in its final form so that page numbers for each section are accurate.

TABLE OF CONTENTS

LIST OF ILLUSTRATIONS. The **list of illustrations** follows the same format as the table of contents. Illustration numbers and titles are used instead of headings. A report may group all types of illustrations and graphics in one list or may have one list for tables and another list for other illustrations (called *figures*). **Figures** may be such items as charts, graphs, drawings, or photographs.

EXECUTIVE SUMMARY. An **executive summary** briefly restates each section of the report emphasizing findings, conclusions, and recommendations. Other names for an executive summary are *summary*, *abstract*, *overview*, and *synopsis*. This section presents essential information in abbreviated form so that the reader has an idea about the content of the report before it is read. A summary should not exceed one or two single-spaced pages. Its length may be determined by the organization's guidelines for preparing the report.

PREPARING A REPORT TITLE PAGE AND LETTER OF TRANSMITTAL

1. Use one of the business situations from Checkpoint 8-1 to create a report title. Use a computer and word processing software to prepare an attractive title page. Be sure to include information such as title, author, and date.
2. For the same situation selected for No. 1 above, write a letter or memorandum of transmittal for the report.

Body of the Report

Formal reports of a research or investigative nature contain all of the parts presented in this section: introduction, procedures or methodology, findings or results, analysis, conclusions, and recommendations. Proposals, however, vary somewhat in format as well as included components. Proposal writing is described in the last section of this chapter.

A report introduction gives the background and the purpose of the study.

INTRODUCTION. The **introduction** gives background for the study so that the reader can understand the rest of the report. The introduction begins with a general description of the problem and the main issues related to it. Next, there is a brief statement that describes how the problem or issue affects the organization followed by the goal or purpose of the study. The purpose may be stated as a question *(Which word processing software package best meets our needs?)* or a statement *(The purpose of this study is to provide information on word processing software packages so that a software package may be selected that meets the needs of the organization).* Next stated is the scope of the research as defined by the boundaries of the study. In this section, the researcher informs the reader of the extent of the research and any limitations. For example, a limitation on a study of word processing packages may be that the packages described are only those that are compatible with Macintosh computers.

Terms used in the report that may be unfamiliar to the reader are included in the introductory section. If the list of terms is extensive, however, a glossary of terms would be in the supplementary section.

Related literature may also be included in the introduction. These information sources should represent reliable sources known to people knowledgeable in the field of study. The literature section should be an integrated discussion based on major topics rather than a summary of each resource included. A review of related literature can be included in the introduction if only a limited amount of literature is available on the topic. When extensive literature sources are included, this topic should be a separate section of the report.

The procedures and methodology portion of a report describes how the study was conducted and how the results were analyzed.

PROCEDURES OR METHODOLOGY. This section describes the steps taken to conduct the study and to analyze the results. The detail in the procedures section should be descriptive enough to enable someone else to conduct a similar study that could validate or invalidate the results of this study. This section also allows readers to judge whether or not all essential aspects of the problem were adequately researched.

FINDINGS OR RESULTS. This section presents the facts found in the research on the topic. These facts should be presented in an objective manner without interpretation or opinions. Both positive and negative findings are presented. Tables, charts, and graphs are used to present detailed data in the findings from the study.

ANALYSIS. The **analysis** section is an interpretation of the study's findings by comparing the results with findings in other related studies and with knowledge about related organizational information. The analysis helps the reader determine important relationships among data in the findings.

Conclusions and recommendations in a formal report have a logical connection with the background and findings from the study.

CONCLUSIONS AND RECOMMENDATIONS. Based on the analysis section of the report, the writer briefly summarizes major findings and interpretations based on logic. All conclusions should have basis in facts found through the research. No new data are presented in this section. The conclusions are the basis for recommendations. These recommendations may be in the same section with the conclusions or, if lengthy, may be placed in a separate section. A recommendation is the writer's opinion of action that should be taken to resolve the issue or problem studied. These recommendations should have a logical tie with the findings, analysis, and conclusions. Recommendations can be listed and numbered if more than two are presented. This section may contain only the recommendations, or it can have both recommendations and supportive reasoning.

Supplementary Section

Material indirectly related to the main topic of the report is placed at the end in a supplementary section. Items in this section may include a glossary, an appendix, and a bibliography or reference list.

GLOSSARY. A **glossary** is an alphabetical list of specialized terms used in the report along with definitions or explanations of what the terms mean within the context of the report. However, if the report uses only a few specialized terms, you would define them in the introduction or with their first use in the body of the report, and not include a glossary.

APPENDIX. An **appendix** contains supplementary information omitted from the body of the report to improve readability. Different items of information are labeled as separate appendixes; e.g., Appendix A: Questionnaire, Appendix B: Table 12, Appendix C: Data Printout. All appendixes should be referenced in the body of the report.

A bibliography is an alphabetical list of references used as information sources; a reference list includes only those resources cited in the report.

BIBLIOGRAPHY OR REFERENCE LIST. A **bibliography** is an alphabetical list of references used as sources of information for the study, including those cited within the report as resources as well as other sources of information on the topic. A **reference list** is an alphabetic list of only those resources cited within the report. Items in a bibliographic or reference list include the author's name, publication year, title of book chapter or title of article, name of the publication, edition (if applicable), book publisher's location and name, and page numbers for an article or a chapter in a book.

CITING REFERENCES

References are represented in essentially two ways in a report. Reference citations are used within the body of the report to support content. In the supplementary section, include a reference list or bibliography. The specific order and format for reference citations follow the guidelines of a style manual. Examples of reference citations in this section are formatted according to the *Style Manual of the American Psychological Association*, 4th Edition.

The **Style Manual of the American Psychological Association,** ***commonly referred to as the APA Manual, gives guidelines for citing resources used in developing a report.***

A reference citation is placed in the text material where major concepts or ideas from other sources are used in your writing, even though the wording may be different. When the wording differs from the source, the author's last name and the date of publication are placed in parentheses at the end of the sentence or within the sentence if the source applies only to part of the sentence.

Example of a magazine or journal citation within the text:

> The Galaxy Bar and Grille in Ocean City, Maryland, is a gourmet restaurant that is trendy and fun (Campbell, 1999). When I visited the restaurant last year, . . .
>
> Reference list or bibliography format for this citation:
>
> Campbell, D.A. (1999, June). Beyond the boardwalk, *Southern Living*, *34*(6), p. 44.

When the month is given, it follows the year. If the magazine or journal has a volume and issue number, they are placed at the end of the magazine name as shown.

Example of a magazine or journal citation in text when the article has multiple authors and uses a quote from the source:

> Character education, which was popular in the 1930s, has seen a resurgence in schools "as a response to a growing perception that American society is in a state of crisis. . . ." (Bebeau, Rest, & Narvaez, 1999, p. 18).

When exact quotations are used, the page number is added to the citation. The paragraph could continue discussing the information from this source without listing the reference citation again, unless this citation is separated from the second use of material or is on a different page.

Example of multiple authors in the reference list or bibliography:

> Bebeau, M.J., Rest, J.R., & Narvaez, D. (1999, May). Beyond the promise: A perspective on research in moral education, *Educational Researcher*, *28*(6), pp. 18-26.

> ***"The quality of the organization can never exceed the quality of the minds that make it up."***
>
> —Harold R. McAlindon

Note that only the first word of the title and the first word after a colon in the title are capitalized; however, each word of the magazine or journal name is capitalized just as shown on the publication.

Example of a book citation within the text:

> Selecting the proper filing storage equipment and supplies is a major key to efficient storage and retrieval of records (Ricks, Swaford, & Gow, 1992). Several options are available for all types of records formats. Vendors are competitive, and product specifications in this field change rapidly.

Example of this book in the reference list or bibliography:

> Ricks, B.R., Swafford, A.J., Gow, K.F. (1992). *Information and image management.* (3rd ed.). Cincinnati, OH: South-Western.

The title of the book is underlined or italicized, but only the first word and the first word after a colon in the book title begins with a capital letter. The publishing location precedes an abbreviated version of the publisher's name.

Example of a book chapter citation for an edited book:

> Zeliff, N.D. (1998). Internet applications related to national standards for business education. In D. LaBonty (Ed.), *Integrating the Internet into the business curriculum*, pp. 33–43. Reston, VA: National Business Education Association.

The reference citation in the text would follow the same pattern as other types of sources (Zeliff, 1998).

For examples of different types of resources used as references, consult the *Style Manual of the American Psychological Association*. Other examples may be on the Internet at *http://www.vic.ub.edu/ac/apa_main. htm* or may be found by using a search engine such as Alta Vista, selecting Education and References, keying in the words APA References, and beginning the search. A search engine locates numerous sites that give examples of APA reference citations.

DETERMINING THE CONTENT OF A REPORT

1. On a separate sheet of paper, make a list of the kinds of information and data that might be included in a report.
2. Select a journal article and a book. Write a reference list entry for each one following guidelines from the *Style Manual of the American Psychological Association.*

   Journal Article:

   Book:

CONDUCTING RESEARCH

Research is conducted to gather information for solving problems or planning future action. Information may come from primary or secondary sources or both. The use of **primary sources** refers to gathering original information directly from the people or situations under study through surveys, observations, or experiments. Using **secondary sources** means reviewing and analyzing published information relevant to the topic of the study. Quite often, research uses both primary and secondary sources. In such cases, first complete the search and review of secondary sources. The information obtained from these sources provides a background for determining specific questions to be answered through information gathered from primary sources. However, the basic step that must precede information gathering from any source is the statement of the problem to be studied.

Primary research gathers information directly from people or situations through surveys, observations, and experiments. Secondary research sources are published literature or documents related to the topic studied.

Research Problem Statement

Organizational planning and problem solving cannot proceed without the gathering and analyzing of pertinent data. Informed decisions are based upon knowledge of relevant facts and logical interpretation of those facts. All types of organizations (for example, businesses, education groups, civic and community groups) use a needs analysis as a basis for planning and solving problems. A needs analysis consists of gathering, interpreting, and reporting information that can be used for decision making. But before the needs analysis and data gathering can begin, there must be a clear statement of the problem or question to be studied.

The *problem statement* forms the basis for gathering information and for preparing a report. The request for a report may state the problem or the purpose to be researched. The *what* and the *why* should be understood clearly before research begins. The answers to these two questions will help you frame a problem statement that has the following characteristics: written in language that can be easily understood by the readers, narrowed in scope to be sufficiently covered by the research, fitted within current knowledge and research of the topic, and identified as a problem that makes a significant contribution to knowledge about the topic. Reports of descriptive research may list objectives rather than use a problem statement. The following examples show three ways to state the research problem for a study of accidents in an organization. The purpose of the research is to identify accident causes for development of an accident prevention program.

WORKPLACE CONNECTIONS

Examples of essential problem-solving skills for employees are improving product quality and solving problems with machines, computers, and other technologies.

PROBLEM STATEMENT. The paragraph below clearly states the what and why based on facts that are already known.

> In 1999, a total of 75 employees of XYZ Manufacturing suffered minor or major injuries as a result of accidents that occurred on the work site during their working hours. This total number of injuries represents 10 percent of our employees, an unacceptable accident rate for worker safety. This study identifies the types of accidents that occurred and contributing causes. This information will be used to develop an accident prevention program.

PROBLEM STATEMENT AS QUESTIONS. The example below states the problem and the purpose in question format. It, too, clearly identifies the what and why.

> What kinds of accidents occurred to employees on their work site during 1999?
>
> For each 1999 accident, what factors do the injured employee and the supervisor believe contributed to its occurrence?
>
> What implications do the 1999 accident data have for reducing employee accidents?

PROBLEM STATEMENT AS OBJECTIVES. The example below states the problem and identifies the what and why by listing objectives.

> Objectives for this study of 1999 employee on-the-job accidents are the following:
>
> - To identify the types of employee accidents that occurred on the work site in 1999.
> - To analyze and describe contributing factors for each of these accidents.
> - To recommend work site improvements for reducing employee injuries, based on findings.

Primary Sources

Primary sources include a description of an occurrence or of data collected by the individual who conducted the research. Data not previously published are considered a primary source. Data are statistics, research results, or other factual information used for decisions, discussion, or calculation. Surveys, scientific observations, and experiments are examples of primary sources.

Surveys use questionnaires, checklists, rating scales, and interviews to collect data.

SURVEYS. **Surveys** use questionnaires, checklists, rating scales, and interviews to collect data. Records can be used to gather factual information such as ages, occupations, grades, and organizational memberships. The most common ways of collecting data for surveys are questionnaires or interviews. A **cross-sectional survey** collects information from a sample group that comes from a research population. The research population is made up of all individuals or units applicable to the question(s) under study. A sample group serves as a study group that is representative of the total research population.

Sample size and random selection of participants are important for data reliability.

Reliability. Two critical issues regarding the reliability of data from a sample population are the sample size and random selection of participants. If the total size of the research population is known, a published sampling table may be used to determine sample size. A randomly selected sample ensures that each member of the population has an equal chance of being selected for the sample. Selection of such a sample might be attained by numbering each population member and using a random numbers table to select the numbers for the sample. For example, let us consider a study of the readers' degree of satisfaction with different sections of a particular newspaper. Subscribers to the newspaper would be the research population. A subscriber list of 10,000 could use a random sample population of 370 subscribers with a high degree of reliability that their responses would be representative of the total population of readers. Table 8-1 is an abbreviated example of a random sample-size table.

TABLE 8-1

Example of a Random Sample-Size Table

Population (N)	Sample (n)	Sample % of Population 100(n/N)
50	44	88.00
100	80	80.00
200	132	66.00
500	217	43.40
1,000	278	27.80
5,000	357	7.14
10,000	370	3.70

Data from survey research presents a snapshot of a particular group at a specific time. Understanding this basic premise of survey findings alerts the researcher to a cautious interpretation of results, taking care not to overstate or over-generalize their applicability to different populations or to different time periods. Survey research cannot establish causal relationships with any certainty but can be used to explore relationships. In the example of the newspaper subscriber's satisfaction with sections of a paper, you might find an apparent relationship (called a **correlation**) between readers' ratings of the editorial page and the same readers' ratings of national news.

Survey validity means that it measures what it was intended to measure.

Validity. Construction of the survey instrument is another matter of importance for valid survey results. **Survey validity** means that the survey measures what it is intended to measure. One means of improving validity is to assure that the questions cover content applicable to the research and that the wording is clear enough that participants understand what the researcher is asking. Review of the instrument by a panel of people who are knowledgeable in the content area helps validate question content. A **pilot study** further validates the instrument by administering it to a small group following the same process to be used for the larger study.

Method. Surveys can be mailed to participants, conducted on the telephone, or completed in personal interviews. E-mail or Internet surveys are other possibilities. Survey questions may be of either closed or open form.

Types of Questions. A **closed survey** form is a forced-choice from a list of possible responses. Multiple responses are provided and the participant selects the best choice. In contrast, an **open form** is similar to an essay question and allows the subject to word the response. Closed-form questions provide for more efficient data tabulation and analysis. Numerous resources are available on constructing survey questionnaires. The following books are examples of these resources:

McNamara, J.F. (1994). *Surveys and experiments in education research.* Lancaster, PA: Technomic.

Babbie, E. (1990). *Survey research methods* (2nd ed.), Belmont, CA: Wadsworth.

Observations should focus on specific behaviors pertinent to the study and that occur in a defined time limit.

SCIENTIFIC OBSERVATIONS AND EXPERIMENTS. Like surveys, observations and experiments are primary data sources. Surveys and scientific observations have different uses because they capture different kinds of information. Surveys rely on possibly biased and inaccurate self-reports of participants as the basic source of data, while scientific observation is a powerful research method that increases objectivity.

Scientific Observations. Scientific observations can yield more accurate quantitative data than surveys. For example, a study of interactions of individuals in group settings is likely to be more accurate with objective recording through observation of these interactions than by self-report of participants. Observations should be focused on specific behaviors that pertain to the study and that occur according to a defined time unit. To ensure accurate recording, observers should be required to score one behavior at a time. Other types of observation such as a case study or participant observer involve more intensive researcher time spent in the setting. Observation research limitations may result from such factors as lack of training for the observer or an observation that requires more information than can be accurately observed.

Experiments. Experiments establish controls so that changes can be observed within a controlled environment. Treatment effect may be measured by pre-test and post-test, with the results of a control group compared with the results from the experimental group receiving the experimental treatment. Results from experimental research can be generalized only from the sample to the larger research population from which the sample was drawn.

Experimental research compares a control group with an experimental group that has received a specific treatment.

Reference books are available that further describe procedures for a variety of data collection methodologies and data analysis. Organizations often employ consultants with expertise to assist with design and collection of primary source data.

Secondary Information Sources

Secondary information sources are found in libraries and on the Internet. Librarians can be helpful to you in locating appropriate information once you have determined the questions that you are trying to answer with research. Secondary resources may include a multitude of reference books, periodicals, books, directories, and audiovisual materials. On-line computerized databases available through the library provide many types of information, even full-text materials in electronic format.

Verify the integrity of information resources: Who is the author? Is the methodology sound? Is the article biased? Is it up to date?

Computerized searches for information on the Internet can locate information on a variety of topics. Search engines such as *www.yahoo.com* allow you to key in the words for a search through multiple databases and Web sites.

Not all information that is printed or in electronic form is accurate. Just because a book or a screen shows the information does not mean that what you are reading is fact. The following questions will help you determine the integrity of the information you have found:

1. Is the information up to date and specific to my research questions and problem statement?
2. Who is the author? What are the author's credentials and reputation in the subject area? Is the research complete and does it describe the methodology in detail? Was the methodology statistically sound and appropriate for the research?
3. Is the article biased or is it objective in presenting the information? Is the publication reputable? Who is the publisher or Web site sponsor?

DEVELOPING A PROBLEM STATEMENT AND SELECTING A DATA COLLECTION PROCEDURE

1. Write a brief, clear problem statement for the report to go with the title page you prepared for Checkpoint 8-2.

2. Identify the types of primary data (factual information) to collect for the problem and determine whether you would use a survey, observation, or experiment. Tell why you chose the method.

DISPLAYING DATA IN A REPORT

Collected data must be presented in a way that makes it easy to read and interpret. Tables, graphs, or charts help explain material that would be difficult to interpret from descriptive information. Studies show that the use of visual aids or illustrations increases retention of information by 10 percent. Charts, graphs, and tables can be powerful communication tools, but their effectiveness depends on how well they are prepared and presented. Good communication principles must be kept in mind:

1. Be sure that each visual element has a specific purpose and message.
2. Match the visual content to the needs, interests, and background of the readers.
3. Use a variety of visual elements such as pictures, graphics, charts, and diagrams to appeal to a wider audience.
4. Keep the message simple and understandable.

Visual illustrations in a report are numbered as *Table 1* or *Figure 1*, with the number for each type of illustration increasing consecutively. Most tables show exact numerical values and display data in columns and rows for comparison. However, tables may be word tables that illustrate relationships of words or terms by placing them in rows and columns. Illustrations other than a table are generally categorized as figures. A figure may be a chart, graph, drawing, photograph, or other visual display.

Tables

Tables allow for the presentation of large amounts of data in a relatively small amount of space. They can replace, in an accessible format, pages of text replete with numbers and explanations of numerical relationships. Tables should be used for essential data directly related to the report content. Detailed supplementary data should be placed in tables in an appendix to the report.

Tables present large amounts of precise data in a relatively small amount of space.

Tables should be arranged so that their meaning is obvious to the reader. Keep in mind that rounded-off values may display relationships more clearly than precise values. In most cases, no more than two decimal places should be used in tables. Be aware that numbers are more easily compared down a column than across a row and that column and row averages help inform the reader.

The title of the table should be brief but should convey clearly the table's content. Use the table function in your word processing software package to prepare tables. Figure 8-2 demonstrates a table format

Demographics of Subscribers to the *Daily News*

Category	Subscribers Total No.	Subscribers Percent	% of County Population
Adults	100,000	100	75
Gender			
Females	56,000	56	83
Males	44,000	44	67
Age			
18–34	30,000	30	61
35–54	42,000	42	83
55 and older	28,000	28	84
Household Income			
$50,000 and over	31,000	31	78
$35,000 to $49,999	21,000	21	56
$20,000 to $34,999	38,000	38	89
Under $20,000	10,000	10	75
Education			
College graduate	17,000	17	71
1–3 years of college	30,000	30	70
High school graduate	32,000	32	80
Less than high school	21,000	21	79

Note: Category totals and percentages may not equal 100% due to rounding.

Figure 8-2
Table

recommended in the *Style Manual of the American Psychological Association* (APA), 4th edition.

Graphs and Charts

Webster's Dictionary defines a **graph** as a diagram that represents variations with a series of points, lines, line segments, curves, or areas. A **chart** is described as an outline map, a sheet giving information in tabular form, a graph, or a diagram. Today most spreadsheet and word processing software uses the term chart to mean the same thing as a graph. Therefore, in this section, the two terms are used interchangeably.

> **"One picture is worth more than 10,000 words."**
>
> —Chinese proverb

Tables present exact quantitative data; charts or graphs usually require the reader to estimate values. However, a carefully designed chart shows the reader relationships and patterns. When deciding to use a figure to display data, you must determine the type of chart that clearly and efficiently conveys the intended message. These are three of the most commonly used charts or graphs and their primary purposes:

- Bar graphs show differences in quantities in one set of data (Figure 8-3).
- Circle or pie graphs show percentages and proportions. An exploded pie graph calls attention to one part of the whole (Figure 8-4).
- Line graphs show changes over time, so they effectively illustrate trends (Figure 8-5).

Figure 8-3
Bar Graph or Chart

Figure 8-4
"Exploded" Circle or Pie Graph

Total Employees of Marketplace, Inc.

Figure 8-5
Line Graph

Three other types of charts that may be appropriate for a report are *organization charts*, *flowcharts*, and *pictographs*. An **organization chart** shows the structural lines of authority within the organization. Line positions of supervisory authority are shown with solid lines, and staff support and coordination are represented by broken lines.

Flow charts illustrate steps in a procedure. Complicated written instructions often can be simplified through the use of flow charts. Boxes of different shapes are connected by arrows to illustrate the direction that the action flows during the procedure. Standard flow-chart shapes represent different types of activities. The size of the box is dependent on the number of words in the label and does not indicate the importance of the procedural step. Figure 8-6 shows a sample of a flow chart that depicts the steps in the process of report preparation.

Symbols or pictorial images of items may be used in pictographs to emphasize differences in statistical data. Computers make it easy to integrate pictures or symbols in a graph to illustrate value differences (see Figure 8-7).

Figure 8-6
Flowchart of Report Preparation

Figure 8-7
Pictograph Chart

PREPARING TABLES AND CHARTS

1. Use the table function in a word processing software to make a table. Use actual data for the table or fictional data based on your best estimate.
2. Use a spreadsheet software package to prepare a chart showing data. Use actual data or fictional data based on your best estimate. You may choose a line graph, a bar graph, a circle graph, or a pictograph. Tell why the type chart you selected is appropriate for what you want the data to convey.

WRITING A PROPOSAL

Proposals are a special type of formal report. They offer a service or product, request funds to conduct research, or request support to initiate a program. In each case, the proposal is based on analysis of a problem and describes a possible solution for the problem.

A proposal is written to persuade the reader to approve or fund a recommended action or project.

Purpose

The general purpose of all proposals is to *persuade* the reader to approve the solution presented or the funding requested. Proposals often have multiple readers. Proposals are typically read by managers with the power to approve or disapprove and by technical personnel who have specialized knowledge in the topic of the proposal. Therefore, the technical details of the proposal must be described sufficiently for reviewers to determine the technical merit and soundness, while the rationale, benefits, and the budget justification must be described for managers.

If the proposal is written in response to a grant request for proposal (RFP), be sure to read and understand the purpose and objectives of the grant description. Frame the language of the problem statement, purpose, and objectives in terms that clearly show the relationship to the RFP description and the project outcomes that contribute to the grantor's purposes. Consider the proposal to be a sales document that creates interest in the product, service, or program and persuades the reader that approval of the proposal will produce results that match the reader's needs.

Audience

Proposals may be written for individuals outside an organization **(external proposals)** or may be sent to managers within an organization **(internal proposals)**. In either case, fitting the proposal to the needs and purposes of the approval audience is critical. If guidelines for the proposal are available, be sure to follow all specific directions and include all requested information. Proposals may be automatically eliminated as incomplete if requested information is omitted or if an explanation for an omission is not included. Proposals for private philanthropic foundations may not have a specific format to follow. In such cases, be sure that the proposal has a clear statement of the problem, the purpose, the objectives, and a brief overview of the proposal procedure, as well as how the proposed program or project presents a new approach or solution to the problem.

Content

Most guidelines for writing proposals call for inclusion of similar elements: introduction, need for the project, goals and objectives, project design and activities, evaluation plan, budget, and budget narrative.

A proposal introduction begins with a statement of purpose.

INTRODUCTION. The introduction begins with a statement of purpose. The purpose statement establishes the rationale and nature of the proposal. This purpose is followed by a brief overview of the organization, department, or division submitting the proposal and the link to the person or organization receiving the proposal. Descriptive information should establish credibility for carrying out the project or program. Demonstrated expertise in the field and/or previous success with experiences similar to those projected in the proposal, as well as demographics that show access to the population to be served by the proposed project or program, are types of information to include in the introduction. The introduction may be preceded by a proposal summary or abstract. This summary gives a brief but complete overview of the most vital information from each major section of the proposal.

NEED FOR THE PROJECT. The next section establishes the need for the project and presents quantitative and qualitative data that are relevant to the purpose of the proposal. These data are gathered from primary and secondary research sources applicable to this proposal. Statements from experts in the field and from national research reports help establish needs. For example, in a proposal that a company build a fitness center, data on absences and the cost of absences, and research that shows health benefits of exercise would be a part of the needs rationale. The description of need leads logically to goals and objectives of the project.

GOALS AND OBJECTIVES. The goal or goals state how the project or program will address the established need. This goal should be supported by clear, concise, measurable objectives that reflect what the project was designed to accomplish. To be measurable, objectives must establish:

1. An observable action to be performed
2. The conditions under which the action takes place
3. The standard used to measure success of the action

Measurable objectives state the action to be performed, conditions for the action, and the standard for measurement.

The following examples illustrate a goal statement and objectives that might be written for a proposal to implement an employee health and fitness center. For the purposes of checking the three stated conditions for a measurable objective, the observable action is in bold type, the conditions under which the action takes place is italicized, and the standard of measure is underlined.

Goal:
The purpose of this proposal is to reduce the number of employee absences due to illness by providing a health and fitness center as part of an employee benefits package.

Objectives:
As part of each work week, all **employees will be allowed** one and one-half hours of paid time **for activities in the on-site health and fitness center.**

By the end of the first year, 70 percent of **employees shall use the health and fitness center** for an average of at least one hour per week.

By the end of the second year, **the average number of absences due to illness shall be reduced** by 5 percent for those employees who average at least one hour per week in the health and fitness center for at least 18 months.

The plan states how each objective will be measured.

Project Design and Activities. The primary basis for evaluation of the proposal is the description of the solution to the problem identified in the needs statement. This section will give procedural steps that make the project operational. Specific information should describe the overall design, along with specific activities, timelines, and personnel requirements. This section tells the reader exactly what you will do and how you will do it. The reader must understand the design and be convinced that it will achieve the objectives and goals of the project.

Evaluation plan. The **evaluation plan** describes what data will be used to measure achievement of the stated objectives. Data should be specified for measurement of each objective. In addition, a final report will give an accurate and detailed account of project implementation and results. For some projects, an external evaluator with expertise in the project area may conduct the final evaluation as part of the project cost.

Budget and Budget Narrative. Funding to support the project is described as part of the proposal. If provided by the funding agency, the budget will be detailed on a budget form; otherwise, the budget will include categories such as personnel salaries, fringe benefits, travel, equipment, supplies, postage and phone, contracted services, and miscellaneous. Budget projections should be based on realistic cost estimates. Be sure that the costs are reasonable in relation to the benefits and services to be provided. If cost guidelines were provided with a request for proposal (RFP), follow these guidelines carefully. In addition to budget figures, a narrative description should explain all cost items, how they were calculated, and their contribution to the proposed project.

Attributes for Approval

Keep in mind the importance of a strong introduction, concrete details in the design, and a sales focus on benefits and feasibility. The introduction attracts the reader's attention and is an important element in a decision for approval. The introduction should help the reader defend the proposal to others. The design section shows your expertise as a project manager by providing concrete, specific details. A personnel summary section may be a part of the design or, if lengthy, may be placed in an appendix. This summary should briefly state for each project staff member the qualifications and experience directly related to project responsibilities. If project personnel are not yet identified, include a personnel section that specifies duties and qualifications for each personnel position in the proposal. The proposal should end by bringing the project focus back to the benefits expected and how it addresses current and future needs.

PLANNING A PROPOSAL

1. Write a statement of purpose for a proposal to request funds for a childcare center for your local high school or for purchase of a new computer system for the local library.

2. Write a general goal and at least two measurable objectives for a proposal that fits the statement of purpose written in No. 1 above.

   Goal:

   Objectives:

   a.

   b.

CHAPTER SUMMARY

- Reports can be formal or informal. They are prepared for top-level management for a specific purpose. As such, they address the interests and concerns of the audience in factual, precise, and straightforward language.
- Formal reports have these major sections: preliminary section, body, and supplementary section.
- Reference citations and reference lists or bibliographies follow a standard format according to a style manual. Types of information used in text citations may include author's last name, publication date, and journal page. Types of information used in reference lists or bibliographies include author's last name, author's first and middle initials, publication year, title of article or book, name of publication, volume and issue number for journals, book publisher location and name, and page numbers for journal articles or chapters in books.
- Investigative or research reports gather, analyze, and interpret data; describe the results; state conclusions; and make recommendations.
- Tables, graphs, or charts help the reader interpret data. Each visual element has a clear, specific message and addresses the readers' needs.
- A proposal is a special type of formal report that analyzes a problem and describes a possible solution for approval and/or funding.

1. For each of the following situations, write a general purpose and one or more specific purposes for a formal report:

   a. An automobile repair shop owner plans to expand her facility from four stalls to eight stalls.

   b. A volunteer organization is writing a summary of last year's activities and accomplishments and next year's goals.

2. For each of the above situations, decide on the audience and how this determines the tone and language for the report.

   a.

   b.

3. Use one of the situations from Application No.1 above to determine a report title. Write this report title in the space below; and then use word processing software to prepare an attractive title page including appropriate information.

4. Using the same situation as No. 3 above, write a letter or memorandum of transmittal for the report.

5. Using the guidelines from the *Style Manual of the American Psychological Association*, correct the following bibliography or reference list entries.

   a. ITHAKA: A DAUGHTER'S MEMOIR OF BEING FOUND. SARAH SAFFIAN. BASIC BOOKS. 1998. NEW YORK, NEW YORK.

   b. BIG BASS by KEN KURZAWSKI and DAVE TERRE in TEXAS PARKS AND WILDLIFE. Pages 4A to 8a. VOL. 57, NO. 6—JUNE 1999.

   c. ALL TOO HUMAN: A POLITICAL EDUCATION by GEORGE STEPHANOPOULOS. LITTLE, BROWN AND COMPANY. 1999. BOSTON, MASSACHUSETTS.

   d. TRAILBLAZING PAINTER'S WORK YIELDS A HARVEST OF HISTORY by LORI STRATTON in COUNTRY WOMAN. Page 14 VOL. 29, NO. 2—MARCH/APRIL 1999.

   e. BUSINESS COMMUNICATION by A.C. KRIZAN, PAT MERRIER, CAROL LARSON JONES, AND JULES HARCOURT. SOUTH-WESTERN COLLEGE PUBLISHING. 4th EDITION. 1999. CINCINNATI, OHIO.

6. You are applying for a scholarship that requires you to submit a report on your financial needs and your academic progress. Include in the report your past year's income, expenses, and academic achievements. If a computer is available, write the report using word processing software; print it; and save it on disk. If no computer is available, write the report on paper.

7. Using a spreadsheet application, construct the most appropriate graphic aid to show how income has changed for Jackson's Appliances in the past five years. Send this graphic as an e-mail attachment to your instructor.

1995	$421,965
1996	494,870
1997	463,110
1998	595,500
1999	710,000

8. Estimate your personal expenses for a semester. Use a graphic aid to illustrate the distribution of the expenses. Your graphic aid should show the relationship of each expense to the other expenses.

9. The following paragraph contains the statistics for the Almo High School basketball team for a four-game series. Construct a graphic aid that will best illustrate the statistics for the four games.

   Jeff made 2 of 8 shots in game 1; 1 of 5 in game 2; 4 of 7 in game 3; and 2 of 4 in game 4. Lamont made 3 of 7 shots in game 1; 5 of 8 in game 2; 2 of 5 in game 3; and 2 of 6 in game 4. Steve made 1 of 2 in game 1; 0 of 1 in game 2; 1 of 3 in game 3; and 1 of 4 in game 4. Al made 2 of 5 in game 3 and 3 of 6 in game 4. Ted made 1 of 3 in game 1; 2 of 6 in game 2; 1 of 3 in game 3; and 2 of 5 in game 4. Derrick made 0 of 3 in game 1; 1 of 4 in game 2; 0 of 2 in game 3; and 1 of 3 in game 4. Simon made 4 of 9 in game 1; 3 of 6 in game 2; 5 of 9 in game 3; 4 of 7 in game 4; and 6 of 10 in game 4. Roger made 1 of 5 in game 1; 0 of 2 in game 2; 2 of 5 in game 3; and 1 of 3 in game 4.

10. You won first place in a competitive event at a student organization state conference. You would like to attend the national conference so that you could compete in the same event. Write a proposal to the student organization adviser requesting the necessary funds to cover your expenses for this national conference. Be sure to include in your proposal the cost of the airline transportation, parking at the airport, taxi from airport to the hotel, hotel accommodations, food, conference registration, and other related expenses.

Correct the grammar, spelling, capitalization, punctuation, sentence structure, and word choice errors in the following sentences. Write *Correct* for sentences containing no errors.

1. When Sharon and me gone to the movies we ate to much popcorn.

2. Sherry placed the pictures of she and I in her family album.

3. Malcolm treated his date to a stake dinner, took her to the movies, and than took her for a buggy ride thru the park.

4. I wish that I saw you when you preformed in the play.

5. Mr. Jones donated 3 goats, 4 bears, 2 deers, and 4 lamas to the Petting Zoo.

6. I saw the yellow car speeding away from the curb in front of the bank, said the beautiful young girl.

7. The three prisoners who were Trustees excaped from todays work detail.

8. Understanding systems means knowing how social; organizational; and technological system work

9. The vegetable truck spilt lettuce; spinach; and onions on the highway.

10. The guest chef showed my class and me how to make reel italian pasta.

APPENDIX A

BASIC GRAMMAR

A written message conveys more than just facts and ideas. It also creates for the reader a mental image of the writer. The message is the representative of the writer, therefore, you want your messages to carry a positive image as well as mirror your intended meaning. Grammatical errors and improperly used words detract from the meaning of the message and the reader's image of the writer. This appendix reviews word usage in sentences, to aid you in constructing messages that will clearly convey your message and reflect well on you.

IDENTIFYING PARTS OF SPEECH

Each word of every sentence can be classified as a specific part of speech. The English language identifies eight parts of speech. Recognizing parts of speech and the function of each word in the sentence helps you to write effectively. The forms and functions of these parts are described in greater detail in the following pages, but to start, here are the eight parts of speech and their definitions:

Knowledge of the parts of speech improves the effectiveness of the writer.

1. **Noun**—a word that names a person, place, or thing; for example, *child*, *James*, *home*, *France*, *number*, *courage*, *response*.
2. **Verb**—a word or a group of words that express action or state of being; for example, (action) *run*, *talk*, *learn*, *will have written*, *did create* or (being) *is*, *has been*, *feels*, *seems*.
3. **Pronoun**—a word that is used as a substitute for a noun; for example, *he*, *they*, *it*, *her*, *who*.
4. **Adjective**—a word that gives you more information about a noun or pronoun (describes, modifies, identifies, or limits); for example, *good*, *heavy*, *beautiful*, *these*, *first*.
5. **Adverb**—a word that gives you more information about a verb, an adjective, or another adverb (describes, modifies, or limits); for example, *directly*, *originally*, *creatively*, *very*.
6. **Preposition**—a word that connects an **object** (usually a noun or pronoun) and any modifying words to some other word in the sentence; for example, *to*, *in*, *from*, *of*, *by*, *at*, *with*.
7. **Conjunction**—a word that joins one part (word, phrase, or clause)

of a sentence to another part of a sentence; for example, *and*, *but*, *while*, *since*, *or*.

8. **Interjection—**a word or words used as an exclamation to show strong feelings such as happiness, anger, or fear; for example, *Oh! Great! No! Help!*

Sentences

A sentence is a group of words that expresses a complete thought. In order to do this, there must be, at the very least, a **subject** (the person or thing that is acting or that has being) and a **verb** (the word that expresses action or state of being); for example, *He* (subject) *left* (verb). Though short, it is still a sentence because it has both a subject and verb and expresses a complete thought. A **phrase** or sentence fragment is a group of related words that do not have both a subject and a verb.

A **clause** is a group of words that has both a subject and a verb. An **independent clause** expresses a complete thought and could stand alone as a simple sentence. In fact, the only difference between a simple sentence and a clause is that a clause is part of a larger, more complex sentence. A **dependent clause** is, as the name implies, dependent on another clause to make its thought complete. A dependent clause is also often called a subordinate clause.

For example, here are two simple sentences: *It was late. The store was closed.*

Combined into *It was late and the store was closed.* the two simple sentences become clauses within a more complex sentence.

In the sentence *When we got there, the store was closed.* "When we got there" has both a subject and verb but cannot stand alone. It is dependent on the next clause to make a complete thought.

Verbs

The verb is the action part of the sentence.

Verbs may express either action or state of being.

Every sentence must have a verb. Each sentence should be built around the verb. A verb gives meaning and direction to a sentence.

VERB TYPE. Verbs express action or a state of being. As noted above, in complete sentences, for every verb there needs to be a subject. **Action verbs** tell what the subject of the sentence is doing. Action can be physical (walk, sing) or mental (think, dream). **State-of-being verbs** are also called **linking verbs** because they link the subject of the verb with a word that describes the subject or means the same thing as the subject. The following sentences give examples of action and state-of-being verbs. The subject of each verb is in bold, and the verbs are italicized in these sentences:

The **senate** *debated* the appropriation amendment.
(*Debated* **is an action verb; the senate is the subject of the verb and is performing the action.)**

Robert *writes* three novels every year.
(*Writes* **is an action verb; Robert is the actor.)**

The **lawyer** *appears* knowledgeable about collection procedures.
(*Appears* **expresses a state of being and links its subject,** *lawyer*, **with an adjective,** *knowledgeable*, **which describes the subject**.)

The **party** *was* a joyous occasion.
(*Was* **expresses a state of being and links** ***party*** **with** ***occasion***.)

AUXILIARY VERBS. A verb may be a single word or may be comprised of a **verb phrase.** A verb phrase has a main verb expressing action or state of being that is combined with *auxiliary* or *helping* verbs and used as a single unit. Examples of helping verbs include *is*, *are*, *was*, *were*, *been*, *have*, *has*, *had*, *will*, *would*, *shall*, *should*, *must*, *can*, *could*, *may*, *might*, and *ought*. The following sentences illustrate the use of helping verbs; the action or state of being verb (main verb) is in bold, and the helping verb is in italics:

Margarita *had* **earned** the respect of her co-workers.

Jacob *should* **wait** for the next train.

Mildred *will* **audit** the financial records for the organization.

The party *should* **be** a joyous occasion.

VERB TENSE. The **tense** of a verb expresses the time of the action or state of being. The word form of the main verb depends on the timing of the action expressed in the sentence. The word used for the verb may have one of four forms: *present*, *present participle*, *past*, or *past participle*. The following example shows these four forms of the verb *go*:

Time is indicated in the sentence by verb tenses.

Go (present)	Going (present participle)
Went (past)	Gone (past participle)

The **present form** of the verb is used to show current action or state of being: *I go to the store every day*. The **present participle** uses the present form of the verb plus *–ing* combined with a helping verb: *He is going to the ballgame*. The **past form** of the verb indicates completed action: *He went to the park yesterday*. The **past participle** indicates completion of the action at an indefinite time or past repetition of an action and requires a helping verb: She *had gone to the park many times in the past*.

Verb forms are either *regular* or *irregular*. The past tense and past participle of most verbs are formed by adding *–d* or *–ed* to the present tense; these verbs are called **regular verbs.** The past tense and past participle of other verbs are formed by changing the spelling of the present tense instead of adding *–d* or *–ed*; these verbs are **irregular verbs**. Table A-1 shows examples of the forms of regular and irregular verbs. Table A-1 does not show the present participle because it has no irregular form; it is always created by adding *–ing* (eat/eating) or replacing an

The past tense of regular verbs is formed by adding -d or -ed; for irregular verbs, the spelling of the verb is changed.

TABLE A-1

Examples of Regular and Irregular Verb Parts

Present Tense	Past Tense	Past Participle	Classification
wash	washed	washed	regular
praise	praised	praised	regular
play	played	played	regular
gather	gathered	gathered	regular
vote	voted	voted	regular
begin	began	begun	irregular
catch	caught	caught	irregular
speak	spoke	spoken	irregular
eat	ate	eaten	irregular
find	found	found	irregular

"e" at the end of a word with *–ing* (vote/voting). The dictionary gives the past tense and past participle for all irregular verbs. Check the dictionary when you are unsure about the correct form of verb to use.

Verb tenses can be categorized as *simple tense* and *perfect tense*. **Simple tenses** are *present, past,* and *future*. **Perfect tenses** are *present perfect, past perfect,* and *future perfect*. Remember that the tense and the form of the verb indicate the time of the action or state of being. The paragraphs and examples in the remainder of this section review the use of verbs for each of the six tenses.

A present tense verb describes current action.

Verbs in the **present tense** indicate that action is taking place now or on a continuing basis. In the following examples, verbs in the present tense are italicized:

The ball team *arrives* two hours before every game.

A programmer *outlines* the project's steps.

A deer *sleeps* during the daytime.

Car phones *are* useful in emergencies.

The principal *makes* announcements every morning.

The past tense of a verb shows past action.

Past tense verbs indicate action that has been completed. In the following examples, the verbs in past tense form are italicized:

Leroy *completed* the survey in record time.

The bear *chased* after the two hikers.

The auditor *recommended* that the books *be reviewed* in three months.

Future tense verbs indicate action that will happen in the future and are formed by placing *shall* or *will* in front of the present tense form of the verb. Italicized words in these examples show verbs in the future tense:

Anticipated action is expressed by verbs in the future tense.

When *will* you *submit* the invoice to accounting?

I *shall stop* at the hospital on the way home from work.

I *will jump* from the airplane after I complete the skydiving class.

The **present perfect tense** indicates an action that was completed at an indefinite time before the present or an action repeated in the past. Adding *has* or *have* to the past participle of the verb forms the present perfect tense. Italicized words in the following sentences illustrate verbs in the present perfect tense:

Has *or* have + *past participle = present perfect tense.*

Jon *has completed* all requirements for graduation.
(Action completed at an indefinite time before the present. If the time of completion were stated, the sentence would be simple past tense and would read, "Last semester Jon *completed* all requirements for graduation.")

Julie *has made* A's in all classes during the past four semesters.
(Action repeated in the past)

Jack *has presented* 45 seminars to professional groups.
(Action completed at an indefinite past time)

Bonnie *has watched* television for two hours.
(Action repeated in the past)

The **past perfect tense** indicates an action completed in the past before some other past action. It is formed by combining *had* with the past participle of the verb. Examples of verbs in the past perfect tense are italicized below:

Had + *past participle = past perfect tense.*

Antonio *had sold* his common stock before the recession began.

He *had gone* to Texas before the letter arrived.

She *had finished* her English term paper before she started her mathematics assignment.

The **future perfect tense** is used to indicate an action that will be completed before a specified time in the future or before another future action. It is formed by adding *will have* or *shall have* to the past participle of the verb. The following italicized words are verbs in the future perfect tense:

Shall *have or* will *have + past participle = future perfect tense.*

By the end of the week, U.S. forces *will have flown* more than 9,000 sorties.

The skiers *will have left* the hotel before the blizzard arrives.

I *shall have gone* to the party before you arrive in town tonight.

In addition to these primary tense forms, both simple and perfect tense groups have what is called a **progressive** form, which uses the present participle as a base. This tense form, as its name implies, indicates progress. Examples of the progressive form of each of the six primary tenses would be: present progressive: I am going; past progressive: I was going; future progressive: I will be going; present perfect progressive: I have been going; past perfect progressive: I had been going; and future perfect progressive: I will have been going.

The subject performs the action in the active voice. The subject receives the action in the passive voice.

VERB VOICE. Verbs are in one of two voices: **active** or **passive**. A verb is in the active voice when the subject is performing the action. When the subject is receiving the action, the verb is in the passive voice. The effective writer uses the active voice more often than the passive. The active voice is more direct and carries a stronger message. Examples of verbs in the active and passive voices are italicized in the following sentences:

Paula *wrote* the poem.
(Active voice/past tense)

The poem *was written* by Paula.
(Passive voice/past tense)

Paula *has written* a poem.
(Active voice/present perfect tense)

Marty *had finished* her assignment before the class ended.
(Active voice/past perfect tense)

Barry *will photograph* the deer.
(Active voice/future tense)

The deer *will be photographed* by Barry.
(Passive voice/future tense)

Barry *will have photographed* the deer before we arrive.
(Active voice/future perfect tense)

Nouns

Nouns name people, places, or things.

Nouns name the people, places, or things about which you are writing. Nouns and pronouns (words that replace nouns) have several jobs in sentences, including subject (which acts or has being) and object (which receives action). An example would be "Bill threw the ball;" both *Bill* and *ball* are nouns, but Bill is the subject and ball is the object.

Because sentences require a subject, most sentences have a noun or a pronoun. The only exceptions would be sentences in which the subject is understood, such as a command. For example, in the sentence *Go away.* the subject *you* is understood—but the sentence still has a subject.

Nouns may be classified into two categories: *proper* and *common.* **Proper nouns** refer to specific people, places, or things and are capitalized. Examples of proper nouns are *George Bush*, *Dallas*, *Canada*, and *Buick*. **Common nouns** are general classifications of people, places, or things. Examples of common nouns are *man*, *city*, *country*, and *car*.

PLURAL NOUNS. Plural nouns are used to name two or more people, places, or things. Most plural nouns are formed by adding *-s* or *-es* to the singular form of the noun; for example, *automobiles*, *flowers*, *wishes*, and *tornadoes*. Some nouns are made plural by changing the last letter or two and adding *-es*; for example, *duty-duties*, *enemy-enemies*, *life-lives*, and *leaf-leaves*. The spelling of some nouns changes when the nouns are made plural; for example, *child-children*, *datum-data*, *mouse-mice*, and *person-people*. A few nouns are spelled the same in both singular and plural form; for example, *deer*, *fish*, *sheep*, and *salmon*. When you are not certain how to form the plural of a specific noun, you should consult a dictionary.

Most nouns are made plural by adding* -s *or* -es *to the singular word.

Collective nouns are nouns that represent a group of people or things. They can be a little tricky because, even though they represent a group, they are singular nouns and, therefore, take a singular verb. Examples of collective nouns are *herd*, *pack*, *team*, and *family*.

POSSESSIVE NOUNS. The possessive form of nouns shows ownership. Possessive nouns end with *'s* or just an apostrophe. The general rule for possessives calls for adding *'s* if the noun is singular (John's, teacher's) and just the apostrophe if the noun is plural and ends in *s* (dogs', friends'). However, there are several exceptions to this rule. Some of these exceptions are fairly recent, however, so in older writing you will probably see the rules observed more often than in current writing.

***Generally, singular nouns form the possessive by adding* 's.**

First, though a singular noun generally gets an *'s*, exceptions are made when the word already ends in "s" and is long or the pronunciation is awkward. For example, it is not a problem to write or pronounce Charles's or boss's. In fact, pronunciation is one of the current guides—if you would pronounce the extra *s* of the possessive, you would write it. Hence, you might see *Samuel Clemens'* or *Samuel Clemens's* when reading about Mark Twain, but the first form is becoming more common. If the name is ancient, such as *Moses*, it is also common to use only the apostrophe to make the noun possessive.

The other exception is for plural nouns that do not add an *-s* or *-es* to become plural. So while *girls* gets only the apostrophe to become possessive (girls'), *women* gets *'s* (women's). Other plurals treated this way include men's, children's, and people's.

Possessive nouns are italicized in the following examples:

the *girl's* jacket	the *boys'* stereo	the *Jones's* car
the *boss's* request	the *singers'* voices	the *people's* voice

Pronouns

Pronouns substitute for nouns.

Pronouns replace nouns so that the nouns are not repeated in a sentence or paragraph. There are seven different types of pronouns: personal, relative, interrogative, indefinite, reflexive, intensive, and demonstrative. Each type performs a different function in a sentence.

The noun that is replaced by a pronoun is called an **antecedent**. For example, in the sentence *When I called Maria, she wasn't at home. Maria* is the noun antecedent and *she* is the pronoun with which the antecedent is replaced in the second part of the sentence.

There are two important things you need to remember about antecedents and pronouns. First, it must be clear what noun each pronoun replaces. For example, if you wrote *My father, my brother, and the dog were playing in the yard, and he was running all over the place*, no one would be able to tell if *he* refers to your father, your brother, or the dog. Second, the noun and pronoun must "agree;" that is, they must be the same in gender and number. This seems obvious, but it is a frequently broken rule. A common example would be, "I saw someone, and they appeared to be studying." *They* is a plural pronoun and doesn't agree with the singular *someone*. If you cannot identify the gender of the someone, you could write "*he* or *she* appeared," or you could substitute a different noun, such as *the individual.*

Personal pronouns change form in first, second, and third person.

Personal Pronouns. Personal pronouns are pronouns that change form in the three different "persons" of communication. The three "persons" are first person (the person speaking: *I*, *we*), second person (the person spoken to: *you*), and third person (a person or thing other than the speaker or person spoken to: *he*, *she*, *it*, *they*).

Personal pronouns change form when they perform different functions in a sentence; for example, *he* or *she* is used as the subject of a verb, but *her* or *him* is used as the object of a verb or preposition. They can also show possession: *my*, *mine*, *his*, *hers*. The different forms of a personal pronoun to fill these different functions are called the **pronoun case**.

A predicate nominative follows a linking verb.

A personal pronoun used as a subject or as a predicate nominative is said to be in the **nominative case**. A **predicate nominative** is a word which repeats or renames the subject and follows a linking verb. Examples of pronouns in the nominative case are italicized in the sentences below:

It was *she* who formed the committee.
(*She* is a predicate nominative; it follows *was*, a state-of-being verb.)

She sent two dresses to the cleaners.
(The pronoun is used as the subject of the verb *sent*.)

Pronouns may be in the nominative, objective, or possessive case.

Pronouns used as an object of a verb or preposition are said to be in the **objective case**. Examples of personal pronouns in the objective case are italicized in the following sentences:

Did you see *me* at the meeting?
(The pronoun is used as the object of the verb *see.*)

Marlena gave the book to *him*.
(The pronoun is used as the object of the preposition *to.*)

A pronoun is in the **possessive case** when it shows ownership or possession. Examples of possessive pronouns are *my*, *mine*, *our*, *ours*, *her*, *hers*, *his*, *their*, *its*, *your*, and *yours*. The italicized pronoun in the sentence below is in the possessive case:

Jill and Joseph had *their* house painted.
(The pronoun shows ownership of the house.)

Note that for possessive pronouns an apostrophe is *not* used. This is a common area of confusion. Since nouns take an apostrophe to create the possessive, it is easy to imagine that *their's* or *it's* would be possessive. However, an apostrophe with a pronoun does not signal possessive, it signals a contraction (for example, *it's* is a contraction of *it is*—*their's* is simply wrong but is misused for *there is*). Another area of confusion is between *their* (possessive of *they*), *they're* (contraction of *they are*), and *there* (a place), so be alert to your word choice.

Table A-2 lists personal pronouns and the forms used for the nominative (subject or predicate nominative), objective (object of verb or preposition), and possessive (shows ownership) cases.

TABLE A-2

Personal Pronouns

Nominative Case	Objective Case	Possessive Case
I	me	my, mine
you	you	your, yours
he	him	his
she	her	her, hers
it	it	its
we	us	our, ours
they	them	their, theirs

RELATIVE PRONOUNS. **Relative pronouns** begin dependent (subordinate) clauses and connect (relate) them to nouns and pronouns elsewhere in the sentence. Relative pronouns include *who*, *whom*, *whose*, *which*, and *that*.

Relative pronouns join clauses to nouns or pronouns.

The form of the relative pronoun is determined by the antecedent or the function of the pronoun in the sentence. For example, *who*, *whom*, or *whose* is used when the antecedent is a person or people. If the pronoun serves as the subject of a verb, *who* is used. *Whom* is used as the object of a verb or preposition. *Whose* is the possessive form. *Which* generally refers to things, not people or animals. *That* is used to refer to animals, collective nouns (nouns that refer to a group, like *committee*), and both people and things. Relative pronouns are italicized and antecedents are underlined in the following sentences:

The representative *who* sells the most cars will get a free trip to Hawaii.
(*Representative* is the antecedent; *who* is the subject of the verb *sells*.)

Julia is a teacher for *whom* we have great respect.
(*Teacher* is the antecedent; *whom* is the object of the preposition *for*.)

We went to the canyon, *which* turned out to be a good choice.
(The entire phrase *we went to the canyon* is the antecedent; *which* is the subject of the verb *turned*.)

Interrogative pronouns ask questions.

INTERROGATIVE PRONOUNS. **Interrogative pronouns** are used to ask questions. You will note that most of the interrogative pronouns are the same as the relative pronouns. It is their use in the sentence that establishes the type of many of these pronouns. Unlike most other pronouns, interrogative pronouns don't have an antecedent. In a question like "Who took my pencil?" the pronoun *who* does not refer back to an earlier noun.

The interrogative pronouns are *who*, *whom*, *whose*, *what*, and *which*. They are used in both direct and indirect questions. For example:

Who forgot to lock the door when they left?

To whom did you send the package?

Which of the troops are missing? (direct question)

He asked *which* troops were missing. (indirect question)

Indefinite pronouns refer to people or things in general.

INDEFINITE PRONOUNS. A pronoun that does not name a specific person, place, or thing is referred to as an **indefinite pronoun**. Among the most commonly used indefinite pronouns are *all*, *another*, *any*, *anybody*, *anyone*, *both*, *each*, *either*, *everybody*, *everyone*, *everything*, *few*, *many*, *most*, *neither*, *nobody*, *none*, *no one*, *one*, *other*, *several*, *some*, *somebody*, *someone*, and *such*.

Indefinite pronouns usually refer to a quantity (*one*, *few*, *many*). Pronouns such as *anyone*, *everyone*, *each*, *anything*, *something*, *everybody*, *nothing*, and *one* are usually singular. If they are referred to by another pronoun, that pronoun should also be singular. (***Everyone** paid for his or her own meal.*) In this example, each person acted individually; therefore, *her* or *his* is used rather than *their*. If the indefinite pronoun represents collective action by a group, the pronoun that refers to it should be plural. (***Everyone*** *liked the music, and they applauded at the end of the concert.*) Pronouns like *such*, *some*, *most*, *any*, and *all* are usually plural but may be singular depending on the usage. The following sentences illustrate the use of indefinite pronouns:

Anyone can come. (Singular)
Everybody should have an opportunity to continue *his* or *her* education. (Singular)
All the dancers made *their* own costumes. (Plural)

Such are risks involved in the sport. (Plural refers to *risks*)
Such a one as he cannot be replaced. (Singular refers to *one*)

A common error is to use *you*, *it*, and *they* as if they were indefinite, but this should be avoided. (An example of this would be "In some countries, *you* (or *they*) can't state political views." Use either a specific noun like "the citizens" or "the people," or the true indefinite pronoun *one*.)

REFLEXIVE PRONOUNS. **Reflexive pronouns** reflect the action of the verb back on the subject. They always end with *-self* or *-selves*. The reflexive pronouns are italicized in the following sentences:

***Reflexive pronouns always end with* -self *or* -selves.**

We have satisfied *ourselves* that we did a good job.

I know that I can do it *myself*.

A reflexive pronoun must agree (singular or plural) with the antecedent to which it refers. A common error in the use of reflexive pronouns is a lack of agreement between the pronoun and its antecedent.

Each **department** must support themselves.
(Incorrect: The antecedent, *department*, is singular.)

Each **department** must support itself.
(Correct: The pronoun *its* agrees with the singular antecedent.)

INTENSIVE PRONOUNS. **Intensive pronouns** also end with *-self* or *-selves*. They are used to emphasize the noun or pronoun that they follow in the sentence. Intensive pronouns are italicized in these example sentences:

Intensive pronouns emphasize a noun or pronoun in a sentence.

The mayor *himself* was on hand for the event.

The company *itself* is responsible for going bankrupt.

DEMONSTRATIVE PRONOUNS. **Demonstrative pronouns** are used to point out specific persons, places, or things. *This*, *that*, *these*, and *those* are the demonstrative pronouns.

Demonstrative pronouns point to specific nouns.

That was not an easy test.

Are *those* the pants you want to take on your trip?

These rules are easy to follow.

Adjectives

Adjectives make nouns and pronouns more precise.

Adjectives describe the words they modify or make the meaning more precise. They give additional information about nouns and pronouns. The adjectives are italicized in the following sentences:

Julia is a *competent reading* teacher.

A beautiful rainbow appeared after *the* storm.

ADJECTIVES AS ARTICLES. The three adjectives *a*, *an*, and *the* are called **articles**. The articles *a* and *an* are used to identify or modify a noun in a general way (any person or thing). The article *the* is used with a noun to indicate a specific person or thing. Use *the* also with a noun that names a category or class (for example, the *public*).

A, an, and the are known as articles and are used as adjectives in a sentence.

Use the article *a* before words beginning with a consonant sound and the article *an* before words beginning with a vowel sound. The beginning sound, not the actual first letter, of the word, determines whether *a* or *an* is used (*a home*, *an hour*). Use *a* when a word begins with a *u* and has the sound of *you* (for example, *unicorn*). Use *an* when the beginning letter *u* has a different sound (for example, an *uncle*).

Examples of articles used in sentences are shown below:

The teacher ate *an* apple and *a* plum.

She sent *a* letter with *an* article to *the* editor.

Janet was given *a* unit of blood.

Can you come see me in *an* hour?

An editor of *a* magazine has many responsibilities.

Do not use *a* or *an* after such expressions as *sort of*, *kind of*, or *type of*.

What sort of a fish is that? (Incorrect)

What sort of fish is that? (Correct)

Adjectives have three degrees of comparison.

DEGREES OF COMPARISON IN ADJECTIVES. Adjectives have three degrees of comparison: *positive*, *comparative*, and *superlative*. The adjective in the **positive degree** describes one noun; for example, *smart person*. Adjectives in the **comparative degree** show differences between two nouns or pronouns; for example, *Judith is **smarter** than Mazie*. Three or more nouns or pronouns are compared using the **superlative degree** of the adjective; for example, *Sue is the **smartest** person in the class*.

Adding **-er** *or* **-est** *to the root word shows comparison for shorter adjectives. For longer adjectives, add* **more, most, less,** *or* **least** *before the adjective.*

Degrees of comparison are made by changing the forms of adjectives. Adjectives may be of two types, **regular** or **irregular**. Regular adjectives can be formed one of two ways. For most adjectives that contain one or two syllables, *-er* is added to the root word to show the comparative degree. *(The woman wore a **smaller** shoe.)* For longer adjectives, the comparative is usually formed by adding the word *more* or *less* before the root word; for example, *He drives a **more expensive** car* (not *expensiver*). You may find that even some shorter adjectives sound better formed the second way; for example, *more eager*, rather than *eagerer*.

Superlative forms of regular adjectives are also formed two ways. As with the comparative, for adjectives of one or two syllables, *-est* is added to the root word; for example, *Her sports car is the newest automobile*. The superlative degree of longer adjectives is usually formed by using *most* or *least* before the root word; for example, *She wore the* ***most colorful*** *costume in the parade*.

Irregular adjectives, like irregular verbs, do not follow the regular methods of forming comparative and superlative degrees. The following are irregular comparisons:

Positive	Comparative	Superlative
bad	worse	worst
good *or* well	better	best
many *or* much	more	most

ABSOLUTE ADJECTIVES. Some adjectives are always in the superlative degree. These adjectives cannot be compared. An example of an absolute adjective is *essential*. A writer can state that food is an *essential* item; however, it is incorrect to state that food is *more essential* than water. Other absolute adjectives include *unique*, *dead*, *round*, *correct*, *wrong*, and *exact*.

Absolute adjectives cannot be compared.

Adverbs

Adverbs are used to describe or modify verbs, adjectives, or other adverbs. Adverbs can be used to answer questions such as *when*, *where*, *how*, or *to what extent* the action of the verb is done.

Adverbs modify verbs, adjectives, or other adverbs.

Most, but not all, adverbs are formed by adding *-ly* to an adjective. Some common adverbs that do not have the -ly ending are *very*, *almost*, *hard*, and *well*. The key is not the form, but rather the use. If the word is used to modify a verb, adjective, or adverb, then it is an adverb. Even nouns can sometimes be used adverbially; for example, in "We are meeting him *tomorrow*" or "He left *yesterday*," nouns are used to modify the verb and tell when the action of the verb takes place.

PLACEMENT OF ADVERBS. It is normally best to place the adverb close to the word that it modifies. Adverbs are italicized in the following sentences:

Adverbs should be close to the word modified.

She *calmly* read the evacuation plan. (read *how*?)

They will deliver pizza *anywhere*. (deliver *where*?)

She arrived *early*. (arrived *when*?)

He worked *hard*. (worked *how*?)

Martha walks *daily*. (walks *how often/when*?)

Ian can *almost* ride that horse. (rides *to what extent*?)

In these examples, the adverb *very* modifies an adjective (hot) and an adverb (badly):

That fire is *very* hot.

He drives *very* badly.

Sometimes adjectives and adverbs are identical: a *fast* ball (adj.), he ran *fast* (adv.). Another example is *well. Well* is an adjective if it is referring to your health (*I feel well.*), or means things are satisfactory (*All is well.*). When it refers to how something is done, it is in adverb (*She played the piano well.*). *Good*, however, is always an adjective—no one does things good, one does them well. *Bad* and *badly* are also often confused. *Bad* is an adjective. If you are expressing how something is done, use the adverbial form, *badly*.

Slow is now commonly used as an emphatic adverb; for example, Drive slow! or Go slow! However, in general use, when you want an adverb, you are always better off using the -ly form, *slowly*.

Adverbs also show degrees of comparison.

DEGREES OF COMPARISON IN ADVERBS. Adverbs, as well as adjectives, may have degrees of comparison. These degrees of comparison are **positive**, **comparative**, and **superlative**. Adverbs that end in -ly usually form their comparative and superlative by adding *more*, *most*, *less*, or *least* before the adverb. Table A-3 shows adverbs in the three degrees of comparison.

TABLE A-3

Degrees of Comparison of Adverbs

Positive	Comparative	Superlative
Regular adverbs		
rapidly	more rapidly	most rapidly
likely	less likely	least likely
fast	faster	fastest
slowly	more slowly	most slowly
quickly	more quickly	most quickly
loudly	more loudly	most loudly
Irregular adverbs		
well	better	best
badly	worse	worst

A preposition requires an object.

Prepositions

A **preposition** shows the relation of a noun or pronoun to some other word in the sentence (the object of the preposition). Prepositions always appear in a phrase. A **prepositional phrase** consists of a *preposition* and the *object of the preposition*, plus any adjectives that apply to the object. A prepositional phrase almost always begins with a preposition and ends with a noun or pronoun. A prepositional phrase is generally used as a modifier—an adjective or an adverb—but may occasionally be used as a noun.

There are numerous prepositions. Here are some common ones: *about, above, across, after, along, at, before, behind, below, beside, between, beyond, but, by, for, from, in, into, like, of, on, over, since, through, to, toward, under, until, up, upon, with.*

In the following sentences the prepositions are in bold, the objects of the prepositions are in italics, and the prepositional phrases are in parentheses:

Lawrence went (**to** the *store*) (**after** *school*).

The deer grazed (**on** the *grass*) and watched (**over** their *fawns*).

As noted earlier, a pronoun that is the object of a preposition should be in the objective case. This is fairly clear with simple objects: *I gave the book to her* (to is the preposition and her is the object of the preposition). It is most commonly confused with a compound object: *Sulinn was seated between Claudia and me* (*between* is the preposition so *me* needs to be in the objective case).

UNNECESSARY PREPOSITIONS. Sentences should not contain prepositions that are unnecessary. Use only those prepositions that make a message clearer or more precise. Examples of sentences with unnecessary prepositions and the same sentences with out them are shown below:

Unnecessary prepositions should be removed from sentences.

Rocky ran *up* to the top of the mountain. (Unnecessary preposition)

Rocky ran to the top of the mountain. (Correct)

The child asked where her mother was *at*. (Unnecessary preposition)

The child asked where her mother was. (Correct)

The equation was erased off *of* the chalkboard. (Unnecessary preposition)

The equation was erased off the chalkboard. (Correct)

SENTENCES ENDING WITH PREPOSITIONS. Writers should avoid ending a sentence with a preposition. Often the sentence needs to be rearranged to make it read more smoothly. Examples of incorrect and rearranged sentences are given below:

Sentences should not end with a preposition.

Whom is the advertisement written *for*? (Incorrect)
For whom is the advertisement written? (Correct)

Which cities are you going *to*? (Incorrect)
To which cities are you going? (Correct)

Conjunctions connect words, phrases, or clauses.

Conjunctions

Conjunctions are connectors. They connect words, phrases, or clauses. The three types of conjunctions are *coordinate*, *correlative*, and *subordinate.*

Coordinate conjunctions join equal parts of the sentence.

COORDINATE CONJUNCTIONS. **Coordinate conjunctions** connect sentence elements that are grammatically equal. For instance, nouns are connected to nouns, prepositional phrases to prepositional phrases, and independent clauses to independent clauses by coordinate conjunctions. The coordinate conjunctions are *and*, *but*, *or*, *nor*, *for*, *so*, and *yet*. Coordinate conjunctions are in bold in the following examples and the words, phrases, or clauses joined by the conjunctions are italicized:

> You *may walk* **or** *drive* to the picnic. (Joins two verbs)
>
> She went *to the game* **and** *to the dance*. (Joins two prepositional phrases)
>
> *I attended the meeting*, **but** *Tom went home*. (Joins two independent clauses)

Correlative conjunctions are used in pairs.

CORRELATIVE CONJUNCTIONS. **Correlative conjunctions** join two sentence elements of equal rank and are used in pairs. Correlative conjunctions include *both/and*, *either/or*, *neither/nor*, and *not only/but also*. Examples are shown in the following sentences:

> *Neither* males *nor* females want to fight a war.
>
> They can send *both* an administrative assistant *and* a supervisor to the seminar.

Subordinate conjunctions join dependent clauses with independent clauses.

SUBORDINATE CONJUNCTIONS. Dependent clauses are connected to independent clauses with **subordinate conjunctions.** Since a dependent clause does not express a complete thought, it must be joined to an independent clause. Examples of subordinate conjunctions are *although*, *because*, *unless*, *while*, and *though*. The subordinate conjunctions are in bold type, the independent clauses are underlined, and the dependent clauses are in italics in the following examples:

> The meeting was canceled ***because*** *it snowed.*
>
> ***If*** *I make the honor roll this semester*, my employer will pay half my tuition.

Interjections express strong emotion.

Interjections

Words that express strong emotion in the form of an exclamation are **interjections**. They are not related grammatically to other words in the sentence. Interjections are normally followed by an exclamation point; however, weak interjections may be followed by a comma. The interjections are italicized in the following sentences:

Wow! That's a beautiful waterfall.

Well, I will stay home for the holidays.

Ouch! That fire is hot.

USING PARTS OF SPEECH CORRECTLY

In this appendix, you have reviewed the parts of speech and practiced choosing the proper form of words. This section covers troublesome areas of word usage and will help you avoid common usage pitfalls.

Practicing proper word usage avoids pitfalls.

Agreement of Subject and Verb

The verb and its subject must both be singular or both be plural. In most verbs, even most irregular verbs, only the third person singular form is different from the other forms within the same tense. *(I go, you go, he/she/it goes, we go, they go).* The following sentences illustrate singular forms of subjects (nouns) and verbs. Nouns used as a subject are in bold type, and verbs are italicized.

The verb and its subject must agree.

A **man** *creates* his own fashion.

The **river** *runs* dry in the summer.

Each **market** *determines* the advertising campaign.

Plural subjects below are in bold type; the corresponding plural verb is in italics:

Men *create* their own fashion.

The **rivers** *run* dry in the summer.

Markets *determine* the advertising campaign.

To be is the verb that is most irregular, and is therefore the one that has to be watched most carefully when matching subject and verb. Here is *to be* conjugated (note that only present and past are irregular):

Present: I am, you are, he/she/it is, we are, they are

Past: I was, you were, he/she/it was, we were, they were

Future: I shall be, you will be, he/she/it will be, we will be, they will be.

Collective nouns may be singular or plural.

Identifying the subject may be difficult in some sentences.

COMPOUND SUBJECTS. When two or more words connected by *and* or *both/and* are the subject of a verb, the verb takes a plural form; e.g., *Maureen and Jolene* ***were*** *sisters*. When multiple subjects joined by *or* or *neither/nor* serve as the subject of a verb, the verb agrees with the closest one. In the following examples, the **compound subject** is in italics; the verb is in bold type:

My friend or your brother **is** invited. (Singular)

My brother or your friends **are** invited. (Plural)

COLLECTIVE NOUNS AS SUBJECTS. Collective nouns, such as *class*, *group*, *committee*, and *number*, are plural if the members of the group are considered in the sentence as acting individually. If the usage of these words indicates that the group is acting as a unit, they are considered singular and take the singular form of the verb.

The committee **makes** the decision. (Singular)

The committee **were** unable to agree. (Plural)

OTHER SUBJECT-VERB DECISIONS. It is not easy to identify the subject and to determine if the verb should be singular or plural if the subject follows the verb or if other words or phrases come between the subject and verb. In the following sentences the subject is bold, and the verb is italicized.

That *is* the best **book** in the series. (Singular)

Benjamin, the best of the ballplayers, *was* my friend. (Singular)

If the subject is part of a construction that is plural, the verb is plural.

Most of the games **were** difficult.

Half of the games **were** difficult.

(*Games* is plural; therefore, *Most* and *Half* would be plural.)

If the subject is part of a construction that is singular, the verb is singular.

Most of the course **was** over.

Half of the course **was** over.

(*Course* is singular; therefore, *Most* and *Half* would be singular.)

Commonly Misused Words

In conversation, some words are often misused. Good writers practice precise usage of words, so check a dictionary or grammar book for any words of which you are unsure or which you know are frequently misused. This grammar review covers the following troublesome words: *lie*, *lay*; *sit*, *set*; *shall*, *will*; *whose*, *who's*; and *its*, *it's*.

Some words are often misused and confused.

LIE AND LAY. The verb **lie** does not have an object; it describes an action taken by the subject. The past tense of *lie* is *lay*; the perfect tenses are *have* or *has*, *had*, and *shall* or *will have lain*.

The verbs* lie *and* lay *differ;* lie *does not take an object.

I *shall lie* down for an hour. (Future tense)

Yesterday I *lay* down for a short nap.
(The past tense of *lie* is the same as the present tense of lay.)

I *have lain* down at the same time each day. (Present perfect tense)

Lay means "to place" and is a verb that takes an object. Remember, an object answers the question *who* or *what*. The past tense of *lay* is *laid*; and the perfect tenses are *have* or *has*, *had*, and *shall* or *will have laid*.

I *lay* my purse on the desk when I arrive at work. (Present tense; *purse* is the object)

I *laid* the book on the table. (Past tense; *book* is the object)

I *have laid* the book on the table each morning. (Present perfect tense)

A summary of the forms of *lie* and *lay* is shown in Table A-4 below.

TABLE A-4

Verb Tenses for Lie and Lay

Present Tense	Past Tense	Future Tense	Present Perfect Tense	Past Perfect Tense	Future Perfect Tense
lie	lay	shall or will lie	have or has lain	had lain	shall or will have lain
lay	laid	shall or will lay	have or has laid	had laid	shall or will have laid

SIT AND SET. *Sit* and *set* follow the same rules as *lie* and *lay*. *Sit* does not have an object; it describes an action taken by the subject of the verb. *Set* requires an object (which answers the question *who* or *what*) and has the meaning "to place." The following examples illustrate the simple tenses of each verb:

Present, past, and future tenses for *sit*:
I *sit* in this chair each day.
I *sat* in that chair yesterday.
The cat *will sit* on the windowsill at midnight.

Present, past, and future tenses for *set*:
Please *set* the vase of flowers on the table.
Yesterday I *set* the vase on the table.
I *shall set* flowers on the table this afternoon.

Table A-5 summarizes the forms of *sit* and *set* for each tense.

TABLE A-5

Verb Tenses for Sit and Set

Present Tense	Past Tense	Future Tense	Present Perfect Tense	Past Perfect Tense	Future Perfect Tense
sit	sat	shall or will sit	have or has sat	had sat	shall or will have sat
set	set	shall or will set	have or has set	had set	shall or will have set

***Shall** is used with the first person.*

SHALL AND WILL. *Shall* and *will* show future tense. *Shall* was once considered the only correct form for the simple future for the first person *I* and *we*. This usage has changed, and *will* can be used in most speech and writing; for example, *I will go to the party* is as well accepted as *I shall go to the party*. In a few expressions the use of *will* in place of *shall* changes the meaning; for example, *Shall I go to the party* may be asking whether it is appropriate to go to the party. *Will I go to the party* may be expressing indecision about going. In these cases, the meaning would determine the usage.

Contractions and possessive pronouns should not be confused.

CONTRACTIONS. Contractions are commonly overused and misused. Contractions are acceptable only in informal writing. Often, the possessive form of a pronoun is confused with a similar-sounding contraction; for example, *whose/who's* and *its/it's*. *Who's* means "who is," and *it's* means "it is." Remember—the possessive of a pronoun is never formed with an apostrophe.

Whose book is that? (possessive)

Who's in the library now? (contraction)

Although we sometimes see the *'s* used to form the plural of capital letters and numbers, such as *C's* or *80's*, it is preferable to omit the apostrophe; the plural would be *Cs* or *80s*. The apostrophe is used to form the plural of lowercase letters, as in *c's*. An apostrophe is also used to show that letters or numbers are missing. This is obvious in contractions. Other cases are when you see a date with the first two digits dropped—'99, instead of 1999—the apostrophe lets you know that numbers are missing. You sometimes see *and* rendered as *'n'*—the apostrophes replace the *a* and *d* (though you will often see this used incorrectly, because not everyone is familiar with these rules).

VERBALS. Verbals look like verbs but have a different use in sentences. They may serve as nouns, adjectives, or adverbs. Verbals are *infinitives*, *gerunds*, and *participles*.

Infinitives combine a verb form with *to*; i.e., *to run, to buy, to pay*. Infinitives are used most often as nouns. In the following examples, the infinitive is italicized:

She always wanted *to play* basketball.

(used as a noun object of the verb *wanted*)

To run a marathon was his dream.

(used as a noun subject of the verb *was*)

Gerunds are verb forms that end with *–ing* and are used as a noun in a sentence. The following sentences have the gerund italicized:

Watching too much television contributes to a lack of exercise.

(used as a noun subject of the verb *contributes*)

She enjoys *decorating* the house for holidays.

(used as a noun object of the verb *enjoys*)

Participles are verb forms that use the present participle or past participle of a verb but function in the sentence as an adjective.

The letter, *written* last month, did not arrive until today.

(used as an adjective to modify the noun *letter*)

Whispering to one another, they missed the sports news.

(used as an adjective to modify the pronoun *they*)

SUMMARY

You have learned to identify the parts of speech and have practiced using them in sentences. Incorrect basic grammar detracts from your message and causes it to lose credibility with the reader. In Appendix B you will review capitalization and punctuation, which also are critical elements in constructing sentences and paragraphs.

APPENDIX B

WRITING MECHANICS

The English language has rules of writing mechanics that writers should follow. These rules are not arbitrary. They contribute to the meaning of the message as well as the reader's ability to understand your message. You must understand these rules and know how to apply them in order to be an effective writer. When you do not follow these rules, the reader may give your message different meanings.

This appendix will review the rules for writing mechanics and give you examples of how they are applied.

PUNCTUATION

The tone of voice and pauses give meaning to oral communication. Punctuation provides pauses and emphasis to written communication.

End-of-Sentence Punctuation

When we speak, we stop at the completion of a sentence. When we write, we end the sentence with a period, a question mark, or an exclamation mark.

Statements end with a period.

PERIOD. The **period** is used at the end of a sentence that makes a statement. *Look at that beautiful azalea bush.*

QUESTION MARK. Sentences that ask a question should end with a **question mark**. *What time is the meeting?*

Questions end with a question mark.

EXCLAMATION POINT. A sentence that expresses a strong feeling is called an exclamation. An exclamation ends with an exclamation point. *That was a dazzling performance! What a great dress! Wow!* However, it is important not to over use the exclamation point, because it weakens your emphasis if it appears too often.

Exclamations end with exclamation points.

Within-the-Sentence Punctuation

Internal punctuation can be used in a variety of ways to aid the reader in better understanding the message. Punctuation marks used within a sentence include the comma, semicolon, colon, dash, hyphen, apostrophe, quotation marks, and parentheses.

Internal punctuation assists the reader in interpreting the message.

Commas signal a pause for the reader and separate items in sentences.

COMMA. The **comma** is a mark of separation, signaling a pause for the reader. Commas separate items used in a series. A series consists of more than two similar words, phrases, or clauses.

> Jennifer takes classes in history, English, math, and computers.
> (Commas separate a series of similar words—in this case, types of classes.)
>
> Mark will spend his vacation canoeing on the river, horseback riding in the country, and working at the park.
> (Commas separate a series of phrases.)
>
> Melody made reservations on an airline, Johnny bought a bus ticket, and Melvin planned to drive his automobile.
> (Commas separate a series of independent clauses.)

A comma comes before a conjunction separating two independent clauses.

When two independent clauses are joined by a conjunction, a comma comes before the conjunction.

> Charles is an outstanding teacher, and he has friends in all parts of the state.
> (Two independent clauses are joined by a conjunction.)

A dependent clause is often followed by a comma.

In a variety of situations, a dependent clause will be separated by commas from an independent clause. (As you learned in Appendix A, an independent clause expresses a complete thought and can stand alone as a sentence. A dependent clause does not express a complete thought and cannot stand alone; it needs an independent clause to make a complete sentence.)

An introductory dependent clause used as an adverb is separated from the independent clause by a comma. This clause is italicized in the following sentence:

> *If we continue putting money in our savings account*, we will soon have enough for a down payment on a new car.
> (The introductory clause acts as an adverb explaining *how*.)

A nonrestrictive clause is a dependent clause that is nonessential to the sentence; that is, it adds extra information but could be left out without changing the meaning of the sentence. These clauses are italicized in the example sentences:

> Mr. Smith, *who lives near the college*, plans to run for city council.
>
> My diligent studying, *which lasted all through high school*, enabled me to go to college.

Appositives and appositive phrases are generally set off by commas.

Commas are usually used to separate an appositive or appositive phrase from the rest of the sentence. An **appositive** is a word that follows a noun and identifies or explains the noun. When modifiers are included with the appositive, it is an **appositive phrase**. A nonrestrictive appositive could be left out of the sentence without changing the meaning.

My supervisor, Claudia, will vacation in Florida this summer. (The appositive, *Claudia*, identifies the noun *supervisor*.)

John Smith, my doctor, recommended I exercise more regularly. (Here, the appositive phrase *my doctor* explains something about the noun it follows.)

An appositive is not set off by commas when it is so closely related to the word it modifies that it is essential to understanding the sentence. This is called a **restrictive appositive**.

My friend George painted the old home on Sycamore Street. (Since the appositive *George* is essential to identify which friend is being discussed, it is not set off by commas.)

A comma separates a word or words of direct address from the rest of the sentence.

Words of direct address are separated from the rest of the sentence by a comma.

Victoria, please leave your essay on my desk.

My friend, I will miss you when you leave.

A phrase at the beginning of a sentence is followed by a comma unless it is short or serves as the subject of the sentence. Even with a short introductory phrase, a comma is used if it is necessary for clarity.

An introductory phrase is sometimes followed by a comma.

In the early hours just before dawn, I enjoy sitting on the patio in the cool morning air.
(Introductory prepositional phrases)

In the spring flowers bloom everywhere.
(Short introductory prepositional phrase—though you may see even a short phrase like "in the spring" followed by a comma in older writing)

Laying flat rocks in the sand makes a sturdy walkway.
(Phrase used as the subject of the sentence)

To Mary, Turner seemed happy.
(Comma needed for clarity)

In a date giving the month, day, and year, a comma before and after the year separates it from the rest of the sentence. Similarly, when a city and state are together in a sentence, the state is separated by commas.

April 25,1990, is a special day to me.

Williamsburg, Virginia, maintains a historic section replicating colonial history.

A comma may indicate omission of a conjunction between two adjectives.

A comma is used to indicate omission of a conjunction when two or more adjectives of equal rank precede a noun.

The historic, friendly city attracts many tourists each year.
(Both words modify the noun *city*; the sentence could read *The historic and friendly city . . .*)

If the two adjectives relate to one another as well as modify the noun which they precede, the comma is omitted.

The historic old city attracts many tourists.
(*Historic* and *old* are related; the word *and* has not been omitted.)

Semicolons separate closely related independent clauses.

SEMICOLON. A semicolon can be used in several different ways in written messages. Its more common uses are to separate short, closely related independent clauses; to replace a coordinate conjunction between independent clauses; to precede a coordinate conjunction between two independent clauses when either or both contain internal punctuation; to create a break and produce a contrast; and to separate items in a series containing commas. However, though there are many uses for semicolons, this punctuation should not appear too commonly in your writing. Semicolons should be used carefully and sparingly, when ideas are closely related and there is a good reason to not separate them into two separate sentences, or when there is no other way to effectively present the information.

The rains fell; the grasses grew.
(Separates short, closely related independent clauses)

Bob watched television; Diana took a nap.
(Replaces a coordinating conjunction)

For my soup, I use homemade broth; and I add fresh herbs.
(Precedes a coordinate conjunction when an independent clause contains internal punctuation)

A gazelle is fast; a turtle is slow.
(Creates a break and produces a contrast)

Mr. Berg's hobbies include investing in stocks, bonds, and mutual funds; reading newspapers, magazines, and short stories; and playing golf and tennis.
(Separates items in a series containing commas)

The semicolon is also used before a *transitional word* or *phrase* between independent clauses. **Transitional words** and **phrases** link independent clauses and help to show how one is related to the other. The following italicized words illustrate transitional words or phrases:

We eagerly await your visit; *however*, we realize that you may be unable to come.
(A semicolon is used before the transitional word *however*. Note that a comma follows the transitional word.)

A good education helps in many ways; *for example*, it opens career opportunities and increases earnings potential.
(A semicolon is used before the transitional phrase *for example*. Note that a comma follows the transitional phrase.)

Transitional words and phrases function as adverbs and conjunctions when they join independent clauses (Table B-1).

TABLE B-1

TRANSITIONAL WORDS AND PHRASES

then	however	otherwise	in fact
next	finally	therefore	on the other hand
also	likewise	as a result	by the way
besides	meanwhile	at the same time	in other words
consequently	nevertheless	for example	in addition
accordingly	hence	on the contrary	after all

A semicolon may also be used before the following words and expressions within a sentence to introduce enumerations, lists, and explanations:

for example (abbreviated *e.g.*)
for instance
such as
that is (abbreviated *i.e.*)
namely
that is to say

The department chairperson had three meetings on the agenda this week; *namely*, an advisory board meeting, a chamber of commerce meeting, and a faculty council meeting. (Note that a comma is placed after *namely*.)

If the above words or expressions are part of a **parenthetical expression** (an expression not necessary to the structure or meaning of the sentence, such as *in fact*, *indeed*, *of course*), the parenthetical expression should be set off from the rest of the sentence by commas or dashes, not with a semicolon.

Game birds; for example, quails; may build their nests on the ground. (Incorrect)

Game birds, for example, quails, may build their nests on the ground. (Correct)

Game birds—for example, quails—may build their nests on the ground. (Correct)

Colons inform the reader that something of importance follows.

COLON. Colons have various uses in written communication. They may be used to introduce explanations, examples, quotations, and lists. Colons are used to separate hours from minutes when time is expressed in figures and after the salutation in some business letters. Some style manuals require that colons be used to separate cities of publication from the name of the publisher in footnotes and bibliographies. The following examples illustrate some uses of colons in written messages:

The tour includes stops in the following cities: London, Frankfurt, Zurich, Stockholm, and Paris.
(A colon is used after a complete statement to introduce a list.)

If the sentence read, "The tour includes stops in London, Frankfurt, Zurich, Stockholm, and Paris," no colon would be used as the list would not be preceded by a complete statement.

8:35 A.M. (Time)

Dear Ms. Valdez: (Salutation)

Cincinnati: South-Western Publishing Co. (Footnote)

Thoughts are emphasized in a sentence by setting them off with dashes.

DASH. Dashes, like commas, can be used to set off a thought in a sentence. More emphasis is given to the words when they are set off by dashes. No spaces are used before, between, or after the two hyphens that are often used to form the dash. The following example shows how dashes may give emphasis to a clause:

The geese will--if they survive--return to Canada this autumn.
(Two hyphens without spacing form a dash.)

If you are using word-processing software, rather than a typewriter, you should use an em-dash, rather than the two hyphens shown above.

The geese will—if they survive—return to Canada this autumn.
(An em dash is a solid line longer than a hyphen that can be made with word processing software.)

Hyphens are used in some compound modifiers.

HYPHEN. Hyphens may be used in a variety of ways in written communication. The most common uses are in some **compound modifiers** (two or more words serving as an adjective) before a noun, in some **compound nouns** (two or more words combined and used as a single noun), with some prefixes and suffixes, in ranges of numbers, and in word divisions. Each use is illustrated next:

J.R. is a well-trained basset hound. (Compound modifier—but if written *J.R., my basset hound, is well trained*, there would be no hyphen between the modifiers)

Luann plans to be the ambassador-at-large. (Compound noun)

The class conducted a mid-semester survey. (Prefix)

Our senator-elect will assume office in January. (Suffix)

For tomorrow, read pages 124–149. (Range of numbers)

The auction supporting the zoo was held before the presentation of awards. (Word division at end of line)

Words may be divided with hyphens to attain a balanced right margin. Word processors with automatic justification make it easy to have even margins; however, most writers today prefer not to divide words. If you need to divide words, consult a dictionary or a word book to identify syllables and to find the best point for word division.

APOSTROPHE. **Apostrophes** are used in written messages to construct possessives of nouns, to indicate letters omitted in contractions, and to clarify some plurals. Today there is a tendency toward limiting the use of apostrophes. Apostrophes should be employed, however, whenever they make it easier for the reader to understand the written message. Examples illustrating the use of apostrophes are shown below:

Apostrophes help the reader understand the written message.

Karen's boyfriend (Possessive)

Don't, it's, they'll (Contractions—the apostrophes replace omitted letters; e.g., *don't* stands for *do not*, and the apostrophe replaces the missing *o*.)

He knows his a's and b's. (Plurals of lower case letters)

In most usage, plurals of capital letters, such as *ABCs, or* numbers, such as *1990s*, do not take apostrophes.

QUOTATION MARKS. Writers commonly use quotation marks to present an exact quote of an individual, to enclose the title of an article in a publication, and to indicate slang or nonstandard expressions. The following examples illustrate uses of quotation marks:

The exact words of an individual are enclosed in quotation marks.

Mario asked, "When will the homework stop?"
(Exact quote—note that a comma precedes it.)

Her article was entitled "Meeting the Productivity Challenge Through Computer Applications."
(Article in published work)

Catherine won the golf tournament despite the "chit-chat" of spectators around the final hole.
(Slang or nonstandard expression)

Whenever text that is already within quotation marks needs to be enclosed in quotation marks, place single instead of double quotation marks around the inside text.

Jules asked, "Did Ginny write 'The Computer Capabilities of Kentucky,' which appeared in the Micro Journal?"

Nonessential items may be enclosed in parentheses.

PARENTHESES. Nonessential information may be separated from the rest of a sentence by parentheses. Both left and right parentheses must be utilized.

Alfred went to the auction to purchase some cattle (Herefords) for his ranch.

CAPITALIZATION

Capitalization helps identify important words.

Important words in our written messages are capitalized for emphasis and identification. In the remainder of this chapter, commonly accepted capitalization rules will be reviewed.

First Words

Sentences always begin with a capital letter.

You must capitalize the first letter of the first word of each sentence. Also the initial letter of a sentence within a quotation is capitalized.

A bird woke me up this morning with its singing.

The freshman asked, "When is the Orientation dance?"

Proper Nouns and Adjectives

Proper nouns and adjectives are capitalized.

Proper nouns and adjectives are always capitalized. Titles of specific courses and literary works (except for articles, short conjunctions, and short prepositions) are capitalized. General academic subject areas are not capitalized except for languages. Specific names of organizations and institutions are capitalized. Examples of nouns and adjectives that are capitalized are shown below:

Thomas Jefferson	Houston, Texas
Business Law I	The Grapes of Wrath
Zenith Electronics Corporation	courses in French
Benton Chamber of Commerce	U.S. Supreme Court

Here are examples of nouns and adjectives that are not capitalized:

chickens	state government
courses in accounting	office building

The Pronoun I

The pronoun *I* is always capitalized. The other pronouns are never capitalized unless they begin a sentence.

***The only pronoun that should always be capitalized is* I.**

Personal Titles

Titles that precede a name are capitalized. Titles that follow a name normally are not capitalized. A title without a name is not capitalized (unless it is readily identified as one, specific person—for example, in *the President of the United States*, *President* is capitalized because it is very specific even if it doesn't appear with a name, though in *presidents of several nations*, *president* is not capitalized, because it is general). If a name or title is hyphenated, capitalize it, if appropriate, as if the hyphen or hyphens were not present. Examples illustrating the capitalization rules of personal titles follow:

Capitalize titles appearing before a name but not after a name.

Senator Randy Sullivan	Professor Ann Crum
the senator	Professor Croy
Paul Miller, professor	Rebecca Hadley-Smith
Father John Devine	Joan Carr, treasurer

Holidays and Seasons

Names of days of the week, months, holidays, and religious days are capitalized. Names of seasons are not capitalized unless the season is part of a specific title. Capitalization rules for holidays and seasons are illustrated below:

Always capitalize the names of holidays but not the names of seasons.

Wednesday	Thanksgiving Day
Labor Day	September
summer	Winter Ice Festival

Geographic Locations

Names of geographic locations are capitalized when they refer to specific regions or are part of a proper name. Otherwise they are not capitalized. Different uses of geographic locations and appropriate capitalization are shown below:

The names of geographic locations are not capitalized unless they denote precise regions.

north	North Pole
south of town	Southern hospitality
the West Coast	the Northeast

Abbreviations generally follow the same capitalization rules as the expanded form of the word.

Abbreviations

Abbreviations are capitalized if they represent words that are normally capitalized. Abbreviations are not capitalized if they represent words that are not capitalized. The time of day may be expressed with either capital or lowercase letters (*8:15 A.M.* or *8:15 a.m.*).

IBM	NBC	A.M. or a.m.
AT&T	dept.	P.M. or p.m.

SUMMARY

Correct use of punctuation and capitalization contributes to the reader's understanding of the written message. Practice applying the basic rules of punctuation and capitalization until they become a natural part of your writing. When in doubt, check a good reference source.

Checkpoint Solutions

CHAPTER 1

Checkpoint 1-1 Identifying Goals

General Goals	Specific Goals
1. to inquire	receive a price quote
2. to inform and influence	receive a refund
3. to influence	achieve employment opportunities
4. to build goodwill	socialize with chat room users
5. to inform	guide decisions about the system

Checkpoint 1-2 Analyzing the Reader's Needs

1. Although both had an initial interest in sports, Leroy's experience is more recent. Also, Leroy played a contact sport. The message to Leroy would need to appeal to his interest in sports while basing the appeal on his knowledge of football injuries. It is likely that Sally still has some interest in sports, so the value of sports could be a part of the letter. However, the main emphasis would be the danger of injuries from contact sports—perhaps with examples. The letter to Sally could not assume a knowledge of contact sport dangers; therefore, more detail would be needed. The letter to Leroy should be respectful of his experience in football since it is likely he still enjoys the sport.
2. Luisa has a higher level of education but may have less interest in classical music than Cathy. The appeal to both could highlight community interest and civic concern while acknowledging their interest in music and the importance of music. Perhaps Luisa's letter should also address the importance of different forms of music to fit different interests and needs of people.
3. Karen will need a stronger message about the dangers of guns because of her interest in hunting. The appeal might acknowledge acceptability of appropriate and safe uses of guns but address the dangers of not controlling gun use. No information is given about William's opinion

of gun use or knowledge of guns. The letter to William could use the same appeal as Karen's letter but with more information about gun use since he lacks experience with guns and knows nothing about their safety features or ways that gun use might be controlled.

Checkpoint 1-3 Classifying Writing Types

1. Individual responses will vary. Each message should have a 1, 2, or 3 for type; one or more of the letters A–F for Goal; and either an I for Internal communication or O for external communication. Messages may be coded for more than one type as well as for more than one goal.
2. Individual responses will vary. Characteristics of the reader may relate to education and experience, emotional state, socioeconomic and cultural background, and interests and opinions.

CHAPTER 2

Checkpoint 2-1 Selection of Writing Options

1. J	6. D
2. I	7. C
3. G	8. B
4. A	9. H
5. E	10. F

Checkpoint 2-2 Software Features for Changing and Editing a Document

1. Use a ruler to check the width of the left and right margin for 1.2 inches.
2. Check that the font is CG Times or Courier 12 pt.
3. Spellcheck should have been used to correct "competative" to "competitive." The student should have changed "Buy" to "By" and "sittings" to "settings." Spellcheck does not catch these two errors.
4. The second word may have been changed to attribute, nature, property, substance, essence or any other synonym judged appropriate by the instructor.
5. Words in the paragraph: 57
6. The teacher would need to check a disk to be sure the paragraph was saved under the file name SCANS.

Checkpoint 2-3 Software Features to Enhance and Print Documents

1. Picture and style of word art may vary. Heading should be centered and 14 pt. font size. Picture should be at the right margin.
2. Solutions may vary but should have three features listed in column 1 with the description of the features in column 2. These features may come from any terms in this chapter under formatting, editing, or refining the appearance of the message. The following table is an example. Sentences below the table should be the same as the example.

copy and paste	moves words, sentences, and paragraphs from one place to another
landscape orientation	places the paper horizontally with the 11-inch side across the top
thesaurus	gives synonyms and related words

3.(a) Microsoft Office® 97 is a software package that includes programs for word processing.

(b) The copyright symbol © is used with printed material to indicate that unauthorized copying is illegal.

(c) The temperature yesterday was recorded at the airport at 75° F.

Checkpoint 2-4 The Internet and Web Pages

1. The page printed is from the University of Illinois at Urbana-Champaign Bibliography Styles Handbook with the sub-heading "APA Format: Typical book entry in a bibliography."

2. The page printed may be any picture from an art museum that does not have a copyright notice or legal restrictions stated at the site that prohibit a copy being made for personal use. If such a restriction is on the site, the student may write the URL for this checkpoint rather than printing the picture.

CHAPTER 3

Checkpoint 3-1 Word Choice

1. Choosing words that are clear (accurate and easily understood), concrete (exact and specific or appeal to the senses), and simple (words not long and obscure):
   a. fluttered—concrete and clear
   b. reduces—clear and simple
   c. seen—clear and simple
   d. rolled—concrete and clear
   e. silver-haired—concrete and clear
   f. pink fluorescent—concrete and clear
   g. stamped out of—concrete and clear
   h. waved—simple and clear
   i. a trip—clear and simple
   j. glistening—concrete and clear

2. Eliminate unnecessary words, trite expressions, and errors. Wording may vary:
   a. The news came as a surprise to us. (*sort of* is unnecessary)
   b. Tell me exactly what you mean by that statement. **or** Say what you mean. (*just* is unnecessary)
   c. Get the most impact from your writing by careful word choice. **or** Careful word choice in your writing has the most impact on the reader. (*maximize* is trite; *try to* is unnecessary)
   d. She owns her home. (*own* is unnecessary)
   e. I am excited about the new job! **or** I am excited about the new job. (*very* is vague and, therefore, unnecessary; if you want to emphasize excitement, the sentence may end with an exclamation point)
   f. Tell me more about yourself. (*a little bit* is unnecessary)
   g. Come to see the paintings in the art museum. (*by* is unnecessary)
   h. Nothing is so unpleasant as rude behavior. **or** Nothing is so unpleasant as seeing someone behave rudely. (unnecessary wording)

i. Can you eliminate unnecessary words in a sentence by careful word selection? **or** Can you reduce the number of words in a sentence by careful word selection? (unnecessary wording)

j. Students in all schools should learn the essential basic skills and personal qualities that are essential preparation for job performance. (unnecessary wording)

Checkpoint 3-2 Using Unbiased Language

Wording may vary but should avoid stereotypes and overuse of gender pronouns. Each pronoun should agree with its antecedent.

1. Nursing care gives patients good bedside care.
2. All A grades in school do not guarantee that a student has gained necessary job skills.
3. Technology has advanced rapidly in the twentieth century.
4. A scientist spends long hours in the laboratory.
5. A doctor earns patients' respect by a caring attitude.
6. Parents must teach their children to follow rules but still feel loved.
7. Lawyers worthy of their training follow a code of ethics with clients.
8. The task of a teacher is not easy, but student success can be rewarding.
9. Now is the time to come to the aid of your country.
10. Anyone who thinks studying is unnecessary to pass a course will be disappointed.

Checkpoint 3-3 Message Structure

1. Wording may vary. Below is a possible solution. You may have students read their paragraphs and have a class discussion of the effectiveness or ineffectiveness as a beginning paragraph, giving reasons for the choices.

   a. Our bank gives you an up-to-date, accurate record of your funds at all times. Your bank deposits are added to your account the first business day after the deposit. This policy assures the accuracy of each day's transactions in your account.

   b. Are you confident that your job skills will keep you employable for the next ten years? Seventy-five percent of the workforce will need retraining before the year 2010. On October 15, you can attend a conference being held in Miami to help participants gain long-term employability.

2. Wording may vary. A possible solution is illustrated. You may have students read their paragraphs and have the other students use a rating

sheet to rate the effectiveness or ineffectiveness of the different ending paragraphs and explain their ratings.

a. Your prompt response is important. I look forward to receiving information on health care insurance.

b. Learn more about computer programming by talking with people who work in this field. This will help familiarize you with job opportunities as a computer programmer.

Checkpoint 3-4 Verb Usage for Message Unity and Strength

1. Action verbs: exhibits, come, can improve
2. Wording may vary but should use active voice rather than passive. An example solution follows:
   a. A surplus of fish and poultry causes the beef industry to suffer.
   b. Employees who seldom see their leaders view them as ineffective.
   c. A fear of mistakes causes writer's block.
   d. Jamie sewed the emblem on the jacket.
3. Wording may vary; negative statements should become positive. A sample solution follows:

   A good listener relaxes and concentrates on what others are saying. Make the speaker the central focus of your attention, and show an interest in what is being said. Good listening habits are important to career advancement, and developing listening skills should be a self-improvement priority.
4. Wording may vary; verb tense should be consistent.

   Competent workers are skilled team members. They negotiate with others to solve problems. They work comfortably with colleagues from diverse backgrounds. They challenge existing procedures and policies.

CHAPTER 4

Checkpoint 4-1 Generating Ideas and Outlining

1. Student responses will vary.
   a. The response should have 12 thoughts listed that relate to one of these topics: Goal Setting, Heroes of Today, Computer Technology, or Basic Career Skills.

b. Students were to free write for 5 minutes on one of these topics: Peer Pressure and Its Effect on Teenagers, My First-Grade Teacher, Happiness: A State of Mind, or My Favorite Hobby.

2. Student responses will vary.

a. The formal outline for this exercise should have items related to one of the topics in 1.a above and should be in the following format:

I. xxxxxxxxxx
   A. xxxxxxxxxxxxxx
      1. xxxxxxxxxxxxxxxxxxx
      2. xxxxxxxxxxxxxxxxxxx
   B. xxxxxxxxxxxxxxxxxxxxxxxxxxxx
II. xxxxxxxxxxxxxxxxxxxxxx
   A. xxxxxxxxxxxxxxxxxxxx
   B. xxxxxxxxxxxxxxxxxxxx

b. The informal outline developed will be a list of items related to 1.b above.

Checkpoint 4-2 Researching and Writing a First Draft

1. Student responses will vary.

a. One or more sources from the Internet should be printed that relate to the student's topic selected from this list: Goal Setting, Heroes of Today, Computer Technology, or Basic Career Skills.

b. At least one copy of information should be printed from a Web site that relates to a selected topic from this list: Peer Pressure and Its Effect on Teenagers, My First-Grade Teacher, Happiness: A State of Mind, or My Favorite Hobby.

c. This exercise continues the work the student did in researching Web sites in Exercise 1.b of this Checkpoint and develops an essay draft from the formal outline on one of these topics: Goal Setting, Heroes of Today, Computer Technology, or Basic Career Skills.

Checkpoint 4-3 Revising and Editing Your Writing

1. The paragraph should be marked with proofreader marks as follows:

references help writers write to correctly and are invaluable tools when editing and proof reading. For correct format or for a formal paper citing References, use a style manual such as the *Publication Manual ofthe American Psychological Association; A Manual for Writers of Term Papers, Theses, and Dissertations* by Kate Turabian; or the Modern Language Association *MLA Style Sheet*. Use of the dictionary thesaurus, and grammatical reference books help with word choice and cor rect usage of of words, phrases, and clauses.

2. The student will self-edit the first draft completed for Checkpoint 4-2 (1.a).
3. Working with classmates, the student continues to edit the draft of a paper written for Checkpoint 4-2 (1.a).
4. A final edited copy of the paper written for Checkpoint 4-2 (1.a) is to be submitted.

CHAPTER 5

Checkpoint 5-1 Subjects, Verbs, and Modifers

1. The subject(s) are underlined, the verb(s) are in boldface.
   a. She **plays** ball.
   b. The picture **fell** from the wall.
   c. The pizzas **were carried** in by Soolyn and John.
   d. **Learn** computer skills to prepare for the job market. (You is the understood subject.)
   e. An employer **looks** for persons who **can teach** technical skills to others.
2. The subject(s) are underlined, the verb(s) are in boldface, and the modifiers of a subject or verb are double underlined.
   a. **Is** that picture a recent one?
   b. Both Jane and Mary **communicate** well with clients and customers.
   c. **Can** she **work** well with people who **have** a variety of different ethnic, social, or educational backgrounds?
   d. Communication skills **enable** a person to share thoughts, feelings, and ideas.
   e. Improving the quality of goods or products **may involve** modifying or creating production systems.

Checkpoint 5-2 Complete Sentences, Verb-Subject Agreement, and Pronoun-Antecedent Agreement

1. Student responses may vary. Sample solutions are given.
   a. Every little problem noticed by a skilled driver and considered to be important by the automobile makers **is carefully analyzed**.
   b. George and Tammy **have** moved their residence to New York.
   c. Some individuals with a small-town background **have** difficulty working for companies that are located in metropolitan areas.

2. Student responses may vary. Example sentences are given.
   a. Either Andy or Glyn was selected for the computer workshop.
   b. Each of the players on the soccer team plays half of every game.

3. Examples of rewritten sentence for clarity.
   a. John thought that the policies of his company were unfair, so he talked with Jerry about them.
   b. When John became unhappy with the policies of his company, he talked with Jerry who thought the policies were unfair.

Checkpoint 5-3 Parallelism

1. Student responses may vary. Sample solutions are given.
   a. You cannot be rescued from a sinking ship, carried from a burning building, or saved from an earthquake if you have never been in danger.
      OR
      Someone cannot rescue you from a sinking ship, carry you from a burning building, or save you from an earthquake if you have never been in danger.
   b. Reading reports, writing memos, and speaking at conferences are primary functions of a manager.
   c. The organization needs to increase communication and to improve its image.
2. I. To inquire
   II. To inform
   III. To influence
   IV. To build goodwill
   V. To entertain

Checkpoint 5-4 Word Choice and Sentence Structure

1. These correct word choices should be circled.
   a. principal
   b. personnel
   c. fewer
   d. accept
   e. quite

2. Sentences will vary. Examples are given.
   a. Martine, Maurine, and Maury, *respectively*, completed the assignment.
   b. The *effect* of the change was not immediately known.
   c. That brooch *complements* your ensemble.
   d. Can you *cite* an example of research that supports your idea?
   e. The palace guard remained *stationary*.

3. Wording will vary. Sample solutions are given.
   a. She and Jules will barbecue for the holiday cookout. (Simple sentence/compound subject)
   b. Barbara may own the house, but George is in charge of remodeling it. (Compound sentence)
   c. Because of increasing paper and ink costs, the Brenham Banner Press increased its subscription rates. (Complex sentence/dependent clause precedes independent clause)
   d. You may choose the color of paint when you go to the store; after you make your choice, I will purchase the paint. (Compound-complex sentence/2 independent and 1 dependent clause)

Checkpoint 5-5 Emphasizing Ideas and Correcting Faulty Sentences

1. Wording may vary. Sample solutions are given.
   a. The team is the best—the best disciplined and the best trained. (Repeat key words.)
   b. New cars are too expensive for me to buy. (Emphasize high cost.)
   c. The hairdresser dyed the political candidate's hair. (Use active voice.)

2. Wording may vary. Sample solutions are given.
   a. Many college students do not have health insurance. Some colleges require it. Some people do not believe health insurance is a necessary expense.
      OR
      Many college students do not have health insurance. Some people do not believe it is a necessary expense, but some colleges require it.
   b. Every little problem noticed by a skilled driver and considered to be important by the automobile makers received attention when the new models were designed.
      OR
      When new models are designed, every little problem noticed by a skilled driver is considered to be important and receives attention by the automobile makers.
   c. Driving 1,500 miles over rugged mountain terrain, Rene enjoyed the beautiful scenery.

CHAPTER 6

Checkpoint 6-1 Organizing Ideas into Unified Paragraphs and Using Transitions for Unity

Mark a "P" where a new paragraph is needed to indicate a change in thought in the following excerpt. Circle transition words and underline examples of parallel structure or repetition of words and phrases.

The frontier forts of Texas were spearheads of civilization in a primitive land. As settlers poured West—ever eager for new fields to break and sow and new pastures to produce beef—lines of forts were established to secure and to protect the far-flung frontier. (P) The passions of that era were often volatile: frontiersmen on one side, tough and self-reliant, accustomed to taking what they wanted; Indians on the other side, resentful of intruders in a land they had once roamed at will. Often in between was the frontier soldier. His hardships were many and his dangers real. (P) Usually it was the soldier who built the fort, felled trees and shaped crude timbers, quarried stone and heaved both into place with pure muscle. (Then) when it was finished—by the time frayed tents gave way to rude barracks—he looked around to find the nucleus of a town. Farmers were plowing new ground; stores and saloons were being built. Civilization had arrived, and the frontier had moved. But the frontier's edge was still bloody, and the soldier moved with it.

Checkpoint 6-2 Constructing Sentences for Smooth Flow of Ideas

1. Circle the reference pronouns and underline the adverbial clause in the following paragraph:

   When Milburn entered the house at 907 Whitehead Street, Key West, Florida, he had the sensation of stepping back in time—back to the time when this Spanish Colonial house was home to Ernest Hemingway. It was here that this great American author lived with his second wife, Pauline, and their two sons. It was here that he wrote *For Whom the Bell Tolls*, *Green Hills of Africa*, *A Farewell to Arms*, *The Fifth Column*, *The Snows of Kilimanjara*, and *The Macomber Affair*.

2. In the following paragraph, underline transition words, tie-in sentences, or reference pronouns.

   To live and make a living in these changing times will require continuous learning. Such is the wave of the future. Today's middle and high school students will have to be life-long learners. They can expect to attend at least two years of post-high school education at a college, university, or technical school. Even then, their education will not be complete. They will be likely to change jobs at least five times during their career. Each work role will call for new learning. With global interaction via the Internet (and communication advances yet to come), people will be learning as long as they live.

Checkpoint 6-3 Paragraph Components

1. In the following paragraph, the topic sentence should be at the beginning of this message, but it is not. Underline the topic sentence that ties together related ideas in the paragraph. Draw a line through any

inappropriate sentence that is unrelated to the main idea of the paragraph.

Schools throughout the United States spend millions each year for computer equipment. Higher productivity and improved communication are the key benefits of communications technology—both in the work world and in education. It is not uncommon for managers to spend up to six hours per day video-conferencing with colleagues. Many businesses today have cafeterias for their employees. Technology can cut travel costs by 30 percent. Technology can easily get people involved to resolve issues and problems.

2. In the space below, write a sentence that could be used as the last sentence for the paragraph preceeding.

   Answers will vary.

3. Rewrite the complete paragraph so that it includes one or more transitions to bridge supporting sentences and the main idea in the paragraph. Leave out any sentence that cannot be linked easily to the topic sentence and add other sentences, if needed. You can compose the paragraph on a computer or you may write your paragraph on a separate sheet of paper.

   Answers will vary. Paragraph should have at least one transition (word or phrase, tie-in sentence, key word repetition, parallelism, or adverbial clause).

Checkpoint 6–4 Organizing Paragraph Details

1. Read the paragraph below and check the items that best describe the paragraph.

   "According to Peter Senge, systems thinking is a framework for seeing interrelationships rather than things, for seeing patterns of change rather than static 'snapshots.' It is a set of general principles—distilled over the course of the 20th century, spanning fields as diverse as the physical and social sciences, engineering, and management. It is also a set of specific tools and techniques, originating in two threads: in 'feedback' concepts of cybernetics and in 'servo-mechanisms' engineering theory dating back to the 19th century."

   —cited in Everett, D.R. (1995). Teaching SCANS competencies in Business Education. *Delta Pi Epsilon. Instructional strategies: An applied research series*, *11*(3), p. 4.

Length of sentence: Long

Unity of thought: Unified

Type of structure: Direct

Type of Paragraph: Descriptive (to inform)

2. Write a persuasive paragraph that urges parents to get involved with their child's education. They can join the parent-teacher organization at the school, volunteer, or become a member of a school-based council or other committees. Include these facts: Research shows that parent involvement in a child's education improves student achievement. A personalized school setting where teachers know students as learners and as individuals promotes learning. Teacher awareness of students' family cultures and lives outside school is an important key to student achievement.

   Answers will vary.

3. Rewrite the fragment to create a topic sentence. Develop a comparison paragraph from the topic sentence that compares this fear to the fear of going to a dentist to have a tooth extracted.

   Answers will vary. An example of changing the fragment to a topic sentence:

   Standing before a crowd to give a presentation can be as scary as going to the dentist to have a tooth pulled. (The topic sentence would then be developed into a paragraph.)

Checkpoint 6-5 Writing and Refining Paragraphs

1. Use the Internet to research information about a topic that interests you. Use word processing software to develop an outline for a descriptive paper on this topic. Use a computer to write the opening and closing paragraphs.

   Answers will vary.

2. Answer these questions about the opening and closing paragraphs that you have written:
   a. What is the main idea?
   b. What is the hook that will motivate the reader to read the message?
   c. What is the final message of the closing paragraph?
   d. What is the response you want from the reader?

   Answers will vary based on the paragraphs written by the student.

CHAPTER 7

Checkpoint 7-1 Selecting and Developing a Topic

1. Two topics should be listed. Answers will vary.
2. The response should identify *formal* or *informal* as the type essay to be developed. A brief explanation of this choice should be stated.
3. The example from Erma Bombeck is satire (overstatement to make a point in ridiculing human situations).
4. "Cruel kindness" is an example of *paradox* (apparent contradictions).

Checkpoint 7-2 Type and Purpose

1. Answers will vary. Students are asked to give the title, main idea (specific purpose), and general purpose of an essay they have read.
2. Answers will vary. Students are asked to list one of the titles selected in Checkpoint 7-1 and give the topic, main idea (specific purpose), general purpose, and whether or not they would write a formal or informal essay on this topic.

Checkpoint 7-3 Descriptive Writing

1. The following sensory words should be circled in the paragraph: *icy fingers, snowflakes, fluffy cotton, swirling, falling, roaring fire, chill.*
2. Simile example: *snowflakes were like fluffy cotton.* Metaphor: *icy fingers of the wind.* Personification: *wind having fingers.*
3. A description should be written of a pet, a friend, or a favorite place. Sensory words that appeal to at least two of the senses and either a simile or metaphor should be used in the description.

Checkpoint 7-4 Expository and Narrative Writing

1. a. Defoe's point of view: Omniscient.
   b. Emerson's point of view: First person.
2. Responses will vary. A short expository essay or narrative should convey the author's feelings about some event that happened.

Checkpoint 7-5 Persuasive Writing

1. a. Answers will vary. Students are to bring to class an example of persuasive writing and tell whether it appeals to reason, emotion, or both.

b. Each student is to identify facts or logic for an appeal to reason or to describe how an emotional appeal is made by the persuasive writing example.

Checkpoint 7-6 Planning an Essay

1. a. Students draw a web cluster of the main idea and subtopics for the essay topic they selected in Checkpoint 7-2, No. 2.

   b. Students are to use their web cluster to draft an essay.

   c. Students are to exchange their draft with another student for critique.

   d. Students are to edit for technical correctness and wording changes and save to a disk for use in Checkpoint 7-7.

2. Responses will vary. Students are to identify whether their essay that was saved to a disk in 1.d uses a primary writing mode of descriptive, expository, narrative, or persuasive. They are also to identify the point of view from which the essay was written.

Checkpoint 7-7 Using a Style Manual to Format Essays

1. Students are to format the essay that they wrote and saved for Checkpoint 7-6. Spacing, headings, and quotations should conform to guidelines described in Chapter 7.

2. The following headings should be written on the lines provided:

   Landscaping Small Gardens

   Space Considerations

   Use and maintenance.

3. The following revision of the paragraph with quotes should be written on the lines provided:

   According to Malen (1998), "Skilled writers meet certain performance standards. One of these standards is 'Presents logical, coherent pattern to thoughts.' "

CHAPTER 8

Checkpoint 8-1 Identifying Report Characteristics

1. Responses will vary.

   a. The general purpose may be to determine why profits have dropped. Specific purposes may include: identify items which caused profits to fall, determine if menu needs major modifications, and determine if new suppliers need to be contacted.

b. The general purpose may be to determine what it will take to be competitive with the new business. Specific purposes may include: updating information on current hairstyles, updating information on current fashions, and investigating possibility of adding services to current business.

c. The general purpose may be to assess needs for the business during the next year. Specific purposes may include: to determine if expenditures will need to be reduced, to determine if business will need to be expanded, and to determine if products or services need to be updated.

2. Responses will vary.
    a. Audience: Employer or owner; Tone/language: Factual, formal, objective.
    b. Audience: Employer or owner; Tone/language: Factual, technical, objective.
    c. Audience: Chief Executive officer; Tone/language: Factual, straightforward, objective.

Checkpoint 8-2 Preparing a Report Title Page and Letter of Transmittal

1. Title pages will vary depending on the topic selected. Title pages should contain all items that were suggested in this chapter. Title should be in all capital letters, and titles of more than one line should be single spaced as a minimum, the title page should give the title of the report, name or organization receiving the report; name, title, and department of the writer(s); and the date of the report.
2. Letter or memorandum of transmittal will vary depending on the topic selected. The letter or memorandum should contain the issue or problem, funding, and due date.

Checkpoint 8-3 Determining the Content of a Report

1. A formal report has facts and interpretations based on research and investigation of relevant data. Informal reports may be a letter or memorandum describing information that does not require extensive data.
2. Journal Article: Author's last name, author's first and second initials. (year, month). Article title with only first word capitalized, journal name underlined or italicized with capitalization as used on the journal, (volume number), issue number, and page.

Book: Author's last name, author's first and second initials. (year of copyright). Book title underlined or italicized with only the first word capitalized, (edition). City, State: Publishing Company.

Checkpoint 8-4 Developing a Problem Statement and Selecting a Data Collection Procedure

1. The problem statement will vary depending on the topic selected for the title page. The *what* and *why* should be stated clearly in this problem statement and written so that it is clearly understood by the reader. The problem should be narrow in scope.
2. The types of primary information to be collected will depend on the problem selected. The type of primary sources used for the study will depend on the problem that was selected. The response should identify the method of data collection and why this method was selected.

Checkpoint 8-5 Preparing Tables and Charts

1. The information in the tables will vary.
2. The data used in the spreadsheet will depend on the problem selected. The type of graphic selected will depend on the problem being studied.

Checkpoint 8-6 Planning Information for a Proposal

1. Individual statements will vary. The proposal should be written to persuade the readers to create a childcare center for the high school or to purchase a computer system for the local library. The statement should contain the rationale and nature of the proposal.
2. The general goal and two measurable objectives will vary depending on the topic selected.

INDEX